CW00347060

KATSUGORO

And Other Reincarnation Cases in Japan

KATSUGORO

And Other Reincarnation Cases in Japan

**OHKADO
Masayuki**

**Foreword by
Jim Tucker, M.D.**

Afterworlds Press

Santa Fe, New Mexico
www.afterworldspress.com

Copyright © 2024 by Ohkado Masayuki. All rights reserved.

Published by Afterworlds Press; an imprint of White Crow Productions Ltd.

The moral right of the author has been asserted in accordance
with the Copyright, Design and Patents act 1988.

No part of this book may be reproduced, copied, or used in any form
or manner whatsoever without written permission, except in the
case of brief quotations in reviews and critical articles.

A CIP catalogue record for this book is available from the British Library.

For information, contact White Crow Books by e-mail: info@whitecrowbooks.com.

Cover Design by Astrid@Astridpaints.com
Interior design by Velin@Perseus-Design.com

Paperback: ISBN: 978-1-78677-202-2
eBook: ISBN: 978-1-78677-203-9

Non-Fiction / BODY, MIND & SPIRIT / Afterlife & Reincarnation

www.afterworldspress.com
www.whitecrowbooks.com

For Kikuyo, Yuka, and Yui

Acknowledgements

I am deeply grateful to my colleagues and friends who have helped me at various stages of my research presented in this book: Eben Alexander, Kamidi Boudha Aradhana, ARASUNA Masana, ARAYAMA Hiroko, ASAHARA Sumiyo, Michiko Baker, Carl Becker, Frank Bob, Stephen Braude, Stephen Bunyan, Elizabeth Carman, Neil Carman, Khanal Kishor Chandra, Kiat Chanyavilas, Jenny Cockell, Frank DeMarco, Lori L. Derr, Molli Shylaja Devi, Ross Dunseath, Jim Ellis, David Fleming, FUNATO Takashi, Jaya Bahadur Ghalan, Pritivi Ghalan, Bidur Ghimire, Shambhu Ghimire, Bruce Greyson, Michael Grosso, Thomas Gutenberg, HARA Keiko, Erlendur Haraldsson, HASEGAWA Mitsuko, Paudel Kalpana, Khanal Yamuna Kandel, Blair Kane, KAWANO Kimiko, Madhu Sudan Kayastha, Jackie Kew, KIRYU Kazuyuki, Athanasios Komianos, Janice Miner Holden, Patrick Huyghe, ICHIKAWA Kimie, IIDA Fumihiko, IKEGAWA Akira, INAGAKI Katsumi, INOUE Fumiko, INOUE Shuichi, IWASAKI Mika, IYEIRI Yoko, Peter Johnson, KAGAMI Chikako, KAKEGI Ryusuke, Blair Kane, KASHIMA Tanomu, Edward F. Kelly, Emily Williams Kelly, KITAMURA Sumie, KOKUBO Hideyuki, KOISO Takahiro, KOMIYA Hisako, KOMIYA Yutaka, James Matlock, Antonia Mills, MINAMIYAMA Midori, Amit Kumar Mishra, MORIYA Noriko, NAITO Yuka, NAKAMURA Chinatsu, NARITA Maiko, NIGORIKAWA Takashi, NIJIIRO Rumika, NISHIKAWA Haruko, OCHI Nobuaki, OCHI Yoshie, OGIKUBO Norio, OGUMA Isao, OHKADO Kikuyo, OHKADO Yuka, OHKADO Yui, OKAMOTO Satoshi, Mick O'Neil, ONO Sakie, OTSUKI Maiko, Shyamial Panthi, Frank Pasciuti, Titus

vii

P. M. Rivas, Eriko Rowe, Tricia Robertson, TSUTSUMI Akio, Sasaki Tomiko, Cameron Smith, Carolyn Smith, Michael Sudduth, Govindam Venkata Siva Sudhakar, SUETAKE Nobuhiro, SUZUKI Toshiko, Tatyana Snitko, TAKEKURA Fumito, TAKEMOTO Ayaco, Krishna Bhadur Tamang, Sukuman Thing Tamang, Yagya Tamang, Ian Tierney, Jim B. Tucker, UMEHARA Yuki, Alexander Wallace, Usa Wongsangkul, YAMAMOTO Mikio, YANASE Hitoshi, YOSHIDA Hiroko, and the participants of my research.

I am indebted to numerous institutes and organizations for institutional and financial support and am grateful to them: Chubu university, University of Virginia, The Society for Scientific Exploration, The International Association for Near-Death Studies, The International Society of Life Information Science, Japan Psychic Science Association, The Society for Mind-Body Science, The Society for Psychical Research, The Scottish Society for Psychical Research, and The Helene Reeder Memorial Fund for Research into Life After Death.

I would also like to thank my family: my father, Masashi; my mother, Junko; my brother, Yasushi; my father-in-law, SUZUKI Shinobu, my mother-in-law, SUZUKI Etsuko; my daughters, Yuka and Yui; and my wife, Kikuyo, without whose support and encouragement this work would have never been accomplished.

Last but not least, I would like to thank Gregory Shushan, the editor of this book for his support and invaluable comments on earlier versions of the manuscript.

Contents

Foreword

~

As readers will learn in this book, there have been children reporting memories of a past life for a very long time. But such cases only became the subject of prolonged, systematic research when Ian Stevenson began investigating them in the 1960s. Ian had come to the University of Virginia to be chairman of the department of psychiatry in 1957, already with scores of published papers to his credit while still in his thirties. He was an iconoclast even before exploring past lives, challenging, for instance, not only psychoanalysis but even the accepted dogma in psychiatry that events in early childhood affect personality development more than later ones. This willingness to question conventional wisdom then led him to explore greater questions about Mind, including whether it can continue after death, with a particular focus on children's reports of past-life memories.

I had the great privilege of working with Ian before he retired. He was a remarkable man with an undying passion for the research, which he always approached with an open mind but also a critical eye. Ohkado shows some of the same characteristics Ian did. When he joined us for a year at the University of Virginia, I saw firsthand his passion for the work. I also saw the same meticulous attention to detail that Ian showed. Both have sought to be as accurate and precise as possible in establishing what happened in each case. And both have been fair-minded in their reports, presenting the weaknesses of the cases along with the strengths.

Ohkado, however, has also forged his own path. For one thing, we haven't had cases from Japan in our files, so it is wonderful to see an

1

investigator studying them there. In addition, Ian focused much more on the children's purported memories from past lives than on ones from the time between lives, largely because the latter ones were rarely verifiable (with some notable exceptions). But those reports may have much to tell us about the full nature of our existence, and Ohkado is not afraid to go there, as he has looked into all the memories children describe: ones of past lives, the period between lives, and times in the womb or during their births.

As readers of this book will see, Ohkado's analysis of the cases is always sober and logical as he considers the possibility of survival of consciousness. Thus, the careful, systematic study of this phenomenon continues, in keeping with past work while also exploring new aspects of it.

Ian Stevenson would be pleased.

Dr. Jim B. Tucker
Professor of Psychiatry and Neurobehavioral Sciences
University of Virginia

A Note on Japanese Names

Throughout I have rendered names in their Japanese order in accordance with the practice in Japanese: family name first, given name second. This is the standard practice for historical figures since many of the names such as Ono no Imoko, "Ono (family name) + no (possessive particle) + Imoko (given name)" cannot be easily reversed. Also, many names appearing to be the combination of family and given names such as "Murasaki Shikibu" are actually the combination of a nickname followed by a social post. For contemporary Japanese names, to indicate that the first name is the family name, it is written in capital letters as in "OHKADO Masayuki" when the given name (Masayuki) is also spelled out. When only family names are mentioned, only the initial letter is in capital as in "Ohkado."

A Note on Romanizing Japanese

The Japanese writing system has three types of orthographies: hiragana; katakana (mainly used for loan words); and kanji. Hiragana and katakana are syllabic and kanji that originated from China is logographic. So, the same word, for instance, "Nippon" meaning "Japan" can be written as "にっぽん" in hiragana, "ニッポン" in katakana, and "日本" in Kanji.

There are two representative systems for romanizing Japanese: the Hepburn system and the Kunrei system. The advantage of the former is that words written in this system will be relatively easy for foreigners to read correctly. On the other hand, the latter better represents the original writing system of the language and will more suitable for linguistically systematic representation of Japanese.

Considering the nature of this book, it might appear that the natural choice is the Hepburn system. However, there are some complicating factors. First, long vowels are to be expressed by using the macron in the Hepburn system as in "ō" and the circumflex in the Kunrei system as in "ô." The government Regulation for Enforcement of the Passport Act states that the Hepburn system is used for Japanese names although, if there are sufficient reasons, other systems can be used. One issue is that the Hepburn system adopted here is a modified version without the macron so that a name with a long vowel cannot be distinguished from the corresponding name with a short vowel. For instance, "Ōno" (written as "大野" in kanji and "おおの" in hiragana, meaning "Big Field") cannot

3

be differentiated from "Ono" (written as "小野" in kanji and "おの" in hiragana, meaning "Small Field"). To avoid such confusion, for "Ōno," for instance, "Ohno" and "Oono" can also be used. The choice is, however, optional and as a result, "Ono," "Ohno" and "Oono" can represent the same name "Ōno." Furthermore, because of the phonological changes of the Japanese language, some vowel combinations are now pronounced as long vowels, but the changes are not yet reflected in the orthography. For instance, the word meaning "king" written as "王" in kanji is written as "おう" in hiragana, the letter-to-letter transcription of which will be "ou." However, the "o-u" combination reflects the older pronunciation and the word is now pronounced as a long vowel which will best be represented as "o." In other words, if we follow the exact transcription of hiragana, the word "king" will be written as "ou" while if we follow the pronunciation of the word, it will be written as "ō" in the Hepburn system and "ô" in the Kunrei system. Likewise, the word meaning "English" is written as "英語" in kanji, and as "えいご" in hiragana, the letter-to-letter transcription of which will be "e-i-go." However, the "e-i" combination here is actually pronounced as a long vowel, which will better be represented by the letter "ē" in the Hepburn system and "ê" in the Kunrei system. The choice of romanization is not consistent even within the Hepburn or Kunrei systems.

Given this complicated situation, the romanization of Japanese in the book is inevitably "mixed." Basically, I have adopted the Hepburn system without the macron (the system adopted for a passport), but for proper nouns, I have adopted an individual's own version if it is available on his/her website or other places.

Preface

∼

I was born in 1963 in the city of Ise in Mie Prefecture, Japan. Although Ise houses the Ise Grand Shrine, one of Shinto's most important shrines, my parents rarely talked about anything spiritual. My father, who was a junior high school teacher, was a strong advocate of materialistic science, and under his influence, I became a materialist by the time I entered a high school.

I became drawn to parapsychological studies for both academic and personal reasons. I had studied linguistics within the framework of generative grammar founded by Noam Chomsky. The goal of the approach is to reveal the innate biological systems that allow human beings to use language. Various abstract theories have been proposed as such systems, but the shared assumption is that the system is in the brain. This appears to be strongly supported by language-related phenomena such as aphasia: It's quite clear that there are close links between the damaged part of the brain and the damage to one's linguistic abilities. However, if you talk with people who have fortunately recovered from aphasic conditions, they often say that they never lost their thoughts or the will to communicate. The content of their thinking was still there, and although they wanted to put it into language, they couldn't. It's like a person wanting to express themselves in a foreign language which they do not have full command of.

There is also the question of *where* was the language ability which was once lost then recovered? I came to think that, although many linguists were beginning to look into the brain, that it is not the right place to develop a *full* understanding of our linguistic abilities.

The untimely deaths of friends, teachers, and some of my students who had come to talk with me about their family problems led me to seek out many books on the meaning of life and death. Certain highly troubling social issues in Japan also contributed to this interest.

One of these social issues involved one of my students. He became involved in the religious cult, Aum Shinrikyo, which carried out the 1995 Tokyo subway sarin gas attack in which 13 people died and 50 were severely injured. My student was arrested, and although he was fortunately not directly involved in the incident, it was very shocking to me. I had often discussed with him philosophy, religion, and cultural and social issues. He was, in fact, a brilliant person – as were many other members of the cult. The founder of the cult, ASAHARA Shoko, did appear to have some paranormal power; and on reflection, many of the believers, who had been familiar only with the materialistic world views which were (and are) dominant in Japan, were mesmerized and came to believe that Asahara was a living god.

A second shocking incident that led to my soul-searching – and indeed the soul-searching of all of Japanese society – was the Kobe child murder case, in which a 14-year-old boy was discovered to be a serial killer. Many articles and books were published about the case, symposia and meetings were held, and TV programs were broadcast, all trying to understand what had led to such a tragic incident. In one of the TV programs, a number of junior high school students – around the same age as the murderer – discussed the issue with some prominent intellectuals. At one point, a male student blurted out: "But why should we not kill a person?" The very fact that a boy of his age could ask such a question to begin with was shocking, but still more shocking was the fact that none of the intellectuals were able to answer the question squarely. This incident spurred an even deeper soul-searching in myself, and in society overall.

Among the numerous books on the meaning of life and death I read, one of them, *Ikigai no Sozo (Creating the Value of Life)* by IIDA Fumihiko (Iida, 1996), introduced me to studies on near-death experiences, children with past-life memories, and past-life regression therapies. These phenomena appeared to show that we actually don't die with the death of our physical bodies – something that was totally against the beliefs I held at that time, but nevertheless seemed quite convincing and fascinating.

I bought many copies of the book and gave them to whomever I thought it would help, but gradually I came to be frustrated because all the cases introduced in it were by Western researchers such as Bruce Greyson and Ian Stevenson. In vain, I looked for Japanese researchers who worked on the topic. It surprised me that so many people (estimated to be over 800,000!) were involved in research in various fields in Japan, but no one was working on such an important topic as the empirical study of life after death or reincarnation. I decided that I should be the one to start.

Since my background was linguistics, I searched for an opportunity to investigate a case of xenoglossy. One came to me in 2009: the case of a Japanese woman who recalled a past life as a village chief in Nepal (see Chapter 14). I investigated the case in-person, and presented a report on it at the International Conference of Life Information Science in the summer of 2009.

Soon after the conference, I became acquainted with Dr. IKEGAWA Akira, who works on children's prenatal memories from the perspective of a medical doctor. His interest is on the practical values of such memories for child-parent relations, especially womb, birth, and life-between-life memories. He found that parents' attitudes dramatically change if they realize that children might choose them, and that they might be aware of their environment when they were in the mother's belly. It was through this work that Dr. Ikegawa came to know children with past-life memories. He introduced some of them to me; then as word of my research spread, parents began to contact me directly.

After publishing articles on the xenoglossy case and on children claiming to have past-life memories, I sought the opportunity to deepen my understanding of parapsychological studies at the Division of Perceptual Studies (DOPS) at the University of Virginia. When I was granted a sabbatical leave for a year, I wrote to two of the most prominent parapsychologists of their generation: Prof. of Psychiatry and Neurobehavioral Sciences Jim Tucker, who specializes in children who remember past lives (carrying on the research of Ian Stevenson, the founder of DOPS); and Prof. of Psychiatric Medicine Bruce Greyson, who specializes in near-death experiences. I asked them for a research position, and it was generously granted, so I was able to spend an entire year at DOPS as a visiting professor. During the stay I was in a euphoric state – like a Christian coming to Jerusalem, or a Muslim to Mecca, or a Buddhist to Bodhgaya. Since leaving DOPS in 2014, I have retained an association with them and have continued my research – including the book you now hold in your hands.

Introduction

Reincarnation and
Parapsychology

~

Reincarnation Cases in the Context of
Parapsychological Research

This book reports a number of Japanese reincarnation cases. The phenomena themselves are intriguing and fascinating on social and cultural levels, but they are of particular importance for the field of parapsychology. Within this context, reincarnation cases have been investigated with the intention of contributing to long-standing arguments concerning the possibility of the survival of the human consciousness after bodily death. This is exemplified by the landmark article by Dr. Ian Stevenson, "Evidence for Survival from Claimed Memories of Former Incarnations" (Stevenson, 1960a, b) and his subsequent books and articles. Most cases and data discussed in this book were collected in the same spirit, so it might be convenient for readers who are not familiar with this research tradition to briefly discuss the issue of the survival of human consciousness.

"Invisible Gorilla"

In an Ig Nobel Prize[1]-winning experiment, psychologists Christopher Chabris and Daniel Simons dramatically demonstrated that we fail to perceive visual stimuli that appear to be impossible to remain *un*noticed, an example of "selective attention" or "inattentional blindness" (Chabris and Simons, 2010). In the experiment titled the "Invisible Gorilla Test," participants were told to watch a short video in which one group of people wearing white t-shirts and another group of people wearing black t-shirts are passing a basketball within each group. Before watching the video, they were instructed to count how many times the players in white passed the basketball. Partway through the video, a person wearing a gorilla suit walks in, stops, beats their chest, and walks away. About half of the participants, who concentrated on counting passes, failed to notice the "gorilla."

It seems that researchers claiming that consciousness is only a product of the brain are like the participants of the "Invisible Gorilla" experiment who failed to witness the "hard-to-overlook" gorilla. Historical examples of such "half-closed-minded scientists" in various fields of science are discussed by Dr. Ian Stevenson (1958), and some notable examples in parapsychology are discussed by Dr. Stephen Braude (1997).

Recent examples are found in a massive volume collecting papers written by "afterlife nonbelievers" titled *The Myth of an Afterlife: The Case Against Life After Death* (Martin and Augustine, 2015). In Part I of the book, "Empirical Arguments for Annihilation," 11 scholars discuss the dependence of various mental activities on the brain by showing a close connection between them (Martin and Augustine, 2015, pp. 49–292):

- Matt McCormick: the dependence on the brain of human cognitive abilities, memories, personalities, thoughts, emotions, conscious awareness, and self-awareness.

- Jean Mercer: the dependence on biological factors of personality traits such as temperament, psychopathology, and intelligence.

---

[1] A tongue-in-cheek award that celebrates what are seen as trivial or absurd scientific achievements.

- David Weisman: the obvious correlation between brain decline and the decline of consciousness.

- Rocco J. Gennaro and Yonatan I. Fishman: the dependence on the brain of mental life and one's ability to have certain conscious experiences.

- Gualtiero Piccinini and Sonya Bahar: the dependence on the brain of mental functions such as spatial memory and cognitive control.

- Carlos J. Álvarez: the localization of emotions in specific neural structures.

- Terence Hines: the process of different aspects of language in highly detailed anatomical structures.

- Jamie Horder: the disruption of mental functions or removal of one's awareness by brain lesions.

- Keith Augustine and Yonatan I. Fishman: the tight correlations observed between mental states and brain states.

The phenomena discussed by these authors do appear to show a high level of correlation between the state of consciousness and brain activity. However, even within the brain science field, some "Invisible Gorillas" challenge these basic assumptions.

One is the phenomenon of terminal lucidity, which is the "unexpected return of mental clarity and memory shortly before death in patients suffering from severe psychiatric and neurologic disorders" (Nahm, et al., 2012, p. 138). Take the case of a female patient with Alzheimer's disease, an irreversible and progressive brain disorder. She was cared for by her daughter for 15 years and was unresponsive for years, showing no sign of recognizing her daughter or anyone else. However, a few minutes before she died, she started a normal conversation with her daughter. In their 2012 article dealing with the topic, German biologist Michael Nahm and his team collected many similar cases from the medical literature and unpublished sources.

Another challenge is the effect of psychedelic drugs on brain activity and concomitant states of consciousness. Profound mystical experiences induced by these drugs seem to suggest increased brain activity. Contrary to this expectation, however, studies of psychedelic drugs using brain imaging techniques have revealed that the enhanced subjective mental activities are more associated with *decreased* brain activity (Lewis, et al., 2017).

These two phenomena alone are enough to question the assumption that consciousness depends solely on brain activity.

One might argue that researchers attempting to explain consciousness as something beyond a process of brain activity, and those advocating the survival of consciousness after death, overlook a different type of "hard-to-overlook" gorilla: How can such high levels of correlation between the state of consciousness and brain activity be accounted for? For such criticism, I refer the reader to the filter theory of mind/brain relation, which postulates that the mind is not generated by the brain but instead is focused, limited, and constrained by it (Kelly, E., 2007). Therefore, although the brain significantly affects the state of consciousness, it is not the source of consciousness, just as the condition of a TV set affects the program image and sound, but the set itself is not the program source.

I believe we can safely put aside the correlation between the state of consciousness and brain activity for now, and focus on the possibility of survival of consciousness after death.

Arguments Concerning the Survival of Consciousness After Death

A prerequisite for the survival of consciousness after death is that consciousness must be independent of the brain at least at some level. Scientific databases can be a useful source for calculating the number of studies on this topic.

A research group in Brazil led by Jorge Cecilio Daher searched for studies on experiences related to the possibility of consciousness beyond the brain in five representative scientific databases (Pubmed, Web of Knowledge, PsycINFO, Science Direct, and Scopus) up to December 31, 2015 (Daher, et al., 2017). The largest number were on near-death experiences, with 598 contributions in total (including original articles, reviews, and other pieces). They are followed by those dealing with mediumship, which amount to 565. The topics with more than 200 articles are reincarnation (244), possession (244), and out-of-body

12

experiences (223). If we include articles on the topics of end-of-life experiences, spirit encounters, and mind-brain relationship, the total number amounts to 1,956.

The earliest works included in the database are those published in 1896 on mediumship in PsycINFO, but we can add earlier works, especially those on mediumship, by psychical researchers such as William Crookes (1832–1919), Henry Sidgwick (1838–1900), Frederic Myers (1843–1901), and Edmund Gurney (1847–1888), among others. Thus, a substantial number of studies exist on experiences related to the possibility of independent consciousness from the brain. Those who deny the reality of these kinds of phenomena do not explain the existence of the hundreds of scientific studies that deal with them. Or, put another way, what do all these studies actually concern if not the very subjects of their research?

The Survival Hypothesis vs. the Living-Agent Psi Hypothesis

Intensive and cautious research shows that genuine cases suggesting the survival of consciousness beyond bodily death do exist. They cannot be explained in terms of ordinary factors such as fraud, misreporting, malobservation, or hidden memories (cryptomnesia), which Stephen Braude called "The Usual Suspects" (Braude, 2003). Among the remaining possibilities are two main hypotheses that center on how to interpret relevant phenomena:

- *The Survival Hypothesis*: Human consciousness, which is independent of the body as suggested by out-of-body experiences or veridical perceptions in near-death experiences, survives bodily death; thus, communicators in mediumistic and after-death communications, and encounters with the deceased in near-death experiences, are conscious in the discarnate state. Additionally, consciousness can obtain a new body as observed in reincarnation phenomenon.

- *The Living-Agent Psi Hypothesis (or The Super-Psi Hypothesis)*: The observed phenomena *apparently* suggesting the survival of consciousness is actually due to living individuals who acquire the relevant information through their psychic abilities. The manifestations of skills and abilities, which the alleged discarnate appears to have possessed but the person in question does not, are accounted for by the upsurge of their latent psychic potential. As for the information source, there are two interpretations: living psychic people acquire the relevant information from people who know the deceased person or records concerning them, or they are able to somehow access a hypothetical cosmic reservoir of consciousness in which memories are stored.

Note that the survival hypothesis can be of two types: one which accommodates the possibility of reincarnation, and the other which does not. As the reincarnation phenomena strongly support the survival of consciousness argument, in this book I argue for the definition incorporating the notion of reincarnation.

The complicated nature of the arguments concerning the two competing survival hypothesis vs the living-agent psi hypothesis is well illustrated by recent remarks of the neuroscientist Prof. Edward F. Kelly, the leading editor of three monumental works demonstrating that the human mind and consciousness are not generated by physical processes occurring in the brain: (i) *Irreducible Mind: Toward a Psychology for the 21st Century* (2007), (ii) *Beyond Physicalism: Toward Reconciliation of Science and Spirituality* (2015), and (iii) *Consciousness Unbound: Liberating Mind from the Tyranny of Materialism* (2021). Even in the concluding chapter of the third volume, Edward F. Kelly is still cautious and avoids choosing one of the two interpretations of the phenomena (Kelly, 2021, p. 485):

> ... large amounts of credible empirical evidence have accumulated for a variety of human mental and psychophysical capacities that strongly resist or utterly defy explanation in physicalist terms.... There is even direct evidence of multiple kinds for postmortem survival of human mind and personality, coupled with increasing recognition that the only credible explanations for this evidence involve *either postmortem survival itself or unusually complex psi processes involving only living persons*[2] – a dilemma both horns of which are fatal to the physicalist worldview.

---

[2] Italics mine.

Such being the current state of research, presenting evidence and arguments for the superiority of the survival hypothesis over the living-agent psi hypothesis is crucial. Therefore, after presenting the reincarnation cases, we will return to this issue in Chapter 15 to show that they can provide additional evidence for the survival hypothesis.

Framework

Before presenting our reincarnation cases, I will first explain the theoretical and conceptual framework of this book, and the terminology adopted.

Let us assume that human consciousness travels through time, repeating the cycle of conception—birth—life with the body—death of the body—life without the body. This is illustrated in the following figure.

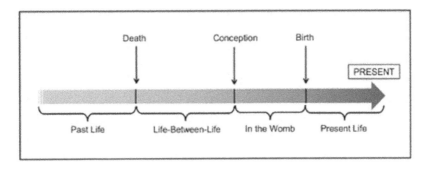

Figure 0-1. Life Cycle Assumed in This Book

Of the nine areas of phenomena related to the possibility of consciousness beyond the brain discussed by Jorge Cecilio Daher and others (Daher et al., 2017), reincarnation (past-life memories) (5) is concerned with the "past-life" section in the figure above. Near-death experiences (1) and end-of-life experiences (3) are concerned with "death," and possession (4), mediumship (6), spirit detection or spirit encounters (7), and transcommunication (8) are concerned with the "life-between-life" state; that is, between physical incarnations. Out-of-body experiences (2) are concerned with the temporary detachment of consciousness while in an incarnate state represented in the "past-life" and "present-life" sections in the figure. Fields (9) include the nature of consciousness and mind-brain relationship, which potentially cover all the stages depending on whether the consciousness or mind can be independent of the brain.

The importance of the reincarnation cases discussed in this book is that some of the subjects reported memories from all four periods: past-life, life-between-life, womb, and birth. This, I argue, strongly suggests the continuation of consciousness after the bodily death. I would also like to point out that, although the number of children (and people in general) having relevant memories does not appear to be large, most of us might actually have such memories subconsciously, which would suggest the universality of the survival of consciousness. This will be discussed in Chapter 16.

Terminology

There are some possible complications concerning the notion of "life-between-life," which should be clarified here.

Ian Stevenson coined the term "intermission memories"[3] for the memories between death and rebirth, and this was later adopted by other researchers. Poonam Sharma and Jim B. Tucker (2004) identified three stages of intermission memories: (1) a transitional stage following death; (2) a stage characterized by marked stability and illustrated by memories of staying in a particular place; and (3) the final stage including memories of choosing parents and being directed to them. They seem to disregard the womb period involved in Stevenson's definition of "intermission memories." James Matlock and Iris Giesler-Petersen added this fourth stage (the missing stage, in the sense of Sharma and Tucker's analysis), (4) memories in the womb, and the fifth and new stage, (5) memories of birth and its immediate aftermath (Matlock and Giesler-Petersen, 2016).

The term "life-between-life" refers to memories at Stages 1, 2, and 3, separately from memories at Stage 4 and 5 in Matlock and Giesler-Petersen's framework, as the first three are qualitatively different from the last two. The last two memories emerge when the new physical body

---

[3] In the first and the second volumes of the four-volume series of *Cases of the Reincarnation Type*, the term included in the index is "'intermission' experiences" (Stevenson, 1975, p. 371; 1977b, p. 370). The term "intermission memories" is included in the index of the third and fourth volumes (Stevenson, 1980, p. 381; 1983, p. 305).

exists while life-between-life memories originate in the discarnate state, that is, without a physical body (Ohkado and Ikegawa, 2014). Memories of being in the womb and those of birth and its immediate aftermath are referred to, respectively, as "womb memories" and "birth memories."

In referring to "life-between-life" memories, Elizabeth and Neil Carman adopted the term "preconception memories" (Carman and Carman, 2019), while elsewhere I adopted the term "prelife" memories" (Ohkado, 2015). Titus Rivas, Elizabeth Carman, and Anny Dirven termed the same concept "spiritual preexistence memories" (Rivas, et al., 2015). The term with the prefix "pre," however, can be confusing as other terms with "pre" refer to a different concept: "prebirth memories," referring to all the memories before birth as well as birth memories, and "prenatal memories," mainly used to refer to womb memories. Moreover, the term "prelife memories" and "spiritual preexistence memories" and "preconception memories" may imply the absence of preceding lives.

Conversely, one potential disadvantage of the term "life-between-life" memories is that it appears to *presuppose* the existence of past-life memories as they appear to be: literally speaking, memories of the period between a past life and the present life. While some children with "life-between-life" memories do have past-life memories, as discussed below there are many children with "life-between-life" memories but *without* past-life memories. If such children do not have past lives, the term "life-between-life" can be misleading. However, due to the lack of better terminology, and owing to the possibility that many of the children (and people in general) who do not consciously have past-life memories may have actual past lives, I adopt the phrase "life-between-life" memories in this book.

Summarizing the Properties of Reincarnation Cases

Over 50 years of intensive and extensive research conducted by Ian Stevenson and other researchers, such as Erlendur Haraldsson (University of Iceland), Antonia Mills (University of Northern British Columbia, Canada), Satwant Pasricha (National Institute of Mental Health and Neurosciences at Bangalore, India), Jürgen Keil (University of Tasmania, Australia), James G. Matlock (Parapsychology Foundation, USA), and Stevenson's successor Jim B. Tucker (University of Virginia), have collected more than 2,500 reincarnation cases. The accumulation of data has revealed recurrent features in the cases, which are listed

17

in (1)-(9) (Stevenson, 2001). For ease of reference, the following abbreviations are used below:

PrP = present personality (the subject of the investigation).
PLP = past-life personality;

(1) Statements: PrP makes statements about PLP.
(2) Desire to Visit PLP's Family: PrP shows a desire to visit PLP's family members.
(3) Desire to Visit Places Related to PLP: PrP shows a desire to visit a place related to PLP.
(4) Behavior:
    a. Emotions: PrP shows emotions toward persons related to PLP appropriate
    for the memories PrP claims to have and behaves accordingly.
    b. Traits: PrP shows phobias related to PLP's death, philias related to PLP, exhibits play that is related to PLP's life. For instance, PrP having a memory of a soldier in PLP likes to play soldier, has unusual skills like performing a dance they claimed to have danced in PLP, but has never learned in the present-life, or being able to speak a language claimed to have spoken in PLP, but not in the present- life (xenoglossy).
(5) Recognition: PrP recognizes persons, places, objects, etc., that PLP was familiar with or their changes.
(6) Acceptance: PLP's family accepts PrP as PLP reborn.
(7) Prediction: PLP predicts that they will be reborn in a particular family (limited to the Tlingit of northwestern North America and the Tibetans).
(8) Announcing Dreams/Departing Dreams: PLP appears in a friend or family member's dream to let them know that PLP will be reborn (Announcing Dream); PLP appears in a friend or family member's dream to inform them that PLP will be reborn in a new family.
(9) Birthmarks, Birth Defects, Diseases, Pigmentation of the Skin and Hair, Facial Appearance, Physique, Posture, and Gait: PrP has birthmarks, etc., related to PLP.

Life-Between-Life Memories

As mentioned above, many children with past-life memories also have life-between-life memories, and those memories can also have verified elements. From the relatively early stages of his investigations, Ian Stevenson recorded some of these cases,[4] though he did not emphasize them. In the first of his monumental 4-volume collection of detailed case reports, *Cases of the Reincarnation Type, Vol. 1: Ten Cases in India*, Stevenson stated that these memories rarely contain any verifiable material and that most feature details of local mythology and culture-bound fantasies. He added that the inclusion of these memories was only because (i) they form part of the record of the whole case and he felt unjustified in suppressing them arbitrarily, and (ii) he felt they may help prepare the reader for similar accounts which would be included in the subsequent volumes. (Stevenson, 1975, p. 50)

Despite his reservations, Stevenson (1975, pp. 312–336) did give an account of a case with impressive, independently verified life-between-life memories: that of Veer Singh, an Indian boy, who recalled his former life as a boy named Som Dutt. Veer Singh correctly talked about various incidents which took place after the death of Som Dutt, such as the lawsuits in which the family of Som Dutt came to be engaged.

Cases of life-between-life memories with verified elements are not limited to that of Veer Singh. Titus Rivas, Elizabeth Carman, and Anny Dirven collected similar examples from scholarly works, and found a total of 22 (including the case of Veer Singh). The authors suspect that the limited number of reported cases is due to the "limited attention that conscious memories of a spiritual preexistence [= life-between-life memories] have so far received from serious scholars" (Rivas, et al., 2015, p. 102).

The DOPS database has two variables for searches on life-between-life memory cases: (i) memory of the funeral or disposition of the body in a past-life, and (ii) memories of a nonearthly realm.[5] A quarter of

---

[4] As stated above, Stevenson classified life-between-life memories with womb and birth memories as "intermission memories," although the majority of the reported cases are life-between-life memories, and not the last two.

[5] The DOPS database also has a variable for memories of terrestrial events other than the funeral or disposition of the subject's body, and one for anything between conception and birth. The first variable is for portion of life-between-life memories and the second for womb memories.

cases include memories of a nonearthly realm, 14% of which are very detailed. A third feature verified elements.

It is true that the number of children with past-life memories who also have life-between-life memories is limited to just one in four. This might seem to indicate that having life-between-life memories is a rare phenomenon – even rarer than having past-life memories. However, this is not the case since there are many children with life-between-life memories, but without past-life memories as shown in Chapter 11.

Children with life-between-life memories (both of being in another realm and of choosing their parents and coming to them) are also reported abundantly in other places. Wayne Dyer and Dee Garnes, for instance, present such reports from all regions of the United States: Arizona, California, Connecticut, Florida, Illinois, Iowa, Kentucky, Maine, Massachusetts, Michigan, Minnesota, Missouri, Nevada, New Jersey, New York, Pennsylvania, Virginia, and Washington (and also from other countries, including the UK, Australia, Canada, etc.) (Dyer and Garnes, 2015). Elizabeth and Neil Carman collected life-between-life memory reports from all over the world, including Australia, Canada, China, Israel, Japan, New Zealand, the Netherlands, the USA, and the UK (Carman and Carman, 2019).

So, when it comes to life-between-life memories, we should not limit our attention to children with past-life memories.

Womb and Birth Memories

Notably, there is a large number of children with womb and/or birth memories, some of whom also have both past-life and life-between-life memories, and some of whom have only one or the other.

Liberated from the traditionally-held belief that "before age three, experience has limited influence over intelligence, emotions, and brain structure," a growing number of researchers emphasize the importance of prenatal or even the preconception period in child development (Verny and Weintraub, 2002). Some experimental studies show that a child learns sounds and language rhythm patterns of their mother in utero (Minai, et al., 2017; Moon, et al., 2013).

Although independent verification is challenging in episodic womb and birth memories because they are mostly related to family matters and independent witnesses are hard to find, some reports are impressive. For instance, Carman and Carman (2019, pp. 106–108) present a case of an American boy who was born at 36 weeks because of premature membrane rupture. At the age of eight, he had corrective surgery of his knee, damaged while in the womb. He told his doctor how the injury occurred in the womb, to which the bemused doctor commented: "I have never heard such a complete and accurate description of premature membrane rupture from a child, in a child's words, and from a child's point of view." His words shocked the parents as the circumstances around the birth were never discussed in the boy's presence.

Therefore, episodic womb and birth memories are other areas that, as in the case of past-life and life-between-life memories, should not sweepingly be dismissed as child fantasies.

The Organization of the Book

Chapter 1 of this book presents the historical background of reincarnation in Japan, beginning with archaeological evidence from the ancient Jomon people, followed by a review of reincarnation cases reported in classical Japanese literature. Chapter 2 introduces the classical case of Katsugoro, which occurred in the early 19th century (and was partly what inspired Ian Stevenson to begin his investigations of children claiming to have past-life memories). Chapter 3 discusses reincarnation cases reported after Katsugoro's case. These partly derive from Japanese folklore, but the majority are more recent and were reported by those with alleged psychic abilities (and mainly concern adults). Chapter 4 through Chapter 9 report cases of children with past-life memories that I personally investigated. Chapter 10 deals with an adult case.

Shifting attention from past-life memories, Chapter 11 focuses on life-between-life memories, as well as womb and birth memories, and discusses their relevance to past-life memories. Chapter 12 reports a case in which a child's talking about her life-between-life and past-life memories led to her mother's spiritual awakening, which is arguably an example of what is called a "Spiritually Transformative Experience." Chapter 13 explores the possible effect of past-life memories on facial features, by comparing a group of Burmese who claimed to have past-life memories as Japanese, with Burmese with past-life memories as Burmese. Chapter 14 reports an adult case induced by hypnotic regression, of a woman who recalled a past life as a Nepali village chief. One of the intriguing features of this case is that apparently the woman was able to communicate in the Nepali language, which was totally unknown to her.

Chapter 15 deals with arguments within parapsychology concerning the interpretation of the reincarnation phenomena: the survival hypothesis, which postulates that the human consciousness survives its bodily death (and may attach to a new body), and the living-agent psi hypothesis, which argues that the phenomena are to be accounted for by the psi ability of the people claiming to have past-life memories. Chapter 16 concludes the book by suggesting that having past-life memories is not a rare phenomenon and that it might even be universal.

A Note on Japanese Religions

The majority of Japanese do not follow any religion. In a survey[6] of 1,434 people, 913 (63.7%) of respondents said that they follow no religion. This was followed by Buddhism (32.1%), Shintoism (2.5%), Christianity (1.2%), and other religions (0.5%). These figures exclude cases in which respondents only attend ceremonial occasions such as weddings or funerals. Furthermore, younger generations tend to not follow any religion. The average age of the "no religion" group is 50, while those of Buddhism and Shintoism are 59 and 60.

Reflecting this general tendency, none of the parents of the contemporary Japanese child cases reported in this book follow any particular religion although most of them attend religious ceremonies, especially Buddhist-type funerals. Thus, their religious backgrounds are only mentioned when necessary.

---

[6] Religion IV-ISSP 2018

PART ONE

Historical Cases

1

Reincarnation in the Prehistoric Period and in Classical Literature

Prehistoric Period and Jomon People

There is some archaeological and cultural evidence suggesting that people in Japan of the Jomon period (14,000-300 BCE) had a belief in reincarnation. WATANABE Makoto, an archaeologist, gives four pieces of evidence for this conjecture (Watanabe, 2013).

First, shell mounds, which are believed to have symbolized regeneration or rebirth, were used for burial sites (see also, Saunders, 2017). Second, many of the *dogu* (clay figures/dolls, mostly of women) of the period appear to have been intentionally broken. This practice is interpreted as representing the wish for a new life to be born (reincarnate).

Third, *umegame*, or buried jars, are found under the thresholds of pit dwellings. In some cases, the jars contained children's bones, and are interpreted as representing the people's wish for the soul of a deceased infant to enter the womb of the mother who stepped over the threshold. This interpretation is apparently supported by the image of a woman drawn on the lower part of a large jar excavated at the Todonomiya archaeological site, 2000 BCE (Figure 1-1).

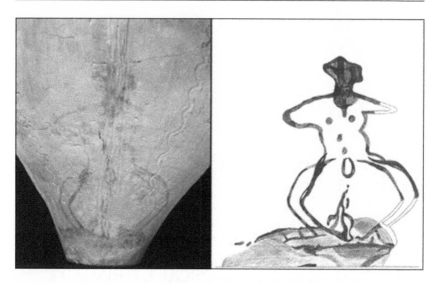

Figure 1-1: An Image of a Woman Drawn on a Pot Found in Todonomiya

The woman is standing with her legs open, with lines depicted under her genitals. WATANABE Makoto interprets the image as depicting the scene of a child's soul about to enter the woman's womb to be reincarnated. The anthropologist TAKEKURA Fumito, however, alternatively suggests that the image is better interpreted as a woman urinating. In a Tlingit custom, a woman wishing for a deceased person to be reborn to her would urinate at a place near the burial, and Takekura suggests that the image on the Jomon jar depicts a similar ancient Japanese custom, (Takekura, 2015, pp. 174-176). Interestingly, the practice of burying the body of infants or stillborn babies under the threshold of a house with the wish that the soul of the deceased would soon return is known in the Tohoku (North-East) region, even in recent years (Moriyama, 2007).

Fourth, there are a number of decorated pots appearing to depict the birth scene of a pregnant woman, such as those from the Tsukimimatsu site (Figure 1-2) and the Tsuganegoshomae site (Figure 1-3).

Figure 1-2: A Pot from Tsukimimatsu

Figure 1-3: A pot from Tsuganegoshomae

Watanabe (2013, pp. 148-150) speculates that the face on top of these pots depict that of a shaman who prays for the return of human spirits.

Ainu People

Based on archaeological, anthropological, and genetic evidence, it has been established that the Ainu in the Hokkaido region are closely related to the Jomon people (Segawa, 2016). It is interesting to note that they (at least up until recently) believed in reincarnation as described in the report of John Batchelor, who was an Anglican English missionary to the Ainu and who spent more than 60 years among their communities in Japan.

> There is an idea among the people that persons are sometimes reborn into this world, especially when God has some particular message to make known to the race. Thus, the old men and women say, "The women ought to be told that people are sometimes reborn into this world. They should therefore carefully examine a baby's ears as soon as it is born, to see whether they have been bored. If they have, it is certain sign that a departed ancestor has come back, and if this be the case, he has returned for some very good purpose." (Batchelor, 1901, p. 237)

In Batchelor's report, no mention of Buddhism is made and the Ainu belief in reincarnation does not seem to be derived from the Buddhist religious concept. Rather, the beliefs may have been cultural remnants from the Jomon period.

In this connection, it is worth mentioning that the Ainu's practice of identifying a "reincarnated" person by a baby's ear is similar in character to some Native Americans' way of identifying a person reborn, as reported in various sources (Mills, 1994, pp. 214-219). Interestingly, this practice appears to have been developed independently due to a lack of common ancestry from Japan to North America.

Figure 1-4: An Ainu man, 19th century

Reincarnation in Classical Literature: The Earliest Examples

The *Kojiki*, dated 712 CE in its preface, is a "collection of mythical, legendary, and quasi-historical material stretching from the appearance of the first gods in the High Heavenly Plain (*Taka-Ama no Hara*) to the reign of the female sovereign later known as Suiko" (592–628 CE) (Lurie, 2016, p. 23) (Figure 1-5).

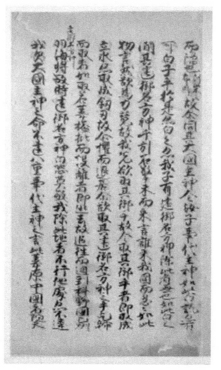

Figure 1-5: A page from the Shinpukuji manuscript
of the *Kojiki* (1371-1372)

In the first book of three, in which the beginning of the world and the workings of various gods are described,[1] the worldview of the ancient Japanese appears to be symbolically expressed: the ultimate life force, which creates everything – including the gods – is constantly working behind the cycle of birth-death-rebirth (Funahashi, 1990). In the *Kojiki*, there is no reference to human or divine reincarnation stories, but it might be the case that the concept of the life cycle depicted in the work implied or reflected the notion of personal reincarnation in these earlier periods.[2]

---

[1] The second book "portrays the origins of rule by legendary sovereigns" (Lurie, 2016, p. 23), and the third book concerns the sovereigns of around the third to seventh centuries.

[2] It is interesting to note that, after his long years of extensive study of Japanese folklore, at the age of over 80 years old, YANAGITA Kunio stated: "I think that the essential part of Japanese beliefs is the notion of rebirth (reincarnation). I

Probably the first written source explicitly concerning reincarnation in the sense that a person is reborn as another person is the *Shomankyo Gisho*, traditionally attributed to Shotoku Taishi, or Prince Shotoku (574-622 CE). This book is a commentary on *Shomankyo*, the annotated Chinese translation of the important Buddhist text, the *Śrīmālādevī Siṃhanāda Sutra*, and is said to have been completed in 611 CE. Because of its character as a Buddhist sutra, the cycle of birth and death is the premised view of the world, and comments are made within that framework. For example, Lady Shoman, the main speaker of the sutra, is considered to have attained her high position of preaching the Buddha's teachings through the good deeds accumulated in her past lives.

Interestingly, in some biographies, Prince Shotoku, arguably the founder of Japanese Buddhism, is portrayed as the reincarnation of the Chinese Tiantai patriarch Huisi (515-577). It seems that the legend was widely accepted by Japanese and Chinese monks,[33] and reincarnation, although it may be confined to prominent figures in this period, appears to have been regarded as a real phenomenon, at least among Buddhist monks.

Apart from commentaries on Buddhist texts or sutras, the earliest reference to the concept of reincarnation in Japanese literary works is found in the *Man'yoshu* (*Collection of Myriad Leaves*) (Figure 1-6). Containing more than 4,000 poems, it is Japan's oldest extant anthology of vernacular verse, believed to have been compiled sometime in the late 8th century CE.

---

think they believed that a person's soul, when the person died young, unless under very specially circumstances, will come back. Ancient Japanese accepted this idea" (Yanagita, 1964, 225-226).

[3] For this legend, see Lin (2018).

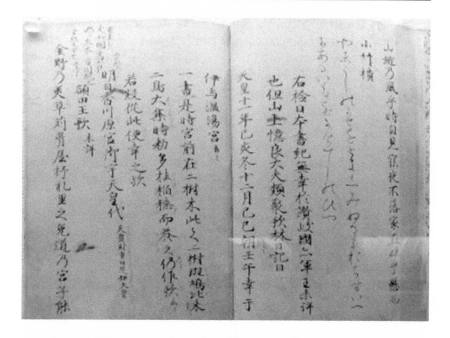

Figure 1-6: Manuscript page of the *Man'yoshu*

The relevant poem is one composed by Otomo Tabito (665-731 CE), Grand Councilor of State, in which he claims that he does not care what happens to him in the next incarnation as long as he can enjoy his present life, alluding to the Buddhist idea of reincarnation or transmigration of the soul.[4]

> If I could but be happy in this life,
> What should I care if in the next
> I became a bird or a worm! (Vol. III, 348)

A possible reference to the concept of reincarnation is found in a poem by Lady Kasa, who fell in love with Otomo Yakamochi (718-785 CE), a statesman of high rank. In the poem, she claims that she could die a thousand times.

> If it were death to love,
> I should have died—

---

[4] The English version is from Nippon Gakujutsu Shinkokai (1965, p. 118).

And died again
One thousand times over. (IV: 603)

From around this time on, the reference to the notion of reincarnation rapidly increases in number.

Reincarnation in Personal Diaries

In the tenth century, diaries written by aristocratic women started to appear and they are excellent sources of information concerning the worldview of elite Japanese people in those days.

In *Kagero Nikki* (*The Diary of Kagero*), written around 974 CE, the author, the mother of Fujiwara no Michitsuna, laments her fate of not being able to have a child by conjecturing that she might have done something wrong in her past life (Totani, 2012, p. 50) (Figure 1-7).

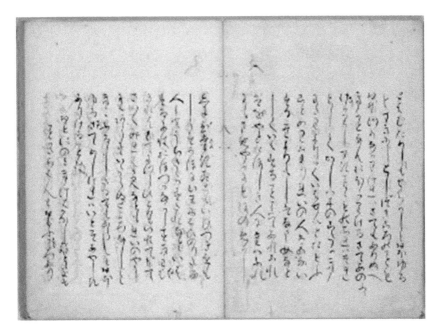

Figure 1-7: Manuscript of *Kagero Nikki*

In *Murasaki Shikibu Nikki* (*The Diary of Lady Murasaki*) (Figure 1-8), Murasaki Shikibu (born between 970-978 CE and lived at least to

1019), the author of the well-known *Tale of Genji* expresses her thought that her miserable situation might be attributed to misconducts she committed in her past life:

> The person of deep-rooted sin cannot succeed even in such a hope [as that]. There happens many a circumstance which makes me think of the [probable] wickedness of my prenatal life and everything makes me sad (Omori and Doi, 1920, p. 137).

Figure 1-8: Murasaki Shikibu Nikki (Picture Scroll, 13th Century)

This worldview is reflected in the *Tale of Genji*. In various places of the story, characters conjecture that their (often lamentable) situations might be due to their past lives.

In *Sarashina Nikki* (*The Diary of Sarashina*) (Figure 1-9) the author, the daughter of Fujiwara no Takasue (her own name is not known), chronicled about 40 years of her life starting from 1020, when she was 13 years old, to 1059. She recorded 11 dreams (Fan, 2013), in one of which she was told by a temple priest that she had been a Buddhist artist in a previous life:

> It would be very difficult even for a saint to dream of his prenatal life. Yet, when I was before the altar of the Kiyomidzu Temple, in a faintly dreamy state of mind which was neither sleeping nor waking, I saw a man who seemed to be the head of the temple. He came out and said to me:

> "You were once a priest of this temple and you were born into a better state by virtue of the many Buddhist images which you carved as a Buddhist artist. The Buddha seventeen feet high which is enthroned in the eastern side of the temple was your work. When you were in the act of covering it with gold foil you died." (Omori and Doi, 1920, pp. 44-45)

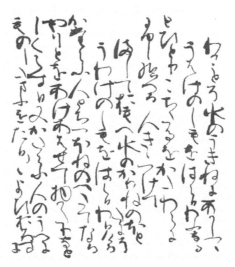

Figure 1-9: Sarashina Nikki (13th Manuscript)

Figure 1-10: Izumi Shikibu by Utagawa Toyokuni (1769-1825)

In *Izumi Shikibu Nikki* (*The Diary of Izumi Shikibu*) (Figure 1-10), the author (b. 978 CE) sends a poem (*waka*) to Prince Atsumichi with whom she fell in love. In the poem, she says that the prince and she had had some relationship in their past lives (Omori and Doi, 1920, p. 153).[5]

It appears that men also shared the similar thought of attributing their ill fate to their possible misconduct in their past lives. For instance, Kamo no Chomei (1153 or 1155-1216), the author of *Hojoki* (*Account of My Ten-Foot-Square Hut*), laments his unsuccessful attempt to become the *Negi* (Shinto priest) of Kamomioya Shrine (Shimogamo Shrine) by creating a poem recorded in the *Shinkokin wakashu* (or *Shinkokinshu*) around 1221.[6]

> Looking at the plant of *Asarum caulescens* [Japanese Wild Ginger], I cannot hold back tears
> What misconducts I made in my past life separated me from the shrine.

In these examples, the writers merely express their thoughts on the notion of reincarnation, appearing to have recourse to the concept in an attempt to come to terms with the harsh realities they are confronted with.

---

[5] The relevant part in the poem is translated as "For on this branch I seem to have exited / From before the birth of the world." This appears to be a mistranslation since the author refers to her relationship with the man in her past life.

[6] For the *Shinkokin Wakashu*, see Atkins (2016, p. 230).

Reincarnation in Setsuwa

Figure 1-11: *Nihon ryoiki* (18th Century Manuscript)

In contrast, ostensibly genuine examples of reincarnation are reported in *setsuwa*, anecdotal stories believed to be true.[7] In *Nihon ryoiki*, "the earliest collection of Buddhist legends in Japan," (Figure 1-11) written by a Buddhist monk named Kyokai in the 8th or 9th century, ten of the more than 100 stories involve "reincarnation cases" which reflect the Buddhist worldview that one's next incarnation is determined by one's karma, the accumulation of merits and demerits, as summarized in Table 1-1, below (Sahara, 1998).

Table 1-1: Reincarnation Stories in *Nihon ryoiki*

No.	Previous Life, Secular or Sacred	Sex	Deed (Good or Bad)	Reborn as
1.	Secular	Male	Bad	Cow
2.	Sacred (Buddhist monk)	Male	Good and Bad	Cow
3.	Secular	Male	Bad	Black cow
4.	Secular	Female	Bad	Red cow

---

[7] In Shirane (2016) the word is translated as "anecdotal literature" and in Kato (1997), it is translated simply as "tales."

37

5.	Secular	Male	Bad	Cow
6.	Sacred (Buddhist monk)	Male	Bad	Venomous snake
7.	Secular	Male	Bad	White monkey
8.	Secular	Female	Bad	Ox-head (*)
9.	Sacred (Buddhist Monk)	Male	Good	Prince
10.	Sacred (Buddhist Monk)	Male	Good	Prince

*A guardian of the underworld.

The latest example is the case of Emperor Saga (786-842 CE). The past-life personalities of seven emperors, including Saga, are reported to be "identified" in various *setsuwa* works (Ito, 2021). Certainly, these narratives, together with others in the work, "served as a source from which his fellow monks might draw 'true stories' to illustrate their popular teaching" (Nakamura, 1973, p. vi).

Not all the reincarnation stories recorded in the work, however, feature the direct karmic retribution of good and bad. For instance, in one story, a man became possessed and eventually killed by the spirit of a fox which he had killed. Then he was reborn as a dog and took revenge on the fox by killing the "new" fox which was the reincarnation of the same fox spirit (Vol. III, 2). In another story, a man's inability to remember a Japanese language character in a scripture is attributed to the claim that the exact character in the copy of the same scripture used by the man's past-life personality was missing because of a burn by a lamp (Vol. I, 18).

Reincarnation in Monogatari (Legends and Folklore)

There are many collections of *monogatari* – incorporating legends, folktales, fiction, and fictionalized accounts of historical events. In some stories, the Buddhist flavor is watered down and the reason for being reborn is not as straightforward as in the cases described above. For instance, in *Hamamatsu Chunagon Monogatari* (11th century) (Figure 1-12), in one of the three reincarnations described in the story, the protagonist's father in the past life, now reborn as a son of the Chinese Emperor, secretly confesses to his mother, saying:

> To tell you the truth, I was a Japanese. The Chunagon [the protagonist who came from Japan because he had heard from a person from China that his father had been reborn there and was now a young boy] was my son in my past life. Since he was my only child, I loved him very much. So, although I wanted to be reborn in the Pure Land, probably I was attracted to this world and was thus reborn (Ikeda [ed.], 2001, p. 49, translated by the author).

Figure 1-12: Hamamatsu Chunagon by Gakutei Harunobu (Edo Period)

In Buddhism, "love for children" can be regarded as an obstacle that prevents people from being spiritually awakened as taught in *The Rhino Sutra*, one of the earliest texts which best reflect the original teachings of Buddha (Nakamura, 1984, p. 18). Here, however, the father's love for his child is depicted in a positive tone.

A more extreme example is found in *Ama Monogatari,* in which the protagonist committed suicide because she wished to be reborn so she could be with the man she loved. This story is recorded in one of the *Nara ehon* (Figure 1-13), illustrated books produced between the late Muromachi and early Edo periods (from 16th to 17th century – although the original stories may go back to the 10th century) (Misumi, 1996). The story is summarized as follows (by the author, after Yokoyama and Matsumoto, 1973, pp. 536-552):

When an officer of Konoefu [Headquarters of the Inner Palace Guards] named Kanemitsu accompanied the traveling Emperor, he fell from his horse and hurt his back. So, he left and went to a hot spring in Naniwa for a cure. In the place where Kanemitsu stayed, *ama* [women who dive into the sea to catch sea food] were called to entertain him. Among them was a beautiful girl aged 15 or 16. He fell in love with the girl, and the girl, who at first was hesitant to accept his love because of the difference in social status, was gradually attracted to him, and they became lovers.

Then, Kanemitsu was ordered to return to the capital, Kyoto, and he reluctantly left the girl. He was unable to forget about the girl and became estranged from his legal wife.

While missing him greatly, the girl found herself to be pregnant. But for fear that the child of the nobleman would not be treated properly because of her social status, the girl decided to commit suicide before the child was born. On the night of August 15th, she threw herself into the sea, wishing to be able to see Kanemitsu again.

On the same night, Kanemitsu had a dream suggesting the death of the girl. In desperation, he sent his attendant to Naniwa to find that the girl had indeed died, which filled him with deep sorrow.

Around that time, the wife of the Great Minister of the Right[8] gave birth to a female child. She grew up to be a beautiful young woman and was chosen to be a wife of the Emperor. She was not happy, however, for she had been wanting to marry Kanemitsu.

On the day of her entry into the Palace, Kanemitsu saw the girl and was immediately fascinated by her. When she saw him, she

---

[8] There were two Great Ministers, the Great Minister of the Right and the Great Minister of the Left.

was so overcome with feelings for him and reluctance to marry the Emperor, that she pretended to be ill, and her marriage to the Emperor was cancelled.

Later Kanemitsu was allowed to marry the girl, and a boy and a girl were born to them. Then, the girl confessed that she was the *ama* of Naniwa reborn, which exalted Kanemitsu. They, then, lived happily ever after.

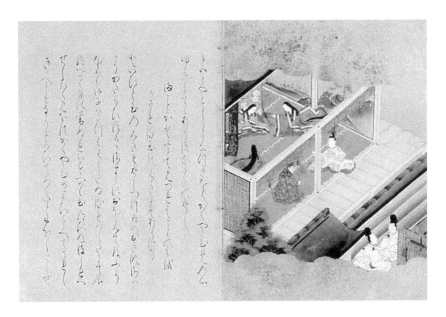

Figure 1-13: A sample of Nara Ehon (1663)

These literary works clearly show that one of the prominent features of the Japanized version of Buddhistic reincarnation is that it transcends the notion of karma (Nitta, 2015). This might be because the concept of reincarnation appears to have existed long before the coming of Buddhism, as we have seen earlier in this chapter.

2

The Case of Katsugoro

~

The case of Katsugoro is the most well-documented classical or historical Japanese case of the reincarnation type. Indeed, such is the importance of the case that it inspired Dr. Ian Stevenson to begin researching the phenomenon. In his seminal award-winning paper (Stevenson, 1960a, b), Stevenson presented seven cases of children with past-life memories to illustrate the phenomenon, and the case of Katsugoro was listed first (Stevenson, 1960a, p. 65). This is Stevenson's summary of the story (with slight modifications by the author):

An eight-year-old Japanese boy named Katsugoro, the second son of Genzo, a farmer in Nakano village, stated that he had been called Tozo in a previous life a few years earlier. He claimed to have been the son of a farmer named Kyubei and his wife Shizu and had lived in a village called Hodokubo. He also stated that Kyubei had died and that his mother had remarried a man named Hanshiro. He said that he, Tozo, had died of smallpox at the age of six, a year after his father had died. He gave details of his burial and described the appearance of his former parents and their house. Katsugoro went to the village he named, and the people he named were found or identified as having lived there. Unaccompanied by any villager, he led the way to his former

43

home in the village, recognized it, and then pointed to a shop and a tree in the vicinity, saying that they had not been there before, which was true. Responsible witnesses made numerous affidavits respecting the facts of this case.

The full version of the story is presented below, following a review of the history of research into the case. Although documented more than 200 years ago, the authenticity of Katsugoro's story is hardly disputable as there are three highly reliable documents corroborating his claimed memories.

The Investigation by a Retired Feudal Lord

In February 1823, Ikeda Kanzan (1767–1833), a retired Daimyo (feudal lord), scholar, and renowned man of literature, visited Katsugoro's house to listen to his story. A couple of months earlier, Ikeda had lost his five-year-old daughter[9] to smallpox (Figure 2-1). Hearing about Katsugoro, he might have felt that the boy's rebirth story would give him some comfort. The visit of the retired Daimyo greatly intimidated Katsugoro, an eight-year-old boy of a farmer, and it made him speechless. Therefore, his grandmother Tsuya narrated the story of Katsugoro to Kanzan, who published Tsuya's narrative in March of that year as *Katsugoro Saisei Zensei Banashi* (*Past-Life Story of Katsugoro*) (Ikeda, n.d.).

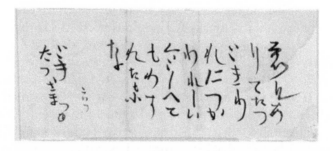

Figure 2-1: Letter from Tsuyuhime to Kanzan, asking him not to drink too much sake.

---

[9] The age is recorded as "6-year-old" using the traditional Japanese system of age reckoning called *kazoedoshi*, and is the equivalent of a 5-year-old in the current Western system.

An Upper Vassal Investigates and Reports

As a result of the article and word of mouth, it was not long before Katsugoro's story became more widely known. An upper vassal (a high-ranking samurai, or *hatamoto*) named Okado Denhachiro, who was in charge of the land where Katsugoro lived, investigated the case and submitted an official report to his superior (Hirata, 2000, pp. 363–367).[10] The report offers detailed information on the two families, Katsugoro's past-life claims, and the origins of the story. The reporter, Okado Denhachiro, explained why he reported the incident: "The story became so well-known that people from various areas came to see Katsugoro. Therefore, I called Genzo (Katsugoro's father) and Katsugoro to investigate. It would not be advisable to suppress the commotion openly, so I secretly report to you what is happening."

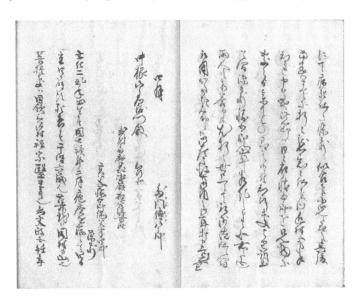

Figure 2-2: The Report by Okado Denhachiro

Okado's report was to his superior, and loyalty to one's superior was highly valued for a samurai. Therefore, the record is a highly reliable source of the story.

---

[10] This document is reproduced in the report written by Hirata Atsutane (Hirata, 2000).

The Investigation by Hirata Atsutane

Hirata Atsutane (1776–1843), a scholar who was regarded as one of the Four Great Men of Kokugaku studies (Japanese philological and philosophical studies), learned about Katsugoro. In April of 1823, he called the boy and his father, Genzo, to his private school and interviewed them. Katsugoro was there on the 22nd, 23rd, and 25th of April, and Genzo only on the 22nd and 25th. Compiling Katsugoro's narratives and adding his scholarly observations, he published *Katsugoro Saisei Kibun* (*Record of the Rebirth Story of Katsugoro*) in June of that year (Hirata, 2000, pp. 359–408) (Figure 2-3).

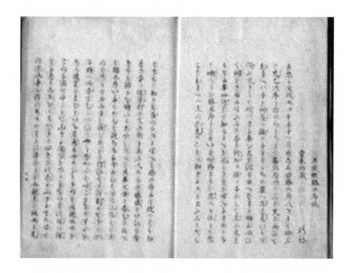

Figure 2-3: Report of Katsugoro by Hirata Atsutane

Hirata Atsutane strived for objectivity and was arguably a precursor of ethnologists and thus, apart from observations that were potentially affected by his philosophy, his record of the story can be judged as reliable.

The Story of Katsugoro Spreads

Other writers and scholars of the period became aware of the story, and at least nine significant works reprinted (sometimes with modifications) or recounted one or more of the three sources of Katsugoro's narrative

(Katsugoro Umarekawari Monogatari Chosadan [A Survey Team of the Reincarnation Story of Katsugoro], 2015, pp. 26–28). Another book, *Chinsetsu Shuki* (*Collection of Strange Stories*), fell into the hands of Lafcadio Hearn via a friend and was translated into English and published in 1897 (Hearn, 1897). The information source for the book Hearn translated was the report by Okado[11] Denhachiro and the book written by Ikeda Kanzan. It was the account in Hearn's book that partially inspired Ian Stevenson to conduct his reincarnation research.

The account provided below, however, is the one written by Hirata Atsutane (Hirata, 2000), for it is considered the most detailed and reliable. It is translated here by the author, with some modifications.

Figure 2-4: Hirata Atsutane

---

[11] The name is transcribed incorrectly as Tamon in the translation.

Report of Katsugoro by Hirata Atsutane

1. How Katsugoro Came to Discuss His Memories

Katsugoro was born on October 10, 1815, in Nakano village [the present-day Higashi Nakano, located about 34 kilometers west of Tokyo], the second son of a farmer named Genzo. His mother was named Sei and his grandmother, Tsuya.

When Katsugoro was eight years old, as he was playing with his elder brother, Otojiro, and elder sister, Fusa, in the rice-field, he said, "Brother, where did you come from before you were born to our house?"

Otojiro said, "I don't know such things."

So, Katsugoro asked his sister the same question. Fusa ridiculed Katsugoro, saying, "How can I know where I had been before I was born? Why do you ask such a stupid question?"

Puzzled by her reaction, Katsugoro asked, "You mean you don't know where you came from before you were born?"

"Well, do you know where you came from before you were born?" asked Fusa.

"I know very well. I used to be a son of Kyubei, named Tozo," replied Katsugoro.

"That's weird. I'll tell father and mother about it," said Fusa.

Katsugoro immediately recanted, crying, "Don't tell father and mother about it!"

"Then, I won't tell. But the next time you behave naughtily and do not listen to me, I will tell," replied Fusa.

After that day, whenever they quarreled, Fusa would threaten Katsugoro, saying, "Ok, I'll tell father and mother," which immediately made him yield to his sister.

Their parents, Genzo and Sei, noticed the exchange and asked Fusa to tell them about the matter. Fusa would not talk, and they worried, thinking that Katsugoro must have been doing something wrong. They asked again and forced Fusa to reveal the truth. Hearing Fusa's story, Genzo, Sei, and the grandmother, Tsuya thought it very strange, and they coerced Katsugoro to talk about his story, until he reluctantly did so:

"I was a child of Kyubei in Hodokubo village, and my mother was named Oshizu.[12] When I was small, Kyubei died, and in his place came a man named Hanshiro. He loved me very much, but I died when I was six. Later I entered mother's womb and was born again."

Since it was such a strange story told by a child, they did not take it seriously at the time.

Now, the mother, Sei, had to suckle her four-year-old daughter,[13] so Katsugoro slept with his grandmother, Tsuya. One night, he asked Tsuya, "Please take me to Hodokubo village, where Hanshiro lives. I want to see my parents there." Thinking it strange, Tsuya did not take Katsugoro's request seriously, but from that night on, Katsugoro made the same request to Tsuya night after night. When Tsuya persuaded him to talk about his past-life memories, Katsugoro recalled what he remembered in detail and asked her never to repeat his story to anyone except his father and mother.

(I heard the following story at Ibukinoya[14] on April 25th. Although I know there is a report written by a person who asked Tsuya for the information,[15] I interviewed Genzo and Katsugoro for thorough information.)

Katsugoro said:

"Until I was around four, I remembered my past-life in detail, but now I have forgotten many things. I didn't have to die, but I died because I didn't take medicine. (He had not known that the cause of his death was smallpox. He said he became aware of it because someone told him so. His date of death was February 4, 1810.)

[12] "O-" in "Oshizu" is an honorific prefix, so "Oshizu" and "Shizu" refer to the same person in this story.

[13] Concerning this part of the story, Hearn (1897, p. 280, note 1) notes: "Children in Japan, among the poorer classes, are not weaned until an age much later than what is considered the proper age for weaning children in Western countries. But 'four years old' in this text may mean considerably less than three by Western reckoning." According to the recent investigation, she should have been two years old at that time (Katsugoro Umarekawari Monogatari Chosadan (ed.), 2015, p. 129–130).

[14] Hirata's private school.

[15] The report by Ikeda Kanzan.

2. Katsugoro's Statements on His Life-Between-Life, Womb, and Birth Memories

"When I expired, I felt no agony. After that, however, it was a little agonizing for a while, and then the agony was completely over. When my body was pushed hard into a coffin, I (my soul) popped out and upwards and stayed aside. When people brought the coffin to a hill to bury it, I was on the white cloth covering it. When they dropped the coffin into a grave hole, it made a loud sound. It resonated in my mind, and I still remember it well. Monks were reading a sutra, but it got me nowhere. I thought they were only thinking about how to steal money, detestable fellows. (His remarks on monks were made when I said to him, "I hear monks are to be respected and that their sutras and prayers will lead you to be born in a beautiful place. Didn't you see heavens or hells?"). So, I came back home and stayed on a desk. I talked to other people, but they made no response. Then, an old man appeared with long white hair, wearing a black kimono, saying, "Come here." I followed, going up to a place which I didn't know where it was. Then, I was in a beautiful field and I played. Flowers were in full bloom, and when I tried to break off a twig, a small crow appeared and threatened me greatly. When I recall this, I still feel scared. ("It must have been the guardian deity of Nakano village," said Genzo, and added "I came up with the idea when Katsugoro said that the bird appeared.")

"As I was playing around, I heard my parents and others talking in my house. I also heard monks reading a sutra, but as I said, I just thought they were detestable. Though I couldn't eat the hot, steaming food they offered, I was able to enjoy the smell. During the ceremony for the dead in July, I went home and saw that dumplings were offered. I was hanging around like this for a while. Then, one day, when we were walking down a street in front of the house (the house of Genzo), the old man pointed to this house and said, "Born to that house." Following his words, I parted from the old man and stayed under a persimmon tree in the yard. After watching the house for three days, I went into it through a window and remained at the wood-burning stove for another three days. I heard my mother talking with my father about leaving alone and going to a faraway place. (Genzo,

Katsugoro's father, said, "It was at the time of new year, about ten months before Katsugoro was born. One night, my wife and I talked and decided that since we were in such difficult circumstances with my mother and two children to support, my wife would go to Edo, the capital city, to work from the coming March. At that time, we didn't reveal our decision to my mother, but in February, we talked about it to her, and in March, she went to Edo. However, when she realized she was pregnant, she took leave and came back. She must have conceived at the time of the new year, and after 10 months, Katsugoro was born. It is unbelievable that Katsugoro talked about this because it was discussed just between us. At the time of the pregnancy and after that, I don't remember any strange things happened.") Then, I went into my mother's belly, I think, but I don't remember very well. However, I do remember that I shifted my position when I thought I was giving pain to her (nearly six years after Tozo's death[16] in Hodokubo village in 1810). I had no trouble when I was born. I had remembered everything until I reached four or five, but then, I began to forget gradually." (The excerpt is a compilation of Katsugoro's words.)

3. How Katsugoro's Past-Life Memories Were Verified

Katsugoro's grandmother, Tsuya, thought his story increasingly strange. When she went to a particular spot where old ladies gathered, she asked, "Do any of you know someone named Kyubei living in Hodokubo village?"

One of them said, "I don't know, but I have some connections in the village. I could ask about that person. But why do you want to know about him?"

Tsuya was unable to remain silent and talked about Katsugoro's story.

Then, on January 7, an old man from Hodokubo village came and said, "I know Hanshiro of Hodokubo village very well. Kyubei was the name of the person who later came to be called as Togoro. However, he died 15 years ago, and nobody knows a living person named Kyubei. The second husband of Kyubei's wife is called Hanshiro. I recently heard about a child who claimed to have

---

[16] Indicating that he was in a disembodied state for nearly six years.

been the child of Kyubei, named Tozo, who died at the age of six and was born in this house. The child's story matches the facts greatly, so they were curious and wanted to know more about it and decided to send me here."

Katsugoro's parents and grandmother told him what Katsugoro had said. Puzzled, they parted, and the old man went back to Hodokubo village. Now many people became aware of Katsugoro's story and came to see Katsugoro. When Katsugoro came out of the house, they teased him, calling him, "Hodokubo kid." Feeling embarrassed, Katsugoro isolated at home. "That's why I said not to tell anybody about my story. Things have become like this because you spoke about it," complained Katsugoro to his parents.

After a while, Katsugoro's desire to return to Hanshiro's home grew stronger and stronger. He even cried all night, begging his grandmother to take him there; but when asked about it in the morning, he said he didn't remember.

These scenes happened every night until the grandmother said to Genzo, "Katsugoro's desire to go to the place where Hanshiro lives is really strong. What he is saying will not be true, but I think I would like to take him to Hodokubo village. It would be inconsiderate for a man to do so, but for an old woman, it will be ok even if ridiculed."

Genzo agreed, and on January 20, Tsuya took Katsugoro to Hodokubo village. (Hodokubo village is about 5.9 kilometers from Nakano village beyond a mountain.)

To Tsuya's queries, "Is this the house? Is that it?" Katsugoro replied, "Not yet. Not yet," and led the way (Figure 2-6).

Then, he announced, "This is the house," and went into the house and Tsuya followed. (Katsugoro had said that Hanshiro's house was the one middle of three houses, which was correct.) Tsuya asked the people living there about the house owner's name. "Hanshiro" was the answer. When asked the name of his wife, "Shizu [Oshizu]" was the answer. Hanshiro and Shizu, although they had heard the story from the villager who visited Nakano village before, hearing it directly from Tsuya made them feel even more strange and sad. They both shed tears. They held Katsugoro, gave a long look at his face, and said repeatedly:

"You do look like Tozo when he was six."

While being held, Katsugoro pointed to the roof of a tobacco shop opposite Hanshiro's house, saying, "That roof was not there before. That tree was not there, either." All this was true, which deeply surprised everyone even more.

Hanshiro's relatives came to see Katsugoro, and one of them was the nursemaid of the younger sister of Kyubei. She said, "This boy even looks like Kyubei" and broke down in tears.

Katsugoro and Tsuya returned to Nakano village on that day, but after that Katsugoro repeatedly said, "I want to go back to Hodokubo village. I want to visit the grave of Kyubei." Genzo turned a deaf ear to Katsugoro's begging, but on January 27, Hanshiro came to Genzo's house to greet him. He asked Katsugoro if he would like to go to Hodokubo village, which delighted Katsugoro, as he wanted to visit the grave of Kyubei. He went to Hodokubo village with Hanshiro and came back in the evening. Then, Katsugoro asked Genzo to take him to Hodokubo village and ask Hanshiro and Shizu to become relatives.

Figure 2-5: Path along Which Katsugoro took Tsuya to Hodokubo village. (now part of Chuo University Campus)

"I agreed, and while I was thinking about when to do so, I was called by the officer," said Genzo.

4. Katsugoro's Attitude Toward Death

Hirata's account continues with the description of Katsugoro's remarkable attitude toward death. He cites words of his father, Genzo (Hirata, 2000, pp. 378–379):

> Since he was born, Katsugoro has not been afraid of ghosts and evil spirits. I took care of a man named Genhichi, who was mentally ill, building a hut for him to live in. While approaching death, his look became horrible. Katsugoro's siblings would not go near the hut. But Katsugoro said, "He is dying. I feel sorry for him. Please prepare enough medicine and food for him. I will bring them to him anytime," and did so even late at night. After he died, his siblings were afraid to even go to the toilet [in Japan, historically, the toilets were in outhouses], but Katsugoro said, "Why are you afraid of the dead?" and showed no sign of fear.
>
> He also said, "I'm not afraid of my death, either." When asked why, he replied, "I realized I was dead because other people said so. At the time of my death, I didn't see my body, and I didn't think I was dead. The moment of death was not as agonizing as it may have appeared to others. After I died, I didn't become hungry, didn't feel hot nor cold. It was not very dark, even at night. No matter how long I walked, I didn't get tired. When I was with the old man, I was afraid of nothing. People say I was born after six years, but I felt it was just a short time." He also said, "Mitake-sama [the name of a god residing on mountains] told me that 'You don't have to be afraid of death.'" I asked, "Where did you see Mitake-sama?" but he didn't answer the question.

The difference in attitude toward death and the dead between Katsugoro and his siblings is remarkable. Hirata Atsutane described Katsugoro's personality as follows: "He doesn't look mature at all and likes boisterous play. He looks more clever than other peasant children. As I heard from Mr. Tani [a steward of Okado Denpachiro, whom Hirata first visited to meet Katsugoro], he likes courageous deeds and showed desire to be a samurai" (Hirata, 2000, p. 376).

Another description of Katsugoro's character is made in an essay titled *Kassiyawa (Stories Started to Be Written on the Night of the Day of the Wooden Rat)*, written by a feudal lord named Matsura Seizan (1760–1841) (Figure 2-6). When Katsugoro visited a house near his, he sent a man to see Katsugoro. According to the man: "He looked sullen. His red hair was close-cropped. He has a long face, is rather slender, and dark-skinned. But he was decent-looking and looked like a clever, smart kid." (Matsura, 1977, p. 178).

Figure 2-6: Matsura Seizan [Kiyoshi] (1760-1841)

Katsugoro's Later Life

In Hino City, where Hodokubo village was located, the story of Katsugoro has remained well-known. In 2006, a research group called Katsugoro Umarekawari Monogatari Tankyu Chosadan investigated Katsugoro's narrative for the Hino City Museum of Local History. The number of researchers was 32, but grew to 62 by the time their investigative report was published in 2015. Among the group members were Katsugoro's and Tozo's living relatives.

Figure 2-7: Report by Katsugoro Umarekawari Monogatari Chosadan
(A Survey Team of the Reincarnation Story of Katsugoro)

The report features some remarkable discoveries, one of which is "A Note of Reborn Katsugoro," which records Oshizu's (Shizu's) words (p. 125). Although who wrote the note is not known, it appears to be a direct transcription of Oshizu's words. It shows how strongly Katsugoro was attracted to his former parents, and how the two families came to be in a close relation because of the incident. For instance, according to the note, when Katsugoro and Genzo were investigated by the officer, they were given some souvenirs and money. When Katsugoro came to Hodokubo village at night, he slept with Oshizu and Hanshiro, held in their embrace as if he were their own child;[17] when Hanshiro went to Nakano village, they treated him to sake.

Other sources reveal that in 1825 when Katsugoro was 11, he became a student of Hirata Atsutane and studied for at least a year. He married twice, adopted a child in 1854, and died in 1869 at the age of 55. Katsugoro appeared to have led an ordinary life as a village farmer where he was born (Katsugoro Umarekawari Monogatari Tankyu Chosadan, 2015, pp. 31–32).

---

[17] It is not uncommon for a Japanese child to sleep with their parents until he/she reaches puberty.

The Cultural Background of the Story of Katsugoro

One might assume that Katsugoro's story was heavily influenced by Japan's cultural background at that time, in which all citizens were affiliated with nearby Buddhist temples, which in turn, were controlled by the central government. The investigator Hirata Atsutane was well aware of the possibility of religious influences on Katsugoro's story and interviewed Genzo, Katsugoro's father, about this. When reading the interview, one must remember that Japanese Buddhism is unique. When it was introduced to Japan in the 6th century, Buddhism became syncretized with the Japanese indigenous religion of Shinto, and absorbed Shinto gods – especially guardian deities of particular places. The land of one's birth was also worshiped. Therefore, although many Japanese were familiar with the notion of reincarnation, they knew it only as a Buddhist dogma and were more sympathetic with the animistic Shinto views of life and death, in which the deceased is merged with their ancestor spirits and may reside in a shrine or household Shinto altar.

Reflecting on this general cultural background, Genzo said that he was not an especially pious believer in Buddhism. Since childhood, however, he donated money to beggars or Buddhist practitioners when they came to his home. In contrast, although his family members worshiped the Shinto guardian god at the shrine only on special days, he did so every day. When he had a chance, he prayed at Buddhist temples, but only with the goal of having a peaceful day. While many people around him joined a Buddhist group that met regularly to pray to the Buddha, he kept a distance. When the story of Katsugoro became widely known, Buddhist monks from various places came and asked Genzo to let them have Katsugoro as a disciple. Some of them even warned that if he made such a special child as Katsugoro a farmer, he would be punished by the Buddha. Genzo declined their offer, stating that Katsugoro hated Buddhist monks, that Genzo himself did not like them either, and if Katsugoro was not intended to become a farmer, he would not have been born to him.

Thus, it is highly unlikely that Katsugoro's statements were fabricated by the influence of household beliefs (Hirata, 1823, pp. 379–380).[18]

---

[18] In the report by Ikeda Kanzan, Katsugoro was described as showing respect to Buddhist monks. Hirata Atsutane asked Genzo whether Ikeda's statement was correct, to which Genzo said, "What I heard from Katsugoro was quite

Notable Features of Katsugoro's Statements

Katsugoro's apparently evidential memories are outlined below. The significant point is that Katsugoro had memories of all four stages of the reincarnation life cycle (see Figure 0-1 in the Introduction), as a person experiencing all events along the flow of time. This is consistent with the notion that consciousness survives bodily death and continues to reincarnate into successive new bodies.

I. The Verified Past-Life Memories of Katsugoro

(1) He lived in Hodokubo village.
(2) His name was Tozo.
(3) His stepfather's name was Hanshiro.
(4) His mother's name was Oshizu.
(5) His father's name was Kyubei.
(6) Kyubei died while Tozo was young.
(7) Oshizu remarried Hanshiro.
(8) He died when he was six.
(9) He identified the house where he said he had lived.
(10) He pointed out that the roof of the tobacco house had not been there before.
(11) He pointed out that the tree had not been there before.

Additionally, according to KOMIYA Yutaka, a modern descendent of Tozo's family, in the area where he lives (the former Hodokubo village), the following story has been handed down by word of mouth from generation to generation: When Katsugoro came to his former house where he used to live as Tozo, he recalled that he had hidden a knife in the mulberry field near the house. When people went to the field with Katsugoro, there was a rusted knife at a stump of a mulberry tree. The same story is also recorded by a local historian named SHIMODA Kyuichi (Katsugoro Umarekawari Monogatari Tankyu Chosadan, 2015, pp. 38–40). Although not recorded in the above-mentioned documents, this story can be regarded as showing another verified element in Katsugoro's statements.

---

contrary. I wonder if he might have said that to his grandmother, but I haven't heard such remarks from him" (Hirata, 1823, pp. 379–380.) It might be the case that Katsugoro's grandmother inserted her own view when she talked about his story to Ikeda Kanzan.

II. The Verified Life-Between-Life Memory of Katsugoro

(1) Genzo and Oshizu talked about the idea of Oshizu going somewhere (Tokyo, to work).

III. The Unverified Life-Between-Life Memories of Katsugoro

(1) At the time of death, he felt no agony. Later, he felt a little agony but only for a while.
(2) His body was pushed into the coffin.
(3) He left the body when it was pushed into the coffin.
(4) The coffin was brought to a hill for burial.
(5) The coffin was covered with a white cloth.
(6) He was atop the coffin.
(7) The coffin dropped into the grave.
(8) The coffin made a loud sound.
(9) Monks were reading a sutra.
(10) He came back home and stayed on a desk.
(11) He spoke to other people, but they could not hear him.
(12) He met an old man with long white hair wearing a black kimono, who called him.
(13) He went to a beautiful place with the man.
(14) There, flowers were in full bloom.
(15) When he tried to break off a twig, a small crow appeared and threatened him.
(16) He heard his previous parents and others talking in the former house.
(17) He heard monks reading a sutra.
(18) There were offerings, some of which were hot.
(19) He enjoyed the smell of the hot offerings.
(20) He went home during the ceremony for the dead in July.
(21) He saw an offering of dumplings.
(22) When he was walking down a street, the old man pointed to the house and said, "Born to that house."
(23) He parted from the old man and stayed under a persimmon tree in the yard.
(24) He watched the house for three days.
(25) He went into the house through a window.
(26) He stayed at the wood-burning stove for three days.
(27) He went into his mother's womb.

Although categorized as "unverified," since no specific descriptions are made in the report(s), items (2)-(5), (7)-(9), (16)-(18), (20), and (21) *could* have been verified had they been investigated.

IV. The Unverified Womb Memory of Katsugoro

(1) In the womb, he shifted his position when he thought he was hurting his mother.

V. The Unverified Birth Memory of Katsugoro

(1) He had no trouble when he was born.
   (This item could have been verified if Katsugoro's mother had been interviewed.)

From an evidential perspective, the verified elements are obviously the most important. However, we can infer that since Katsugoro had such strong memories that he was able to make correct statements regarding his past life (and perhaps regarding his life-between-life state), the other statements might also be correct. Although no definitive justification for such inference can be made, we may slightly strengthen its validity by emphasizing the facts that (i) there are a large number of children with unverifiable life-between-life memories similar to those of Katsugoro (such as meeting a god-like entity, going to an unearthly place, and choosing parents), and that (ii) there are many children with verified womb and birth memories. We will return to these issues in Chapter 11.

Furthermore, Katsugoro not only talked about his memories, but he showed strong emotions toward the people he claimed were past-life relatives. Those people, in turn, accepted Katsugoro as the reincarnation of their relative. He also made some personal recognitions related to his past-life.

VI. Katsugoro's Emotional Features

(1) He showed a strong desire to return to his previous home.
(2) He showed strong affection to his previous mother, father, and stepfather.

(3) He behaved in ways that were appropriate to the affection he showed:
(i) he had a strong desire to visit his father's grave and did so, and (ii)
he slept with his previous parents, being embraced by his previous
mother.

VII. Katsugoro's Recognitions

(1) He recognized the house of Tozo.
(2) He apparently recognized his past-life mother and stepfather.
(3) He recognized the change in the tobacco shop roof.
(4) He recognized the presence of the new tree.

VIII. The Reactions of Katsugoro's Past-Life Relatives

(1) Tozo's parents accepted Katsugoro as reborn Tozo.
(2) The nursemaid of the younger sister of Kyubei accepted Katsugoro
as reborn Tozo.

IX. Katsugoro's Attitude Toward a Dying Person and Death

Katsugoro's attitude toward death and dying were remarkable for a
young boy. Specifically:

(1) He showed compassion for a dying man, of whom his siblings were
afraid.
(2) He was not afraid of death or ghosts.

The features of Katsugoro's story, whose authenticity is hard to
deny, appear to be best explained by the hypothesis that Katsugoro's
consciousness survived death in his past-life as Tozo. He remained in
the life-between-life state for some time and was reborn as Katsugoro.

3

Reincarnation Research
After Katsugoro

~

In later periods, numerous reincarnation stories were reported around the country, though none were as thoroughly investigated as the case of Katsugoro. Nevertheless, before exploring some recent cases in depth, it will be useful to review the rather unsatisfactory state of reincarnation studies between the 19th century and the present.

Reports by Folklorists

In his famous *Tono Monogatari*, a collection of stories gathered in the city of Tono in Iwate Prefecture in the Tohoku (North-Eastern) region, YANAGITA Kunio (1875-1962) (Figure 3-1), arguably the founder of modern Japanese folklore studies, reported that in the area, reincarnation was regarded as a common phenomenon:

> It is said that reincarnation often takes place. A child born in the village of Kamigo in the previous year would not open his clenching fist for a long time. When he was forced to open it by a family member, a piece of paper was found, on which it

was written that the child was a reincarnation of the old man Taro of Tajiri in Kitagami. When family members of the old man heard of the story, they became happy, saying that he had been reborn less than a year after his death. It is also said that willow and other trees that grow on the earth of the graveyard without being planted are signs that the person there was already reborn somewhere (Yanagita, 2013, pp. 193-194).

Figure 3-1: Yanagita Kunio (1875-1962)

In the essay titled "Raisekan (The View on Afterlife)," which Yanagita wrote in his later years when he was 82 or 83 years old, he even said: "I think the most important aspects of the Japanese faith is the concept of rebirth" and cited the following example (Yanagita, 1964, pp. 225-226):

There was a boy named MATSUOKA Benkichi, who was a younger brother of my grandmother. He died when, I believe, he was about six years old. They say he was a smart kid, learning how to read and write letters at a very young age, and that he had big, round eyes. When my father was born, everybody around him said: "You are Benkichi reborn." So it seems that the idea of himself as reborn Benkichi was always in his mind and that he was working not just as himself, but as Benkichi.

Inspired by Yanagita's works on folklore, MATSUTANI Miyoko (1926-2015), a picture book author, collected a great number of folktales in various categories from all over Japan (Figure 3-2). Thirty-one of them are reincarnation stories collected from 16 different regions.[19] Many of these stories describe only the outlines of the events, but some of them are relatively rich in details. One such example is based on the personal experiences of a woman named Kayoko:

Figure 3-2: Matsutani Miyoko (1926-2015)

It was around 1970. I was three or four years old by the traditional Japanese reckoning, so actually two or three years old, around the time when I had become able to speak coherently. One day, I was brought to my maternal grandparents' house to be taken care of while my parents were out. Although I was a quiet child who didn't talk or laugh much, at that time I began to talk incessantly, saying "I am Masako. This is not my house. My house is such and such," and continued talking about Masako's life. My maternal grandparents were at a loss about how to respond. When my parents came to take me back home, my

---

[19] Aichi (1); Aomori (1); Chiba (1); Gunma (3); Fukui (3); Hyogo (1); Ishikawa (1); Kanagawa (2); Nagano (1); Niigata (3); Okayama (1); Osaka (1); Shiga (3); Tokyo (6); Toyama (1); and Yamanashi (2)

mother was just perplexed at my words. But my father changed his countenance and said: "Masako was my elder sister." Masako had become sick and died when she was five years old (by the traditional Japanese reckoning) .... Then, for about a month, I kept on saying: "I'm Masako" and the statements I made about Masako were all correct.... (Matsutani, 2003, pp. 525-527).

Another example involves the so-called "experimental birthmark," a practice observed in Asia in which the body of a dying or deceased person is marked with soot or other substances in the belief that, when the person is reborn, he or she will bear a birthmark and be identified as the person reborn.[20]

> A younger brother of my husband was drowned when he was nine years old. His father (the grandfather-in-law of the reporter), who grieved over his death, smeared the sole of the left foot of his body with soot, and buried him, saying: "Be reborn." We got married and the baby boy was born in 1975. He had a small mole on the sole of his left foot. It kept growing and is now seven or eight centimeters. The elder sisters of my husband are saying: "Since he has a birthmark on the same spot as our father marked, he must be the deceased younger brother reborn." (Matsutani, 2003, p. 516).

Unfortunately, the claims were not investigated by a researcher and therefore this cannot be considered a verified reincarnation case.

Reports by Psychics and Therapists

There are numerous claims of reincarnation cases made by psychics and therapists, based on their counseling sessions. Among them are:

---

[20] Dalai Lama (1962, p. 31) writes that, when his younger brother died at the age of two, his parents made a small mark on his body, and that when another boy was born, he had a birthmark on the spot where the butter had been smeared on the body of his deceased younger brother. Stevenson (1997) and Tucker & Keil (2013) investigated numerous such cases. I have also investigated a Japanese case and reported it in Ohkado (2017).

- EHARA Hiroyuki, the founder of the Spiritualism Research Center and one of the best-known psychics in Japan, who appeared countless times on television and made many past-life readings of popular entertainers.[21]
- ASANO Makoto, the founder of Asano Research Institute, who published five books reporting representative cases of his psychic past-life, or more precisely, Akashic readings like those by Edgar Cayce, the total of which exceeds 15,000 (Asano, 2002; 2003; 2004; 2005; 2006).
- KIRIYAMA Seiyu, the founder of Agon Shu (Agama School), a new Buddhist religion. He conducted numerous past-life readings through psychic abilities gained through his Buddhist training, and published some cases based on his readings in his book (Kiriyama, 1993).
- OCHI Keiko, a psychiatrist and a psychic, who reported numerous cases based on the psychic readings of her patients' past lives (Ochi, 1999).
- OTSUKI Maiko, a Weiss Institute-trained hypnotherapist, who has been conducting past-life regression therapies for more than 20 years and published representative case reports in her books (Otsuki, 2004; 2007).
- MOTOYAMA Hiroshi, a parapsychologist, honorary priest of Tamamitsu Shrine, and founder of both the International Association for Religion and Parapsychology (IARP) and the California Institute for Human Science (CIHS). He focused on cultivating one's spirituality through meditation, yoga, and other eastern practices, and scientifically researching their mechanisms.

From the numerous cases reported by the above-mentioned writers, I introduce a case reported by MOTOYAMA Hiroshi, since it is described through a researcher's eyes, an attempt is made at verification, and it was published in an academic journal (Matsushita, 1984). The primary focus of the story, however, is on eliminating the client's problems.

---

[21] He published his view on past-life readings in Ehara (2010).

The Case of K. M.

K. M., a 21-year-old female, fell into a state of depression, and her mother, who was an avid believer of the teachings of Tamamitsu Shrine for 40 years, came to Motoyama for his advice as a psychic. In the meditative state, Motoyama obtained the following information.

(1) K. M. was a reincarnation of a daughter of a samurai named Nakanose Hachiroemon.
(2) The samurai was a chief vassal of Kato Kiyomasa (1562-1611), a renowned *daimyo* (feudal lord) of Higo (present Kumamoto prefecture) of the Azuchi-Momoyama and early Edo periods.
(3) He later became a vassal of a *daimyo* of Suwa (present Nagano prefecture) and died there.
(4) His grave is in a temple named Kokokuji in Suwa (Nagano).
(5) K. M. and her elder brother were lovers in their past lives.
(6) K. M. was not allowed to marry the man (her brother's past-life personality) and died young in grief.
(7) K. M. fell into depression because her past-life personality had suffered from depression at around the same age.

The investigations conducted by K. M. and her mother revealed that items (2)-(4) were correct, and that the samurai had a daughter, consistent with item (1).

Through the process of investigation and through prayers, K. M. gradually and eventually recovered completely from her depression.

It should be noted that the verified part of the case is limited to the existence of the samurai and his daughter. The identification of K. M. and the daughter of the samurai was made through Yamamoto's psychic abilities. K. M. herself did not recall any memories related to the daughter. Motoyama himself admits that the identification of the soul (consciousness) in two different lives cannot be verified in scientific terms nor through human senses (Motoyama, 1987, pp. 9-10).

Some more examples, for which no verification attempt was made, are given below.

Ehara's Reading

EHARA Hiroyuki performed numerous past-life readings on a TV show and reported some of them in his book (Ehara, 2010). For instance, Ehara writes that ABE Natsumi, a Japanese singer and a member of the Japanese girl group Morning Musume, had lived in East Asia, possibly Vietnam, had lost her parents, had been taken to an orphanage, and had had a lonely girlhood. In her past life, she was with the other members of her musical group. In their hard circumstances, singing had been the only thing they had enjoyed (Ehara, 2010, pp. 119-120).

In the TV show, the singer appeared to have been convinced by Ehara's reading which she believed accounted for her personal traits such as being unusually protective of her family members, which she believed was due to her having been an orphan in her past life. There is, however, nothing independently verifiable about the case, and therefore nothing evidential.

Asano's Reading

ASANO Makoto does not give specific information about his clients' past lives, providing only what is relevant to their present life. Here is a sample of his reading of a 23-year-old male student (2006, pp. 205-207).

> You have enjoyed working directly communicating with people. You have always had purpose in life and had rewarding works. Your mission in life is to give hope and guidance to other people. Bringing courage and hope to others, encouraging and leveraging them to live life creatively with confidence and conviction, these are what you can do.
>
> From your past life, you have been involved in many aspects of human education and guidance, or management and human resources. You have paid attention to the dramas woven by human beings and society as a place where these dramas take place, and have been interested in how to be a social human being. In past lives, you have been particularly involved in education, politics, and management. You also studied linguistics and at times was interested in speeches, editorials, and oratory. At times you were attracted to charismatic individuals who lead people.

You yourself were a single-minded, disciplined, and dedicated person. You were serious and noble, offering support, encouragement, and pep talks to others when you thought or felt something for them. You were willing to work with others, and you used your energy to get along with others and to pursue the same goals with others with the same slogan.

You had a strong will to live. You also aspired to be a painter and at times made highly artistic household utensils and furnishings. You were also quite attracted to singing and reciting poetry. You were also a man of conviction. For you, believing was to put what you believed into action. You were honest, down-to-earth, straightforward, and sometimes naive. You were also open, unable to hide anything, and at times had a strong sense of justice. This sometimes led you to become angry and short-tempered. On the other hand, you were also a generous, long-tempered, hard-working person who set big goals.

You can do this by paying attention to the human way of life, doing what you believe in, and being an example of how to live as a human being.

Although the client appeared to have been impressed by the reading, since the reading consists only of generalizations with no specific information given, we cannot determine its authenticity.

Kiriyama's Reading

A 46-year-old woman came to KIRIYAMA Seiyu for help. Her daughter, who was a second-year high school student, had become so depressed that she was unable to go to school, and even stopped the piano lesson she had been enjoying since she was five years old. She made a couple of suicide attempts. Then she resumed playing the piano, but again stopped after two or three days. Similarly, she started to study hard until midnight for a couple of days, but then seemed to withdraw into a shell. Her mother took her to a mental hospital, but the doctor was unable to find the cause of her condition.

Kiriyama immediately realized that the girl had been a woman living in East Asia, possibly the Philippines, and asked the mother whether the girl and the family had any connection with the country. The mother said that her daughter started to experience her emotional problems after returning from Manila, which they had visited together on a sightseeing trip. She also said that her father (the girl's grandfather) had been a branch manager of a trading company in Manila. He told her that there had been a Japanese employee of the company who had fallen in love with a Filipino and committed suicide with him since they had not been allowed to marry. Kiriyama performed a religious ritual to comfort the girl's spirit (and that of the Filipino), and the girl became well again, returning to school and to her piano lessons. (Kiriyama, 1993, pp. 94-118)

Ochi's Reading

OCHI Keiko uses her psychic ability to identify the cause of her clients' complaints. She often claims that it goes back to past lives. For instance, in the case of a female civil servant in her 30s, who had a back problem, Ochi saw a vision of the woman's past life, in which she was a shaman's apprentice. One day, she got into a fight with a rival shaman apprentice and inadvertently put out the sacred fire when she fell backwards upon it. For her, a shaman's apprentice, putting out the sacred fire was an irreparable mistake, and the guilt from that time had stayed with her until now. When Ochi healed and released the woman's sense of guilt, the pain in her back was greatly lessened. (Ochi, 1999, pp. 55-56).[22]

Regression Therapy Report by Otsuki

OTSUKI Maiko reports a number of cases in which her clients' mental problems were solved or alleviated. For instance, a woman fell in love only with married men, even though she had no intention of choosing them, and kept on suffering the pain of infidelity. The past life she recalled was in Ooku, the women's quarters of the Edo castle where the reigning shogun resided. The place incorporated a system of side-wives to keep the line of succession alive, and there were fierce conflicts among them over the shogun. In the woman's past life, she was one of the side wives, and was loved and cherished very much by the shogun. She was even pregnant with his child. However, she fell victim to

---

[22] Ochi reported another apparently verified past life of the same woman, which, although intriguing, I do not cite here because it is exceptionally complicated.

insidious bullying by some of the other side-wives and was eventually poisoned to death. After her death, the side-wife who poisoned her was chosen by the shogun as the legal wife and came to have immense power in Ooku. The woman's spirit stayed at Ooku after her death, and she witnessed these events with fury.

Thanks to this recall, the woman came to realize her subconscious anger and how it made her choose married men – repeating the pattern of being loved by a man, but provoking the anger of his wife, and eventually being betrayed by the man (Ohtsuki, 2004, pp. 106-108).

It is clear by this brief chapter that despite an encouraging beginning with Hirata's study of the case of Katsugoro, until recently, reincarnation studies in Japan have been largely unscientific or rudimentary – limited to unverified folktales and claims of psychics. It should also be mentioned that the cases reported by psychics involve adults. This is in contrast to the many cases of children who claim to have past-life memories, similar to Katsugoro. Let us now turn to some of these cases which I have personally investigated.

PART TWO

Contemporary Cases Of The Reincarnation Type

4

1 Used to Peel Garlic:
The Case of Como

~

D espite Katsugoro's case inspiring Ian Stevenson to launch his
investigations into children who remember past lives, there was
no report of Japanese children with past-life memories until
2011.[23] I filled this gap initially by investigating two Japanese cases, and
reporting on them in both English and Japanese. This chapter presents
the first, that of Tomo, who was born in January 2000. I interviewed
him twice in the summer of 2010, first with his mother, and again with
his father. He was a very intelligent boy, speaking energetically about
various topics. However, at the time of the interviews, he had lost
most of his past-life memories. The descriptions of his statements and
behaviors are therefore largely based on his parents' memories, much of
which were supported by their documentary records, including diaries
and other memos by his mother, fax exchanges between his mother
and councilors, pictures and video clips.

---

[23] One Japanese case, that of OGURA Susumu, is reported in Stevenson's
monumental book on birthmarks and birth defects (Stevenson, 1997, pp. 519–
520). However, the only feature suggesting reincarnation was his birthmark. It
appeared to correspond to the incision spot behind the ear where his deceased
brother had an operation called mastoidectomy.

I Used to Peel Garlic

"I want to peel garlic," said Tomo, at the age of 3 years and 11 months.

His mother, who was in bed with Tomo as she was putting him to sleep, was puzzled and asked without understanding what her son meant:

"Why do you want to do that?"

Tomo's answer puzzled her even more. "I did this before I came to be called 'Tomo.'"

"What? What do you mean?" asked the mother. Tomo's answer did not make any sense to her.

"I was a child of a restaurant owner in the UK before I came to be called 'Tomo.'"

"When was he born?" she asked.

"He was born on August 9th, 1988. I was called 'Geiris.'[24] I lived in a seven-story building."

If Tomo had been the "Geiris," but not anymore, where did Geiris go? The mother asked, "Where is the former 'Tomo' [referring to "Geiris"]?"

Tomo gave another surprising reply: "He had a high fever of 45 Celsius [113 F] and died."

Tomo's mother had no knowledge of the existence of children claiming to have past-life memories, but since Tomo insisted on peeling garlic, the next day she bought heads of garlic and gave them to Tomo. To her surprise, the little boy very skillfully peeled the garlic (Figure 4-1).

Figure 4-1: Garlic peeled by Tomo.

---

[24] In the diary of the mother, the name is written as "ge-i-ri-i-su" in Japanese letters. The mother, who does not speak English, naturally chose to write it down in Japanese, and if Tomo had pronounced the word in English (or in English-like manner), the transcript might not be very reliable. It could perhaps have been "James." Other names such as "Gary" or "Gareth" suggested by Gregory Shushan (personal communication) are also possible.

Surprisingly, he peeled the garlic with his left hand (Figure 4-2) despite the fact that he is right-handed. He became left-handed only when he peeled garlic.

Figure 4-2: Tomo peeling garlic with his left hand.

Tomo's mother recorded in her diary the conversation they had on that day as follows:

Mother: "Tomo, have you ever peeled garlic?"

Tomo:"Yes. I have done this when I was 'former Tomo.'"

Mother: "Who is 'former Tomo?'"

Tomo:"Tomo who was born on August 9th."

At around the same time, there were some further impressive incidents. Tomo, who had never taken a pill, said to the mother, "'British Tomo' was taking a pill, called EMD."

"What pill?" asked the mother, to which he replied:

"Yellow and round."[25]

Tomo also said: "When my 'British mother' read a picture book before I went to bed, she said, 'This much for today,' and did this [touching his forehead with a finger]."

The mother thought that Tomo was talking about a good-night kiss, which Japanese mothers rarely do.

One day when they went to a do-it-yourself store, they saw a globe. Tomo pointed to the upper region of the UK and said, "Tomo lived around here." After going home, his mother showed Tomo a map of the UK and asked where he had been. Tomo pointed to around Edinburgh

---

[25] There is a pharmaceutical company named EMD Serono. However, it appears to only produce injectable medications, not pills.

and said, "I lived in 'Edinbia.'" This is a fairly close approximation of the 4-syllable Scottish pronunciation of the word, "*Ed-in-bur-ruh.*"

Earlier Events Apparently Related to Tomo's British Life

Before he began talking about his past life, Tomo had perplexed his mother a number of times. When he was 11 months old, he was very attracted by the roman letters he saw on TV commercials such as "AJINOMOTO" and "TOYOTA." Before he learned any Japanese characters, he knew some roman letters. When he was two years and nine or ten months, he signed his name as "tomo" using roman letters (Figures 4-3 and 4-4).

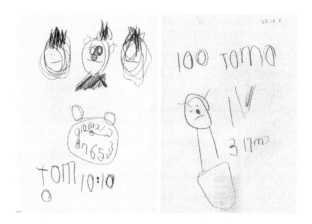

Figures 4-3 and 4-4: Pictures drawn by Tomo.

At around the same time, when Tomo's mother was watching a TV drama, the song by the American duo the Carpenters, "Top of the World" was playing. To the best of her knowledge, Tomo had never heard the song, but he was able to sing along, which greatly surprised her.

Tomo soon started to talk about his past-life memories more intensively, as recorded in the mother's diary (Table 4-1).

Table 4-1: Statements and Behaviors
Tomo Made Between 4 and 5 Years Old

	Age	Statement and/or Behavior
(1)	4 years old	"I had a dog called John. He had yellow or golden hair with a long nose. His ears were on the upper head. We slept in the same room."
(2)	4 years old	"British Tomo went to a school, not a kindergarten [as Tomo does now]. My teacher was a male. I had a friend called 'Suimenli.'"
(3)	4 years old	When he talked about the dog, John, Tomo started to say "John, John, very my John" (*sic*) in English. He kept on saying this for a long time. (He remembered this phrase even when I met him at the age of 10)
(4)	4 years old	When he saw salmon eggs at the dinner table, he said "Gungu!" This might have implied "gungo peas" (or "pigeon peas") which he might have been familiar with if he was a child of a restaurant owner.
(5)	4 years old (cf. (22))	"When 'British Tomo' died between 24th and 25th of October 1997, British mother looked troubled. She was saying 'Now there are only five of us.'" Surprised, Tomo's present mother asked him, "What? Did you see that?" He replied, "Yes, they buried me."
(6)	4 years old	"There was no time before I was born. 'British Tomo' had a watch."
(7)	4 years old	"British mother often said, 'I love you.'" (Japanese mothers rarely say this)
(8)	4 years old	(Pointing to his own legs) "I had a lot of hair here."
(9)	4 years old	"In the UK, I bathed in milk (bath)." (This might have been for his health. See 11, below)
(10)	4 years old	Pointing to the washbasin, Tomo repeatedly said "Washbasin" in English. He also said "pleasure" in English.

(11)	4 years old (cf. (15))	"In the UK, I took 'healing herb.'" Instructing his mother to hold him and imitate giving a glass of liquid to him, he said "British mother said to me, 'Take this, take this. It will help you feel better.' The herb was like trefoil, and it was green liquid when I took it. My [older] brother took leaves [probably medicinal leaves from the garden]. We also used it like this [pretending to put a leaf on his forehead]."
(12)	4 years old	Tomo tried to explain what he ate in his past-life. "With chopped carrots and Japanese radish-like vegetables, with cheese. We heated it for about 4 minutes and when the cheese melted, we ate it." When the mother asked, "Is it gratin?" he said, "Oh, it's difficult to explain."
(13)	4 years and 1 month old	"When I was 'British Tomo,' on February 16th, white liquid came out of my penis for the first time." When his mother asked, "What do you mean?" he said, "From the penis of 'British Tomo,' yellow pee and white juice came out."* (Surprised at Tomo's remarks, the mother asked kindergarten teachers if they gave sex education. The answer was naturally negative.)
(14)	4 years and 1 month old	"I got on a double-decker bus. The money I used was not yen, but pound."
(15)	4 years and two months old (cf. (11))	"My mother made me drink 'healing grass' mixed with pineapple juice, but I knew it was medicine."
(16)	4 years and 2 months old	"There was a special shopping mall in front of our restaurant. They sold Japanese soy sauce." (His mother thought this statement remarkable because it was unlikely that Tomo, who had never been abroad, would know that soy sauce is specifically Japanese seasoning.)

---

* If Tomo's statement is correct, the past-life personality died at the age of 9. This is unusually early for spermarche, but it is not impossible. See Kinsey, et al. (1975, p. 186).

(17)	4 years and 2 months old (cf. (18), (24), (25))	"'British Tomo' was hospitalized at 'Muginba Paresu' [as transcribed in the diary in Japanese letters] hospital. At first no room was available. When room 4 on the 13th floor became available, four of us – father, mother, brother, and me – went there by car. It was 115 kilometers from my house to the hospital. Since it was far away, we used a highway [see Tomo's drawing, Figure 4-5]. My brother was five years older than me and 14 at that time. In the hospital, there was a place like a bath, and there was a doctor who put powder medicine into hot water and massaged me. The treatment didn't work and I had an operation. I had a fever of 40 Celsius* [104 F] and died."
(18)	4 years and 7 months old (cf. (17), (24), (25))	Tomo: [Seeing a picture in a picture book titled *Human Body*, in which food is stuck in a person's throat] "Oh, no! This guy has become 'British Tomo!'" Mother: "Did 'British Tomo' die because something stuck in his throat?" Tomo: "I had throat disorders. I was hospitalized and stayed on the seventh floor of a 13-story hospital.** I felt so sick and died." Mother: "Did you die of asthma, perhaps?" Tomo: "Yes. The healing herb didn't cure me, either. 'The former Tomo' was weak and died young. So, this time I chose a strong body."
(19)	4 years and 7 months old (also 5 years and 6 months old) (cf. (24))	(Watching news of a train crash) "There was also a train accident in the UK, in Southall. I watched the news on TV. It said 'Accident! Accident!' Two trains collided, and a fire occurred. Eight people died."
(20)	4 years 7 months old	Tomo: "The blood type of 'British Tomo' was B. I was weak and couldn't exercise, and there were many things I wanted to do." Mother: "Why did you recall British Tomo?" Tomo: (crying) "I want to meet my British mom."

---

* This figure differs from that given earlier (45 C) regarding his death.

** This is another discrepancy: in (17), (24), and (25) he said he was in "room 4 on the 13th floor."

(21)	4 years 9 months old	(About a meal Tomo ate in his past life) "I ate *chili con carne*. Red kidney beans were in it and it was hot." [He never ate the dish in his present life, and it is unlikely he had ever heard of it]
(22)	5 years old (cf. (5))	Tomo: "I died between 24th and 25th of October, 1997." Mother: "How did you know that you died?" Tomo: "My British mother looked troubled. She said, 'Now only five of us were left.'" Mother: "Did you see that?" Tomo: "Yes, I did." Mother: "Then, what did you do?" Tomo: "I was doing something like riding on a slide or on the escalator of a 25-story building."
(23)	5 years old	When Tomo's family had a coffee break, Tomo pointed out that what they drank is different from what the family of the past-life personality drank. "In the UK, I drank black coffee, my father drank it with milk, and my mother with milk and sugar. Now, I can't drink coffee, but dad and mom can. You (dad and mom) drink coffee with milk."
(24)	5 years 6 months old (cf. (17), (18), (19), (25))	(After a thunderstorm at night) "'British Tomo' was hospitalized in 'Muginba paresu' hospital. At first there was no room available. Then, room 4 of the 13th floor became available, so my father, mother, brother, and I went there. We used a highway because the hospital was far away. It was located 115 kilometers to the north from my house. My brother was 5 years older than I, 14 years old. In the hospital, in a bath-like place, a doctor poured powder medicine into hot water and massaged me. It didn't work and I had an operation. But I had a high fever of 40 Celsius [104 F] and died. My house was about 30 seconds away from the station. There was news of a train crash. TV said 'News! News!' and I saw crashed trains on TV."
(25)	5 years 6 months old (cf. (17), (18), (24), (25))	From room 4 on the 13th floor, I could see fireworks. The hospital had a bath.

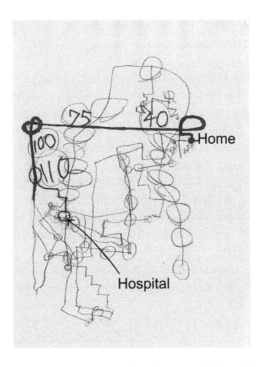

Figure 4-5: A Map Drawn by Tomo as He Explained
How to Get to the Hospital (Item 17)

Most of the statements listed above concerning the life in Edinburgh seem to be compatible with an actual life there, and beyond the knowledge of ordinary Japanese people – including Tomo's parents. Especially striking is Tomo's statement about the train accident at Southall station in the UK (19), which factually occurred on September 19, 1997 (Uff, 2000).

Tomo's mother had been a good listener of his words, but when the boy started talking about his past-life memories, she was frightened, thinking he might have mental problems. She took him to a psychiatrist, who diagnosed him with Asperger's Syndrome (now autism spectrum disorder). Not fully convinced, she searched for further information and eventually came across Dr. IKEGAWA Akira, an obstetrician and gynecologist, who had been working on children's prenatal memories, having conducted a large-scale questionnaire-based survey on children's birth and in-the-womb memories (Ikegawa, 2005, see Chapter 11). Through him, the mother came to know that there are other children who talk about past-life memories and she began to think that Tomo might be one of them.

As for Tomo's father, up until the moment the child talked about the accident at Southall station, he regarded Tomo's statements as mere imagination, and did not pay much attention to them. Since his statement was fairly specific, the father started to search for the information on the Internet. His search in Japanese gave no relevant information, but using English, he found a Wikipedia page titled "Southall Rail Crash," which gives basically the same information as Tomo gave.[26] Because of this incident, the father began to believe that what Tomo had been saying was true.

Because Tomo repeatedly said that he wanted to go to Edinburgh to see his British mother, his father eventually yielded and took him there. On August 1st, 2008, Tomo and his father left for the UK. His mother stayed in Japan because Tomo's brother was three years old and too young to go.

On the day of the arrival, they went around the city of Edinburgh. They found that *chili con carne* is served in many places in town as Tomo had said (21).

According to the diary written by Tomo's father, on the second day, at 6 o'clock in the morning, Tomo woke with a start, saying, "I felt my mother. She must be around here." In the video taken at that time, Tomo commented that some of the buildings had become new although Edinburgh Castle looked the same. He also said that he would go to the station close to his former house. Asked by his father if he remembered the name of the station, he first muttered a word, and then replied, "I forgot. But there weren't many trains."

They spent four full days in Edinburgh, but their search for Tomo's past-life house was not successful. Tomo's father told me, "I thought my son would easily find the way to his house once we got to Edinburgh. If I had known that this would not necessarily be the case, I would have made more preparation."

Although the trip was not successful in the sense that they could not find Tomo's house from his past-life, it seems to have somehow soothed his desire to go back to his "former house." He began to talk about his past life less and less, and soon stopped talking about it completely.

---

[26] See http://en.wikipedia.org/wiki/Southall_rail_crash. *Wikipedia* now has a Japanese page for the accident. The number of people who died in the accident was seven, not eight as Tomo stated.

Yet, Tomo's desire to meet his British mother didn't fade away. In one of the interviews in 2010, when he was 10 years old,[27] he claimed, "I still have a visual image of my British mother," "I still want to go to the UK to meet my mother," and "You'll see, when I become old, I'll go there myself" – all of which I found very impressive.

The Investigation of Tomo's Past-Life Personality

My investigation concerning Tomo's past life personality included an Internet search based on Tomo's statements, seeking information from people connected to the UK – including members of the Society for Psychical Research and the Scottish Society for Psychical Research – and visiting Edinburgh myself in 2011. At present, however, the search for the past-life personality has been unsuccessful.

It turned out that no death comparable to the present case seems to have been recorded in the city of Edinburgh. Since Tomo clearly stated the specific dates of his birth and death, I expected that Internet genealogy database services such as "Scotland's People" or "Ancestry.co.uk" (a subdivision of "Ancestry.com") would allow me to easily trace the past life personality. However, contrary to my expectation, these types of services require the name of the person you are looking for, and, since Tomo did not give the exact name of his past life personality, they were ultimately not useful. Finally, I consulted with the National Record of Scotland, whose role includes the administration of the registration of births, deaths, marriages, divorces and adoptions in Scotland. Mr. Blair Kane helped me with this search, and checked all the death records for the Edinburgh area for the year 1997. According to Mr. Kane, there were no deaths of children around the specified age range. Nor were there any cases of asthma related deaths in those months. He stated that, "It could well have been he died in the Edinburgh area but his death was registered in a different district."

---

[27] In my original article, I erroneously wrote Tomo was 9.5 years old (Ohkado, 2013, p. 626).

Some Discrepancies

There are some discrepancies in Tomo's statements. He stated that his past personality had been hospitalized in a 13-story building (17), (18), (24), (25), which does not match the facts in Edinburgh. According to Dr. Ian Tierney of the University of Edinburgh, "there are no 13 story hospital (or residential) buildings in Edinburgh, nor have there ever been. The only 13 story buildings are a university research building and an office block built since 2000."

If Tomo's statement concerning the hospital location in relation to the residence of his past-life personality is correct (17), (24), and the hospital is indeed in Edinburgh, despite the above-mentioned discrepancy, the place his past-life personality lived cannot have been Edinburgh. On the other hand, if the residence was indeed in Edinburgh, the hospital should be somewhere in the Highlands.

Tomo's Life-Between-Life and Womb Memories

As shown in items (5) and (22), Tomo talked about what had happened after his death in his past life. He also made interesting statements about his brother.

When his younger brother was born in 2005, when Tomo was five years old, he repeatedly said, "That's strange. That's strange." Being asked why, he explained, "I had taken them [= his younger brother's spirit] to Japan from England. She was a girl who died 12 minutes after me there, but she was born with a penis. That's strange." He also said, "She had been with me all the time, but after coming to Japan, her time started to be out of sync with my time."

He also said, "The place where I stayed after I died was always bright. It was not like the sun is shining, but was like it's bright although it's cloudy. No rain, no snow. It's not hot nor is it cold. You don't have to go to the restroom. You don't have to take a bath."

He further described his between-lives experience to his mother: "In the place where I was, there was an old man with a white beard. Together with the girl [= his younger brother], I looked around the world, looking for candidates for our mother and chose you."

It is interesting to note that the place Tomo described appears to be quite similar to the place Katsugoro said he was in after he had died in his past life. Also interesting is that, like many other children claiming to have life-between-life memories, Tomo said that he had chosen his mother. It is also worth pointing out that Tomo said he had chosen a healthy body since he had been weak and unable to do what he had wanted to do in his past life (18).

When Tomo was three years old, looking at the calendar, he said puzzledly, "The February calendar I saw when I was in mom's tummy had the 29th." His mother was surprised by the accuracy of Tomo's words: the year 2000 when Tomo was born was a leap year and the calendar on the wall had the 29th in February.

Tomo's Later Development

After our interviews, Tomo appears to have quickly forgotten the remaining portion of the already-fading memories. When he was interviewed at the age of 14 by a TV director for a program titled *Chojo Gensho (Supernatural Phenomena)*, which was broadcast on NHK in 2014, he said, "I don't remember at all. I don't know why I said that [concerning his past-life memories]" (cf. Umehara and Kanda, 2014).

According to Tomo's mother, around this time he was saying, "I want to be a researcher and examine my brain and make it clear why I said that." Now (May 2022) he is a graduate school student, but the subject he is studying is not his brain. He is planning to be a meteorologist.

5

I Fought on the Battleship *Yamato*: The Case of Takeharu

~

Figure 5-1: The *Yamato* during sea trials, 1941

The Battleship Yamato

Yamato was the name of ancient Japan and of its old Imperial House, believed to have been established in the 3rd to 4th century. The Chinese characters representing the name, 大和 (大 meaning "great" and 和 meaning "harmony"), signify the Japanese spirit of respecting harmony.

Yamato was chosen as the name for Japan's largest and most powerful battleship: 263 meters in length, 49,000 tons in weight, and equipped with the nine of the world's largest guns (460 mm). The pride and the symbol of the Imperial Japanese Navy entered service in the Pacific War at the beginning of 1942. June of that year saw the Battle of Midway, which is generally considered a major turning point in the Pacific War, as it was becoming increasingly clear that the country was fighting a losing battle.

On April 6th, 1945, the *Yamato* and nine other warships departed their base in Tokuyama Bay and headed for Okinawa, which had been invaded by Allied forces on April 1st. It was a naval version of a kamikaze attack: any battleships that managed to survive the attacks of Allied forces would beach themselves and fight until they were destroyed. With a large portion of aircraft having been destroyed, the battleships had virtually no air protection.

The first series of attacks began on the afternoon of April 7th. Around 300 Allied bomber aircraft dropped a countless number of bombs, striking various parts of the *Yamato*. Three torpedoes struck her port side. The *Yamato* listed to port about 5°-6° but the list was reduced to 1° by counter-flooding.

The second series of attacks started less than an hour later. Three more torpedoes hit the *Yamato's* port side and she listed to port about 15°-16°, but the list was reduced to 5° by counter-flooding.

The third and final series of attacks came soon after. Two more torpedoes hit the *Yamato* and it listed to port about 16°-18°, and the list angle increased rapidly. The *Yamato* started to sink and the Commanding Officer gave the order to abandon the ship. The list was increasing and when the ship reached an angle of 120°, the ship exploded and sank. Only 276 of the 3,332 crew members survived.[28]

---

[28] The account is largely based on Skulski (1988, pp. 12-13). For detailed accounts comparing the Japanese and American official records, see Hara (2003).

Figure 5-2: The explosion of the *Yamato*

Takeharu's Strange Remarks and Behaviors

Takeharu was born in Hiroshima in May 2012, the third son of Keisuke (father) and Yuki (mother). Keisuke is a dentist and Yuki a high school teacher. As one of only two cities in history to have been hit by atomic bombs, Hiroshima is a center for promoting peace in education, with the main goal of fostering anti-war values. Takeharu's parents had no interest in military affairs, nor did his two older brothers. The eldest brother loved animals and playing sports, while the second brother liked solving puzzles. Takeharu is the only member of the family with a keen interest in military affairs of the Second World War. He is especially attracted by the battleship *Yamato*.

When he was quite young, Takeharu refused to be called "Takeharu," and asked the other family members to call him by a different name (unfortunately, none of the family remember what that name was).

Takeharu had a mild form of aquaphobia and refused to take a bath. His mother had a hard time forcing him to do so. Often when Takeharu bathed with his two brothers, he asked them to play a battleship war game with him, using bath salt bags or other items as a battleship and making the "battleship" sink. The younger of the two brother recalls that Takeharu asked them to do so every day.

One day, when he was taking a bath with his mother, Takeharu said, "I won't die." Yuki was perplexed by his curious remarks. Later, as his verbal skills developed, he said: "I won't die before mom. You cried a lot, didn't you?" He repeatedly made the same remarks when he took a bath with Yuki.

On his third birthday, Takeharu drew a picture with a big black object occupying the lower part of the scene, with many red ovals above, looking like cocklebur seeds. None of the family members were sure what Takeharu had drawn, but Yuki thought it might be a whale shark.

Figure 5-3: The picture Takeharu drew when he was three years old.

Only later did the family understand that what he had drawn was the *Yamato* being attacked by U.S. aircraft.

Takeharu then started to say, "I want to see *Yamato*," repeating the request over and over again. None of the family members had any interest in the battleship, or anything related to warfare, and they did not understand what he meant.

One day when four-year-old Takeharu came back from kindergarten, he looked very happy and said, "Musashi is in the same class with me. [We are] brothers! [We are] Brothers!" Later, when recalling the incident, Yuki realized that Takeharu was referring to the battleship

Musashi, which was the sister ship of the *Yamato*.²⁹ It is not common knowledge that Yamato and Musashi were sister ships.

Takeharu also sang a song with the following lyrics: *"Getsu Getsu Ka Sui Moku Kin Kin"* ("Monday, Monday, Tuesday, Wednesday, Thursday, Friday, Friday"). Yuki thought that it was a song to help children to memorize the names of the weekdays and that Takeharu had learned it at kindergarten. It turned out that it was a *gunka*, or "military song," which describes hard-working navy men who had no Saturday or Sunday breaks.

Four-year-old Takeharu then began to make the following remarks over and over again: "I made mom cry. I won't make mom cry this time."

"There was a very strong battleship."

"Nobody knew about the ship" (the design and construction of the *Yamato* were top secret and carefully guarded against recognition [Skulski, 1988, p. 8]).

"They got us on the left side."

"It exploded."

"We went to help, but they got us, and I died."

"I drowned."

These statements led his parents to think that Takeharu might have been talking about the famous battleship *Yamato*. In January 2017, when Takeharu was four years and eight months old, he made a 6-page booklet titled, *The Battleship* Yamato *is Actually Alive.*

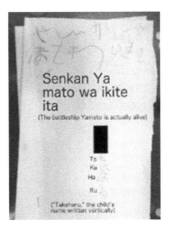

Figure 5-4: The booklet Takeharu made
(Roman letters added by the author)

---

²⁹ In Japanese, the word "brother" not "sister" is used to refer to a "sister ship."

In his child's handwriting, the booklet is not easy to read, but the following sentences are legible:

"Guns bang, bang! Everyone wanted to get on the *Yamato*."

"Let's talk about the strong battleship *Yamato*."

"The *Yamato* exploded, but three of us worked hard." (Takeharu often mentioned "three of us.")

Takeharu sometimes surprised his parents with his detailed knowledge of the *Yamato*. For instance, when he was still four, he told his father Keisuke that the ship had six big guns in the front and three in the back, which is correct. He also said that the *Yamato* had aircraft. Keisuke hadn't thought that the battleship could hold aircraft, so he was surprised when he found that what Takeharu had told him was true.[30]

Takeharu at the Yamato Museum

The city of Kure, located about 20 kilometers south-east of Hiroshima city, was "the best naval port in the Far East, and the biggest arsenal town in Japan" (Yamato Museum, n.d.). Many ships were built there and the battleship *Yamato* was one of them. The city houses the Kure Maritime Museum, which "introduces the History of Kure and a broad range of Science and Technologies, including shipbuilding and steelmaking which have served as a foundation for the modernization of Japan, with a perspective on the efforts of our predecessors and lifestyles and cultures at that time" (ibid.). The museum is better known as the Yamato Museum because, as its symbol, it exhibits a "one-tenth scale model of the battleship *Yamato* measuring 26.3 meters in length" (ibid.). It is about 30-minute drive from the house in which Takeharu and his family lived.

After Takeharu's parents realized that he had apparently been talking about the battleship *Yamato*, in response to Takeharu's repeated request to see the battleship again, they took him to the museum, saying that he would be able to see it there. It was in April 2017, two weeks before Takeharu turned five years old.

The parents expected that seeing the large-scale model of the battleship *Yamato* would delight Takeharu. Contrary to their expectation, however, when Takeharu saw the model, he got angry and cried: "It's a fake! The *Yamato* was much, much bigger!"

---

[30] The *Yamato* was designed to carry seven floatplanes of the F1M2 "Pete" and E13A1 "Jake" types (Skulski, 1988, p. 21).

Figure 5-5: The one-tenth scale model of the
battleship *Yamato* at the Yamato Museum

Various figures and plastic models of the *Yamato* were sold in the museum gift shop. Takeharu first asked his parents to buy him a fairly expensive complete painted replica of the ship, which they were unable to afford. Takeharu then begged them to buy him the biggest plastic model on sale (1/600 scale). They consented and bought it. Surprisingly, 4-year-old Takeharu assembled it accurately – despite it being intended for much older children. From that time on, for about two years, Takeharu brought the plastic model to the bathtub and played with it in the way that the *Yamato* was attacked and sunk.

It is important to emphasize here that Takeharu's first exposure to information concerning the *Yamato* was through the museum's exhibits, which he encountered on the occasion of this visit. There is no possibility that Takeharu learned even general information about the *Yamato* in elementary school, let alone the detailed information he actually expressed.

Attracted by World War II Pictures and Exhibits

On August 6th, 2016, the anniversary of the day that an A-bomb was dropped on Hiroshima in 1945, Takeharu's parents took him to the Hiroshima Peace Memorial Museum. The museum exhibits belongings left by the A-bomb victims, A-bombed artifacts, testimonies of survivors, and related materials. Takeharu was very much drawn to the place, and every year on August 6th he asked his family to take him there.

In 2017, when one of his brothers took him to the museum, he said he liked the place because the exhibits are from the World War II period. The following day, Yuki took him to the Hiroshima and A-Bomb Exhibition at the Gojinsha Wendy Hito-Machi Plaza in the city. He begged Yuki to buy a booklet titled *Genbaku to Taisen no Shinjitsu (The Truth of the A-Bombings and World War II)* (Figure 5-6), which contained many pictures of the period, some of which show very tragic scenes (Shimonoseki Genbakuten Jimukyoku, eds., 2008).

Takeharu said, "These pictures remind me of the old days" [i.e., in his past life].

Figure 5-6: The cover of the book Takeharu wanted.

Takeharu's Taste for Alcohol

Children with past-life memories sometimes display their previous personalities' cravings for alcohol, tobacco, and related adult products. An unforgettable family episode involving two-year-old Takeharu can be regarded as conforming to this pattern.

One evening, Yuki put two glasses of sake on the table, one for her and one for Keisuke. She was away for a while and when she came back, the glasses were empty. She asked Takeharu, who had been there, if he had drunk the sake. Takeharu at first denied having done this, but when Yuki smelled sake on his breath and pointed this out, he admitted that he had drunk it – with red face and singing merrily. Due to this incident, the parents try not to drink sake in front of Takeharu. When he was a kindergartener, Yuki asked Takeharu why he wanted to drink sake. He replied: "I used to drink sake and I loved it."

Takeharu's Unusual Knowledge About the Japanese Era

A "Japanese era" name is a title used for numbering years in the Japanese calendar system. On April 30, 2019, the era of Heisei ended and on the next day of the same year, the new era of Reiwa started.

While watching a TV program reporting the start of the new era, six-year-old Takeharu said, "I died at the age of 19. The first year of Reiwa started [today]. I understand what this means because *wa* in 'Reiwa' is the same as *wa* in 'Showa.' I was born in the first year of 'Showa.' I think it was a cold day, maybe Christmas." The era of Showa was from 1926 to 1989. *Wa* in "Reiwa" and "Showa" means "harmony." Takeharu was born in the 24th year of the Heisei era (1989-2019), that is 2012 of the Christian year, but he was unable to tell in which year of the Heisei era he was born. In other words, he seemed to know his previous personality's Japanese era birth year, but not his own.

Other Remarks and Behaviors After Visiting the Yamato Museum

In the years following, Takeharu continued talking about the battleship *Yamato* and showing behaviors related to his past-life memories. The following statements were recorded by Yuki in her diary.

Five Years Old
    "Americans got me and I died." (February 16th, 2018)
    "I was on the invincible battleship *Yamato*. But on the way to Okinawa, we were attacked and killed. The left (port) side was attacked over and over again. Inside the ship, I calculated using an abacus."

(Takeharu is learning abacus, and appears to be unusually skilled.) (February 20th, 2018)

Six Years Old
"I died, but why am I alive?" (April 23th, 2019)
Takeharu repeated the story of the *Yamato*, though no exact words were recorded. (April 30th, 2019)

Seven Years Old
"Americans were not fair. They kept on attacking the same side. Torpedoes hit the left (port) side and the *Yamato* listed. They put water from the right (starboard) side, but it was no use. Because of the heavy bombings, people got injured and the deck was red with blood. We couldn't fire because it was cloudy and couldn't see the Americans. Eruptions of water vapor occurred. It was scary. It hurt. Nobody helped me. I called mom. Because of the whirlpools, I couldn't swim and sunk with the battleship."
Takeharu created another plastic model ship and airplanes and played with them, this time not in the bath, making the airplanes attack the ship and making the ship sink. For a while, he repeated the same play every day. (September, 2020)
"I want to see the *Yamato* again." (October, 2020)
"I was drowned in the place with a lot of water, probably it was the sea. Nobody noticed and I sank. It was long time ago, but I still remember." (Takeharu had never swum in the sea.) (undated)

My Interview With Takeharu

Takeharu's repeated statements and peculiar behaviors made Yuki think he had been talking about a past life. She began looking for researchers working on children with these kinds of anomalous memories, and contacted me in November 2020. After numerous e-mail exchanges and some telephone conversations, I interviewed Takeharu and Yuki via Zoom. During the exchanges, Yuki took a video of Takeharu's statements and of his reactions to the information I provided concerning his memories. In March, 2021, I visited the family and interviewed Takeharu and his parents in person. Takeharu was eight years old and I found that he:

- Still had a keen interest in the battleship *Yamato*
- Showed emotions appropriate to a crew member of the battleship
- Expressed pride in being a crew of the largest battleship
- Expressed resentment towards Americans
- Expressed a strong desire to see his mother from his past life. He explained that his past-life memories were fading, and that he would like to meet his past-life family before they were completely gone.

During the interview, Takeharu made the following statements about his ostensible past-life personality:

"I had graduated from a school shortly before I got on the *Yamato*."

"When we boarded the *Yamato*, we went there on a small boat." (The *Yamato* was designed to carry boats [Skulski, 1988, p. 21])

"When I was told that the operation was a suicide attack, I thought I would never be able to go back, I have to die; but at the same time, I felt I will fight the Americans and make it!"

"I don't like Americans very much."

"I loved to drink sake and I remember I drank a lot at the farewell party on the night before the final battle." At the time of the interview, Takeharu said that he still wanted to drink sake.

"Before the battle, rice balls were served and I ate them quickly."

"It was cloudy, and we couldn't see airplanes until they came very close."

"During the battle, I don't remember why, but I got hurt."

"During the battle, the deck was filled with blood and bodies of crew members."

"I was in charge of guns. I don't remember which one, but it was not the main ones" (45 Caliber Type 94 naval guns.)

"I want to have the *Yamato* back in shape."

"My memory is fading and before it is gone, I want to meet my [former] mother. If I can, I want to tell her, 'Don't worry. I'm doing fine.'"

In response to my question, "Which life do you prefer, the past life or the present life?" Takeharu replied, "I like the past. Because I was a crew member of the *Yamato*, and knew how to use guns and other things."

Being a crew member of the *Yamato* was a source of pride and honor. Also, if the person Takeharu referred to was a graduate of the Naval Academy, it was likely that he also had great pride in that since they were regarded as elites among the elites (Taiheiyo Senso Kenkyukai (ed.), 2002).

Using plastic models of the *Yamato* and airplanes, Takeharu vividly described how the battle went on, and these descriptions were largely consistent with his previous ones: "Lots of airplanes were coming, they kept on coming, attacking the port side. Lots of bombs and torpedoes hit the *Yamato*. The *Yamato* was listed to the left (port) side, but it was put back (by counter-flooding being commenced), but torpedoes hit again and again on the left side, and it eventually sank" (Figure 5-7).

Figure 5-7: Takeharu explaining how the Yamato was attacked.

The statements concerning the last battle, such as rice balls having been served before the battle, the cloudy weather, the deck having been filled with blood and bodies of crew members, and the *Yamato* having been attacked mostly on the left side, were all true as a number of survivors and official documents reported (Yoshida, 2013; Hara, 2003).

The Person Takeharu Remembered Being

After the Zoom interview with Takeharu, I began to search for the person whose memories he seemed to have based on the information he had provided. The names and ranks of the crew members of the *Yamato* were readily available in a book published by the former Executive Officer of the ship, NOMURA Jiro (Nomura, 1973).

Judging from Takeharu's statement that he had graduated from school shortly before he joined the crew of the *Yamato*, I thought he might have graduated from one of the three representative naval schools: the Naval Academy, the Naval Engineering College, or the Naval Paymasters' School. I obtained audio files of the school songs of each, and asked Yuki to have Takeharu listen to them. As she did so, Yuki took a video of Takeharu's reaction. The order was the songs of the Naval Paymasters' School, the Naval Engineering College, then the Naval Academy. Takeharu showed no reaction to the first two, but when he listened to the third, he became suddenly happy and began to hum along, saying he used to sing the song.

An alumni association directory of the Naval Academy I obtained had pictures of the members. I found that the 73rd graduates included the youngest members of the Naval Academy who participated in the *Yamato* operation. Eight of them lost their lives in the operation, so they were the likely candidates. I asked Yuki to show Takeharu the eight pictures one by one, and to ask him whether they looked familiar. Of the eight people, five of them were crew members of the *Yamato*. Two of them were crew members on the light cruiser *Yahagi*, and the remaining one was on the destroyer *Asashimo*. The *Yahagi* and *Asashimo* were two of the five ships that were sunk together with the *Yamato*.

Yuki showed the pictures to Takeharu on a PC. Again, she took a video of the process. Takeharu picked one of the pictures and told his mother that the person (Mr. K) in it was him.[31] The next day, Takeharu proudly said to Yuki, "Just as I have been saying, the 'old me' did exist." But Takeharu was unable to recall the name (Mr. K).

I then gave Yuki the names of the people in the eight pictures without telling her which name corresponds to which picture. Takeharu did not show any noticeable reaction to any of the names.

I had also obtained the school songs of four old system junior high schools, one of which Takeharu's apparent previous personality appeared to have graduated from. I asked Yuki to have Takeharu listen to them. She did so on January 4th, 2021, but Takeharu was unable to recognize the melody of any of them. He did say, however, that he remembered an episode concerning a word in one of the songs – which was the song of the school Mr. K graduated from. It contained the word *kenji*, an old-fashioned word meaning "brave child." Takeharu said, "I remember it

---

[31] Out of privacy considerations for the families, only the initials are given of the names of the people concerning Takeharu's memories.

was in the lyrics of the school song and that I asked a teacher what it means."

On the same day, Takeharu indicated another picture and said, "I know this person. I'm wondering why." A month later, he added, "This person catching my attention might be one of the three members who were good friends." He appeared to have been referring to one of the three crew members he wrote about in the booklet he created when he was four years old. "I think he was on the cruiser *Yahagi*. The ship was attacked first, so I was worrying, but then the *Yamato* was also listed, and I was unable to get any information about him." It turned out that the person he talked about, Mr. H, was indeed one of the two crew members of the *Yahagi*, who died in the battle.

The only other information I was able to obtain about Mr. K was in the book written by a 73rd graduate of the Naval Academy, who was a Navy pilot. According to the book, Mr. K was in charge of the Secondary armament and was in the Secondary armament transmitting station at the time of the sinking of the *Yamato* (Abe, 2015, p. 50).

On January, 2021, I told Yuki that: (i) the person Takeharu picked out in the pictures was named Mr. K and was one of the five crew members who were on the *Yamato*; (ii) he was in charge of the Secondary armament in the armament transmitting station; (iii) the school song was that of the school from which Mr. K graduated; and (iv) the person who Takeharu described as one of his friends aboard the *Yahagi* was named Mr. H and was indeed on the light cruiser and was sunk in the battle shortly before the *Yamato*. These matches seem to be unaccounted for by any normal means.

When Yuki conveyed all this information to Takeharu, he drew the picture in Figure 5-8, saying that he had been using the trumpet-like pipe to send the captain's orders to the crew members who were directly in charge of the guns.

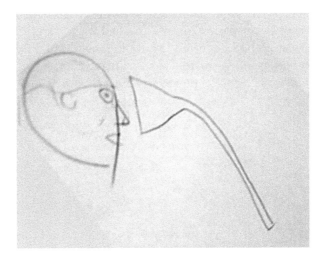

Figure 5-8: A picture drawn by Takeharu, April 9, 2021

It seems he referred to a voice tube of the kind typical on such ships, which was likely to have been used by the person Takeharu identified himself as having been (Abe, 2015, p. 50).

I should add here that there are two possible discrepancies between Takeharu's statements and the facts concerning Mr. K. First, in December 2020, Takeharu said he wore a sailor suit, but later denied this, saying that the uniform he wore was different from a sailor suit. Sailor suits were for sailors and not for officers like Mr. K. Takeharu might have been simply confused, but the detail is worth noting. Second, most of the 73rd graduates of the Naval Academy were reported to be 20 or 21 years old when they boarded the *Yamato*. Since the date of birth of Mr. K is not recorded, we cannot exclude the possibility that he was unusually young when he graduated, though this could also be a discrepancy.

Concluding Remarks

Given that more than 75 years have passed since the destruction of the *Yamato*, the available information concerning the crew members of the ship is limited, especially for non-survivors. So, although Takeharu's unusual knowledge, behaviors, and emotional traits match Mr. K, the identification is, from the objective point of view of scientific research on paranormal phenomena, inconclusive. However, from the subjective point of view of Takeharu, he himself reached the obvious conclusion that the person he had been talking about was found. Although he was sad that he was unable to see his past-life mother and other family members,[32] he was at least happy to have found who he had been in a previous life.

---

[32] The alumni directory had the address of his old house, but a letter I wrote was sent back. I also wrote to an alumni association of the high school, but they had no information on the person. I also contacted the first service school of the Maritime Self-Defense Force, where the information of the crew members of the battleships including the *Yamato* is stored, but I found that they can give the information only to relatives. In my request they "revealed" that all the information they have is the same as in the alumni directory and a picture. As for the picture, I cannot know whether it is the same one as shown to Takeharu or a different one of Mr. K. Privacy protection in Japan is very strict and is often an obstacle to the research.

6

Looking for My Son's Past-Life Mother: The Case of Sakutaro

A Twitter Message

In February 2020, Yu Darvish, a professional baseball player, retweeted a message sent by the mother of a 7-year-old boy. It was then immediately retweeted by more than 900 people. The message read:

> I'm looking for a past-life mother.
>
> My 7-year-old son, who started talking about his past-life mother, is saying: "I want to see my former mother."
>
> The mother might still be in grief and if possible, I want to take him to her.
>
> I think there are those who do not believe in past lives and those who are not comfortable with such requests. To them I apologize and beg to skip this message over.

The sender of the original message was Chie, a nurse living in West Japan. As written in the Twitter message, her son, Sakutaro, had begun talking about his past-life memories and was hoping to meet his past-life mother. Chie, a very caring person, imagined a woman who lost her son and was in deep grief, and felt that if she would be able to meet Sakutaro and know that her dead son was "alive" in a different place, she might be consoled. Chie is also a reserve self-defense official, and is a very brave and active person. She decided to look for her son's past-life mother by using Twitter. The use of Twitter as a medium was suggested by a Buddhist monk whom Chie had become acquainted with. He had lost a baby to stillbirth and upon hearing the story of possible past-life memories of Sakutaro, he told her how painful the experience had been, and how happy the parents would be if they knew that their lost child was still "alive."

Mom's Voice Was Cuter

That night, Chie was putting three-year-old Sakutaro to sleep. Unexpected words came from his mouth.

"The voice of my present mom is not very cute."

"Did I get old?" said Chie, surprised.

Sakutaro quickly corrected her, "No, no. I'm talking about the mom when I was former Sakutaro." He added, "This time, I won't get on a motorbike."

Chie immediately thought that Sakutaro might be talking about his past life. So, without denying anything he said, she just listened. Bit by bit, Sakutaro made the following statements:

(1) "Mom in my past life was very affectionate."
(2) "Mom in my past life had longer hair than the present mom."
(3) "I called her *okasan*." (Sakutaro calls his mother *mama*.)[33]
(4) "I used to ride a motorbike. I began to ride it because my former mother said, 'You're old enough. Why don't you ride a motorbike?'"
(5) "I had an accident while riding on a motorbike. I was as old as my elder brother." (Sakutaro has a half-brother. He was 17 years old at that time. However, he looked much older than he actually was. So,

---

[33] Both *okasan* and *mama* are common Japanese terms of address to one's mother, but *mama* is usually used by children.

106

the past-life personality might have been older than 17 when he had the accident.)

(6) "I was crossing a road. A car came to me from the right side, ignoring the red light, and hit me."

(7) "I got injured on my right leg and was brought to a big hospital."

(8) "My mother, who came to the hospital after the accident, was crying."

(9) "I had an operation, but I died." (However, the cause of death was not the accident injury itself. He is not certain what it was.)

(10) "The motorbike I rode on was a red motor scooter type."

(11) "I loved Famicom from Nintendo [the Nintendo Entertainment System, first released in Japan in 1983] and especially loved to play Super Mario."

(12) "My father was not a nurse like you (Sakutaro's mother). He was not a doctor. He was making medicine."

(13) "I was the only child."

Figure 6-1 is a picture of the accident Sakutoro drew when he was seven years old. A traffic light and tactile paving tiles are seen. The motorbike is crossing from the lower side of the picture and the car is coming from the right.

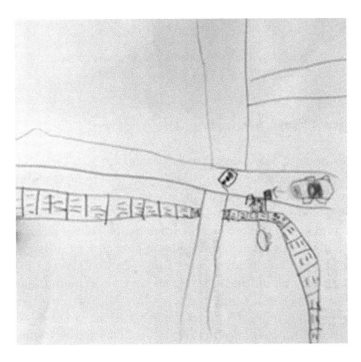

Figure 6-1: Sakutaro's drawing of his past-life accident.

He said that his former house was close to the place drawn in the picture.

Because of the accident, Sakutaro did not like motorbikes and would not ride on them. Although he was born in August 2012, he said he enjoyed playing with the long-obsolete 1983 gaming system, the Nintendo Famicom (Figure 6-2). Although he also loved to play the contemporary version of Nintendo games, he particularly liked to watch YouTube videos in which older versions were played.

Figure 6-2: The Nintendo Famicom, 1983 version

Sakutaro's Vivid Memory of the Accident

I became aware of Sakutaro's case in February 2020, via the Internet, and contacted his mother, Chie. After a couple of exchanges and a Zoom interview, I met Sakutaro and his parents the following month when he was 7 years and 7 months old. Because of the Twitter message posted by Chie, replies claiming to provide information related to Sakutaro's past life had been pouring in and Chie was busy sorting through them.

About a year had passed since Sakutaro had started to go to elementary school, but he appeared to have vivid memories of the accident and repeated to me the story that he had earlier told his mother. His desire to meet his former mother seemed to have lessened. He repeated that he still did not like motorbikes and would not ride on one, and that he liked watching YouTube videos of old Nintendo games being played.

His father, who used to play Nintendo games himself – including those for the 1983 Famicom system – said that he was often surprised by Sakutaro's knowledge of old games which were not available any more. When Sakutaro's father first heard of his past-life recalls, he was surprised and told his son, "Only this mom (Chie) is your mom." However, he gradually accepted what Sakutaro has been claiming, especially because the boy's story had been consistent.

Possible Identification of Sakutaro's Past-Life Family

Messages related to Sakutaro's past life continued to pour in, and one of them appeared to be quite specific. A family had lost a young boy after an accident similar to the one Sakutaro described. The location of the accident was also as depicted in Sakutaro's picture. The father of the family used to be a pharmacist and had owned a drugstore. Furthermore, the drugstore was not very far from where the accident took place. These matches convinced Chie to visit the family.

In October 2020, after obtaining detailed information about the family from the person who had sent her the useful message, Chie visited the city where the family's house is located. She had written a letter explaining why she wanted to visit them, just in case she found herself unable to explain properly in person. Since the idea of reincarnation might not be familiar to the family, she worried that the family might think she was crazy and refuse to even talk to her. Outside the house she found a man who appeared to be the father of the family. She briefly explained to him why she had come and tried to hand him the letter. However, for whatever reason, it seemed the man was not happy to hear her story and refused to even accept the letter.

When Chie told the story to Sakutaro, without seeming upset he said: "Well, if they don't want to see me, it's okay. They don't want to see me, do they?" There is no real way of knowing what Sakutaro felt, but his calmness surprised Chie in view of the fact that he once showed such a strong desire to go back to his former family.

Judging from what the informant told Chie, the dead son of the family could be the person Sakutaro was claiming to have been, but at present this is unconfirmed.

"I Have Come to You Because You Looked Sad"

As early as 4 years old, Sakutaro had started talking about how he came to Chie. He said, "I was in a fluffy place [like clouds]. There was a bigger man. I was looking for mom [a woman who would become his mother] on something like a spaceship. You were [living] on the second floor. So, I went to the second floor, and then to the first floor, and then went out and found you. You were shopping, and when you finished shopping, I secretly entered your tummy."

Sakutaro also said, "I have come to you because you looked sad." The words struck Chie's heart because shortly before she became pregnant, she had been suffering from depression and had been able to go out only for shopping. She felt that Sakutaro had really been watching her and had decided to come to her.

At the time of my interview with him, Sakutaro repeated the same story except for the reason why he came to Chie. This time he said: "Mom looked generous."

I Am with My Sister

Sakutaro has an accessory auricle on his right year – a somewhat rare but minor developmental anomaly (Figure 6-3).

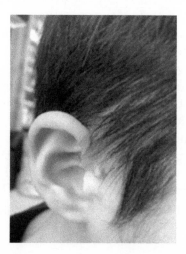

Figure 6-3: Sakutaro's accessory auricle

One night when Chie was putting four-year-old Sakutaro to sleep, he pointed out his accessory auricle and said, "This is my (elder) sister, who has come with me saying 'I want to play with you.'" Sakutaro almost had a sibling: his mother had had an abortion six years before he was born. The fetus was about three months old, and although its sex had not been examined, Chie felt it was a girl.

When she was pregnant with Sakutaro, Chie repeatedly dreamed of a girl who looked like her husband. An image of the girl eating strawberries happily impressed Chie. Because of the dreams, Chie thought the aborted child had returned to now be born. It turned out that the baby was a male, and she wondered why the girl in the dream would not come back. Chie was therefore surprised when Sakutaro talked about his elder sister and she thought that the aborted child had come back when Sakutaro was born.[34] At that time, Chie confessed to Sakutaro that he did have a sister without talking about the abortion.

When his friends pointed to his accessory auricle and asked what it was, he would say: "This is my sister." Sakutaro explicitly said he did not like soccer and baseball, both of which are quite popular among school boys. He preferred playing "shops" with girls – pretending they were shopkeepers and customers, buying and selling goods. His friends often said, "You're like a girl," and at school, girls often talked to him about their personal problems and he would give advice to them. He has been learning ballet since he was around 4 years old. Although he rarely talks about his past life, he still talks about his sister in his accessory auricle, and still loves to be among girls.

---

[34] Chie was not certain whether she thought the girl had been reborn as her baby boy, or the girl was somehow *with* Sakutaro.

Figure 6-4 Chie and Sakutaro

Although we again lack validation in the form of a verified past-life identity, some of the unusual features of this case could indicate that Sakutaro is the reincarnation of a youth who died in a motorcycle accident; and that with his new rebirth he also embodies something of his aborted sister.

7

Mom, Aren't You Lonely?
The Case of Kanon

~

This is a case in which a deceased girl appears to have been reborn as her own brother in the same family. The boy made some striking remarks suggesting that he did have memories as his departed sister. He also played in such a distinctive way as to remind the mother, Yoshie, of the way her daughter played when she was alive.

Kanon was born in a metropolitan area in 2009, and he continues to live there. He has one living half-sister, Ryumi, and the deceased sister, Momoka – his possible past-life personality. I came to know Yoshie, a nurse, through Dr. IKEGAWA Akira, whom Yoshie first contacted, and I started communicating with her via e-mail and private messages on social media in November 2013. After a number of exchanges, I interviewed Kanon and his parents in person in May 2015 – my first opportunity to do so. After the interview, we continued to speak over the telephone and exchange messages, and Yoshie still occasionally updates me about Kanon's development.

Momoka

Momoka (Figure 7-1) was Yoshie's second daughter, born on May 27th, 1997.

Figure 7-1: Momoka aged 2 years and 11 months.

She was an active girl who loved to play with her older sister, Ryumi, using toy rabbits called Sylvanian Families. Such was her enthusiasm for these toys that they were placed in her coffin as she was cremated (those seen in Figure 7-2 belong to Kanon).

Figure 7-2: Kanon's Sylvanian Families toy rabbits

Momoka often "directed" the play, asking Ryumi to adopt the role of a certain rabbit figure and say a certain set of words. For instance, Momoka would say: "Sister, you are this rabbit. Now say 'Let's go to the park.'" When Ryumi said the words, Momoka, acting as a different rabbit figure, would say: "Oh, that's nice. Let's go to the park together."

Her favorite color was pink, which is the most popular color for girls in Japan. But in Momoka's case, the color held a special, personal significance: the name "Momoka" is a combination of "peach" (*momo*) and "flower" (*ka*), and the color pink is also called "peach color" in Japanese. She also loved books and her mother used to read to her at bedtime.

When Momoka was three years old, tumors were found in her adrenal glands and she was diagnosed with cancer. After two years of intensive treatment in hospital, she appeared to have overcome the disease. However, before she was discharged, an examination revealed that she was developing leukemia and she underwent a bone-marrow transplant. The operation was successful (Figure 7-3).

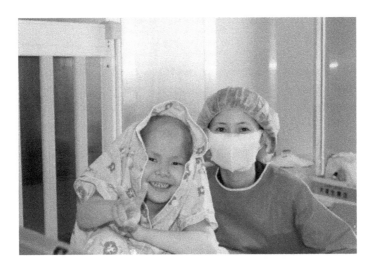

Figure 7-3: Momoka and her mother,
Yoshie, after the successful operation

In the spring of 2003, however, the leukemia returned. There was nothing more that the hospital could do, so Yoshie decided to take Momoka home for *mitori*, the practice of accompanying and caring for someone to the end of their life (Clark and Takenouchi, 2020, p. 189). The doctor was strongly against the idea of taking a child patient suffering from leukemia from the hospital, because her various symptoms – including bleeding – would best be treated at hospital. But Yoshie felt strongly about bringing her daughter home.

In the car heading home from the hospital, Momoka, who Yoshie believed did not know her real condition, said, "I have to go back to the 'Snow World.'"

Hiding her shock, Yoshie replied, "Going back? It's like [the story of] Kaguya-hime[35] [who returns to the moon]; but what will happen if I say: 'Don't go!'?"

Momoka replied, "I will be scolded for being late. But, Mom, I will write a letter to you, saying, 'Are you okay? Aren't you lonely?'"

It was an unforgettable moment for Yoshie.

After returning home, Momoka's condition improved for a while, but ultimately, on January 24th, 2004, she passed away in her mother's arms. She was 6 years and 8 months old.

Incidents Suggesting the Survival of Momoka's Consciousness

A couple of days after Momoka's funeral, her mother and sister were in their living room together. Suddenly, the room lights went out. The breaker for the living room lights had blown for unknown reasons, but Yoshie and Ryumi interpreted the event as evidence of Momoka's return (a notion that has precedence in mediumship research[36]).

About six weeks after Momoka's death, the kindergarten she had attended held a graduation ceremony, and Yoshie was given a graduation certificate on her daughter's behalf. According to Yoshie, some of the

---

[35] "Kaguya-hime" is the main protagonist in *The Tale of Kaguya* or *The Tale of the Bamboo Cutter*, a 10th-century Japanese folk tale. She is found by a bamboo cutter as a baby, inside a bamboo stalk, and raised as his daughter. She turns out to be an otherworldly being from the moon, to which she eventually returns. See Kawabata, Keene, and Miyata (1998).

[36] Research mediums who demonstrate their abilities to obtain verifiable information say that electricity related phenomena can be one of the signs of a deceased person's attempt to communicate (Beischel, 2014). The phenomena may be accounted for in terms of psychokinesis on the part of a disembodied mind (Matlock, 2017).

graduating children said they could see Momoka. At the ceremony, the names of the graduating children were called one by one. When a child's name was called, he or she would reply, "Yes." When Momoka's name was called, however, naturally nobody said "Yes." The ceremony was videoed by a local broadcasting company and was broadcast on a local TV program. To Yoshie's surprise, a strange noise that appeared to sound like *hai* – "yes" in Japanese – was recorded after Momoka's name was called, as if she had replied. I confirmed this by watching a video copy of the program recorded by Yoshie.

Four or five years after Momoka's death, a boy named Mikkun (nickname) and his mother had an impressive experience. Mikkun's mother, a friend of Yoshie, related it to me over the telephone. Mikkun had been in the hospital with Momoka for a number of weeks and was discharged a few months after she had passed away. He was only one year old at the time of discharge. Since Mikkun's mother and those around him had not talked about Momoka, he apparently had no opportunity to get to know about her before her death.

One summer night, however, Mikkun suddenly told his mother, "Someone has come from the entrance."

His mother, who was surprised because she had not seen or heard anything, said, "Who?"

Mikkun replied, "She's saying, 'I'm Momoka. I've come to see you.'" Then Mikkun added, "There's another [child]."

His mother said to him, "Ask for her name."

After muttering something, Mikkun replied, "I asked, but she wouldn't say."

"Then, ask Momoka [who it is]," his mother replied.

"Momoka says [the child is] Yumi." Yumi (pseudonym) was another child who was in the same hospital as Momoka and Mikkun. Although Yumi herself was too young to speak, she took to Momoka who often talked to her. Yumi had died about half a year before Momoka. Since Mikkun's mother had not talked to him about Yumi either, he had had no way of knowing about her.

This incident was an unforgettable one to Mikkun's mother: her child had talked about Momoka and Yumi, two deceased girls with whom he had spent some time in the same hospital but did not know and could not have remembered. When I talked with her over the telephone, she said she still vividly remembers every detail of the incident.

Announcing Dreams

As discussed in the Introduction, an announcing dream is a common feature of cases of the reincarnation type (Tucker, 2005, pp. 27-28). The phenomenon may be interpreted as a disembodied mind's attempt to communicate with the living through extra-sensory perception (Matlock, 2017).

Yoshie was 35 years old when she got a divorce, and she did not expect to remarry or to have another child. However, after receiving an unexpected proposal she did remarry. One day in November 2008, she had a significant dream in which her favorite band, Mr. Children, played a song with a beautiful melody and lyrics. A couple of days after the dream, on November 20th, she turned on the TV to find that in a variety program titled *Utaban*, Mr. Children were about to sing a new song. The title of the song was *"Hana no Nioi"* ("The Scent of Flowers"), which she thought was significant since it appeared to her to imply that Momoka (*ka* in Momoka means "flower" as explained above) was still present. The lyrics of the song also seemed significant with such phrases as:

Even if this is goodbye forever,
I can hear you breathing
I just know that in some other form, with that same smile
You'll come to see me again.

Even if this really is goodbye
I hear your warm breathing
I just know that in some other form, with the same gaze
You'll come to see me again.[37]

Yoshie strongly felt that Momoka would come back. Eleven days after the dream, she found that she was pregnant.

Soon after, her husband, Nobuaki, had a significant recurring dream in which two female children were laughing joyfully in the woods. Although he was unable to see them, he thought they were Momoka and Yumi.

---

[37] The original lyrics are in Japanese, written by SAKURAI Kazutoshi. The English translations are from a fan site with slight modification by the present author. https://ijahlovesmrchildren.wordpress.com/2008/11/16/mr-children-hana-no-nioi-the-scent-of-flowers/.

Kanon's Statements and Behaviors

The baby turned out to be a boy and he was born on July 26th, 2009. He was named Kanon after the classical music piece *Canon* by the 17th century German composer Johann Pachelbel. The name was chosen because it was his parents' favorite piece of music, and because they thought that the musical technique of counterpoint used in the piece symbolized reincarnation or spiritual connections.

Nobuaki, who is an artist, painted a picture of Yoshie in her final month of pregnancy. She is depicted holding a peach symbolizing Momoka. Below her is a portion of the musical score of Pachelbel's *Canon* (= Kanon) symbolizing Momoka's reincarnation (Figure 7-4).[38]

Figure 7-4: A portrait of Yoshie painted by Nobuaki.

While the painting demonstrates that both Momoka and reincarnation were on the parents' minds, a number of phenomena occurred once Kanon was born to suggest something more than just wishful thinking.

According to Yoshie, Kanon's facial features, tone of voice, and behavioral patterns were remarkably similar to those of Momoka.

---

[38] They did not know the sex of the child in advance. "Kanon" can be a name for either sex.

Needless to say, genetic factors must have been at work, but the resemblances were so strong as to seem almost identical.[39]

Up until the time of the interview, however, Kanon had not said that he was Momoka reborn and his parents had not given any indication that they were thinking about such a possibility (at least not deliberately). Nevertheless, Kanon had shown a number of characteristics reminding his parents of Momoka, and he had made some statements that made a strong impression on them.

Kanon's tastes were more typical of Japanese girls than of boys. Like Momoka, he loved flowers. His favorite color was pink and he always chose pink clothes to wear. At the kindergarten he attended, children made their handprints to commemorate their birthdays. They could choose either pink or blue ink to make the handprints. An unwritten "rule" was that "blue is for boys and pink is for girls." Defying this "rule," Kanon insisted on using pink for his 3-year-old and 4-year-old celebrations (Figure 7-5). However, he chose "boy" blue for his 5-year-old celebration.

Figure 7-5: Kanon's handprint for his 4th birthday commemoration

---

[39] The extreme facial resemblance between Kanon and Momoka is supported by an emerging technology of computer science. The "TwinsOrNot" site (http://twinsornot.net), which assesses how similar people in two photos are by giving a score from 0 to 100, gave 82 points to a picture of 5-year-old Kanon and a picture of 5-year-old Momoka. The scores of Momoka's picture and five pictures of other 5-year-old male children, randomly chosen from a kindergarten class with which I was involved as a volunteer, are 44, 62, 67, 71, and 79 points. At present, since the technology is not yet full-fledged, the scores are just for a reference.

He also liked typically "girls'" toys, and had a toy cosmetic set with lipstick, comb, mirror, and ribbons (Figure 7-6). He sometimes asked his mother to tie his hair with a ribbon (Figure 7-7).

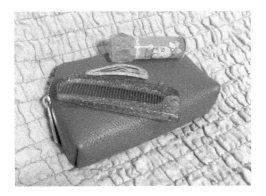

Figure 7-6: Kanon's toy cosmetic set

Figure 7-7: Kanon wearing a ribbon.

Like Momoka, he loved Sylvanian Families, the toy rabbits. As stated above, the ones Momoka possessed had been put in her coffin, so new ones were bought upon Kanon's request. His fondness for playing with dolls, which are generally considered as being for girls (including the toy rabbits), is itself worth noticing; but more interestingly, he played with them in the same way that Momoka did: he called his half-sister to play with him and asked her to say words and behave as he directed.

Perhaps more intriguing, however, were statements Kanon made when he was 4 years and 4 months old: "The wall color of the house used to be different. It used to be much darker." This was a correct statement because the wall color of the house, which had been dark brown when Momoka lived there, had faded and was now light brown.

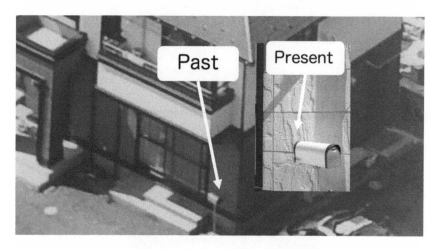

Figure 7-8: The wall color of the house

Five months later, when his parents were present, all of a sudden Kanon said, "I was once burnt." They were so surprised that they did not ask him what he meant, but they believed that he was talking about the cremation of the body of his past life personality, Momoka.

The most memorable and most convincing incident, however, happened when Kanon was 4 years and 6 months old. The necessary background information is that Kanon showed precociousness in reading and writing. He was able to write all the Japanese characters when he was four years old.[40] According to Shimamura and Mikami (1994), of the 432 four-year-old children they investigated, none were able to write all the Japanese letters. By the age of five, Kanon was able to read books written for elementary school children.

---

[40] He wrote some letters in mirror writing. See note 42.

One day, Kanon came to Yoshie saying, "I have written a letter to mom." Rather than actual writing, Kanon had drawn only two horizontal lines.

Yoshie asked him: "What does this say?"

He said he had written, "Mom, are you okay? Aren't you lonely?'"

These words touched Yoshie deeply, recalling the conversation she had had with Momoka in the car on the way home from the hospital 11 years earlier. In addition, it had been snowing for a few days, and it was indeed as if Momoka's letter had come from the Snow World as she had promised.

The next day, Yoshie asked Kanon to write another letter, saying: "Kanon, you can write all Hiragana [one type of the Japanese characters].[41] Could you write the letter you gave me yesterday again?" Thinking that she should not guide him in any way, she was careful to say only "write the letter you gave me yesterday."

Upon her request, Kanon wrote another letter, this time with the actual correct characters. It reads: "Mom, aren't you lonely? Aren't you lonely?"[42] (Figure 7-9). This incident convinced Yoshie that Momoka indeed had come back as Kanon.

Figure 7-9: Kanon's letter echoing Momoka's words.

Kanon's statements and behaviors appearing to be related to Momoka are summarized in the following table:

[41] Japanese has three types of characters: Hiragana, Katakana, and Kanji (originated from Chinese characters). The first two are phonetic symbols.

[42] In the letter shown in Figure 7-9, mirror writing is observed in two letters: "し" and "く". Yet, Kanon's precocity is undeniable.

Table 7-1: Kanon's Statements Apparently Related to Momoka

	Age	Characteristics/Statements
(1)	1 year old (to the present)	Loved flowers and often said, "They are beautiful."
(2)	1 year old–5 years old	Favorite color was pink, for clothes, school birthday handprints etc.
(3)	1 year old–5 years old	Showed interests in girls' toys and fashion (He also loved boys' toys, however.)
(4)	1 year old–5 years old	Asked to buy toy rabbits of the Sylvanian Families, Momoka's favorite toys. Played with his half-sister in the same way as Momoka used to.

Table 7-2: Kanon's Behaviors Apparently Related to Momoka

	Age	Characteristics/Behaviors
(1)	? –present	Precocious in reading and writing.
(2)	4 years and 4 months old	Knew that wall color of the house used to be different.
(3)	4 years and 6 months old	Wrote a letter repeating the promise Momoka had made to Yoshie.
(4)	4 years and 9 months old	Out of the blue he said, "I was once burnt."

Kanon's Life-Between-Life Memories

Kanon also spoke impressively of some apparent life-between-life memories. When he was two years old, at bedtime he said, "I've come to mom's belly from a faraway place. I've come, hurry, hurry! [I've come in a hurry]." Yoshie was 41 years old when Kanon was born, and she interpreted his words to mean that he had cared about her age so he had come to her as quickly as possible.

When he was 6 years and 2 or 3 months old, Kanon and Yoshie were lying on the bed and watching the night sky from the window. Yoshie said, "It's beautiful, feels good."

To this, he replied, "I'm wondering if there is heaven above clouds. I'm not sure whether it was real or in the dream, but there were so many flowers blooming in heaven and a river was running with glistening water. The flowers and the river were much more beautiful than those you see in this world. The color of the river was like pink and orange, and angels the same size as me are flying. Some were male. A god in heaven was sitting on a sort of cushion. There were many masks. You chose your own mask. Some of them were funny like this [he puckered and skewed his mouth to one side]. I chose mine and then my face became Kanon's face."

Some children who remember life-between-life states say that they chose their face or body, even in cases where they had handicaps. For instance, INYAKU Rio, who had to undergo several surgeries and spend a lot of time in the hospital due to a serious heart problem, said that he chose his body because he had thought it exciting to cope with the diseases, almost like playing a game (see Inyaku 2012). Kanon seems to have referred to a similar kind of face/body choice in his life-between-life state.

About two months later, while taking a bath with his mother, Kanon asked, "Do you remember the story of heaven I told you the other day?" (The story just described above). When Yoshie talked about the beautiful flowers and the river, Kanon said frustratedly, "That's not all." He then talked about the story of God and the masks again. Yoshie felt that he did so because he wanted her to believe that it was real, and to emphasize that it was not a fantasy.

Two months later, when Yoshie asked Kanon what heaven was like, he replied: "There was a river or a sea, and the water was glittering and very beautiful." It seems that he still retained life-between-life memories at that time.

His statements concerning life-between-life memories are summarized in the table below:

Table 7-3. Kanon's Statements about Life-Between-Life Memories

	Age	Statements
(1)	2 years old	"I've come to mom's belly from a faraway place. I've come, hurry, hurry! [I've come in a hurry.]"
(2)	6 years and 2 or 3 months old	Described the life-between-life state and choosing his new face there.
(3)	6 years and 5 months old	Asked Yoshie whether she correctly remembered the story he had talked about (2).
(4)	6 years and 7 months old	To Yoshie's question about what heaven was like, he gave a vivid description.

Reincarnation Cases and Sex-Change

Sex-change can sometimes be observed in cases of children claiming to have past-life memories: a female remembers a life as a male or vice versa. In the DOPS database I consulted in 2015, 176 (9.2%) of 1,909 cases are sex-change cases. 126 of them are cases in which females had past-life memories as males and 50 are those in which males had past-life memories as females. These so-called sex-change cases often involve cross-dressing or/and other gender nonconformity. But such traits usually disappear as children grow older just as their past-life memories fade away. This pattern is observed in the case of Kanon.[43]

Sudden Flashback of Past-Life Memories?

In early May, 2020, Yoshie told the author about some very interesting incidents that had just happened. Kanon was 10 years and 10 months old, and had lost most of the feminine tastes that seemed suggestive of Momoka. His parents, especially Yoshie, had not talked about their thought that Kanon might be Momoka reborn, out of consideration for the possibility that Kanon would not be happy with the idea.

---

[43] Past-life memories might account for at least a portion of gender nonconformity observed in children. See Pehlivanova, et al., 2018).

However, one day while Kanon was sitting on the sofa with his parents in the living room, he blurted out: "I am Momo-chan[44] [= Momoka] reborn." They were so surprised that they were unable to ask him why he said that.

On another day, while Kanon was with Yoshie in the morning, he again said, "I am Momo-chan reborn." Again, Yoshie was unable to react to the remarks at that time, but later in the evening, when Nobuaki was present, Yoshie talked to Kanon about twice saying that he was Momoka reborn. He immediately protested, "What are you talking about? How could I say such a thing?"

Yoshie turned Nobuaki for help, asking him, "Kanon did say that, didn't he?"

Nobuaki had been present when Kanon had said it first time, so he replied to Kanon, "Yes, you did."

Kanon continued to deny it, claiming, "No, I didn't say that! I never said that!"

It appears that for a short period of time, his past-life memory had flashed back twice but quickly faded away.

---

[44] "Chan" is a kind of honorific marker attached to what the speaker/writer considers "cute" such as children, girls, pets, etc.

8

I Wanted to Be Born in Japan: The Case of Akane

~

kane (pseudonym) was born in June 2005. In July 2010, I visited her at her home and spent two days interviewing her with her mother. Akane's parents were divorced and she lived only with her mother. She was 5 years old at that time and appeared to retain vivid memories of her ostensible past life. Apart from some incidents that happened before Akane turned three, the statements recounted below were made either by Akane herself, or by her mother and confirmed by her.

When Akane was born, she had an oval birthmark of about 3 x 1 centimeters on her forehead, which was, according to Akane, related to her past life.

Akane's mother described to me how she noticed her daughter's marked attraction to people with dark skin:

The first impressive incident that was related to her past life, or so I found later, occurred when I took her to a kindergarten tour. She was two years old. The selling point of the kindergarten was that children were taken care of in English as well as in Japanese. About 15 children participated in the tour and there were three teachers: a Japanese, a white American, and a black

American.[45] Naturally, most of the children gathered around the Japanese teacher. Some around the white American, though Akane was the only child who went to the black teacher and played with her happily.

The mother said that around the same time, Akane surprised her when they went to an Indian restaurant. Dark-skinned people were serving and cooking, and Akane appeared to be very happy and attracted by them. Later when she was able to talk, she said: "I like people having dark skin."

Akane started talking about her past-life memories just before she turned four. She was a late talker and her mother had been worrying about that, and had even taken her to a doctor who was unable to find any particular problem. One day, the mother talked about Akane's apparent delay in language development with a friend of hers over the telephone. When she got off the phone, Akane protested with broken Japanese. What she said was, in essence: "I used to live in India, and was able to speak English. I'm in trouble because Mom can't speak English. So, I'm reluctantly learning Japanese." Although surprised by her words, her mother, who had read a book about children with prenatal memories, just listened to what Akane said, without judging whether it was true or just the girl's imagination.

When Akane was three years old, her mother took her to a clinic to have the birthmark on her forehead removed (Figure 8-1).

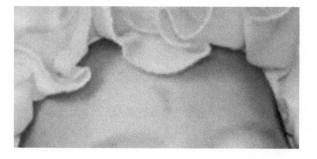

Figure 8-1: Akane's birthmark

---

[45] The mother thought they were Americans, but she did not remember whether the teachers themselves said so.

After the treatment, Akane said: "I hated it all the time even when I was in India," seemingly referring to a *bindi* (a colored dot of religious significance) largely worn by Hindus. "But when I was in the sky [i.e., in the life-between-life state], a goddess put it on my forehead so that I wouldn't forget my life in India." According to Akane, there was a number of goddesses and gods in the sky (Figures 8-2 and 8-3).

Figure 8-2: Goddesses Akane met in the sky.

Figure 8-3: Gods Akane met in the sky.

Notice that the gods and goddesses in the pictures wear bindis on their foreheads. According to Akane, the colors of the bindis vary among the different deities.

Akane also appeared to be familiar with some of the Indian deities. To the interview, I brought a book titled *Hindukyo no Hon (A Book of Hinduism)* (Books Esoterica, 1994), which has pictures of representative Hindu gods and goddesses. I showed them one by one, asking Akane whether they were familiar to her or not. Although Akane did not give the names of the gods and goddesses, she was quick and decisive in answering which gods/goddesses she knew and which ones she did not. She said that she knew Brahma, Lakshmi, and Durga, and that she did not know Vishnu, Shiva, Saraswati, and Kali.

It often angered Akane when her mother wrapped a towel around her head after giving her a bath. She said that it was men's practice, appearing to refer to the turban Sikhs and other religious groups wear. Had she been in India, she would have had ample opportunities to see them, impressing on her that wearing a cloth around the head is only for men. Akane said she still thought that women should not do that.

She remembered the name of her former self in India, and the names of the other family members. She said she had been called Radhi.[46] The name of her father had been "Rai Heiz" and that of her mother "Taiyre" (Figure 8-4).

Figure 8-4: Akane's drawing of her mother from her past life.

---

[46] The spellings of the names are inevitably approximate. "Radhi," for instance, might be "Ladi," "Ladhi," or some other similar forms. Gregory Shushan suggests that it might have been "Radhe," also spelled "Radha," who was Krishna's consort deity.

Akane also said that she had had an elder brother and an elder sister, whose names had been "Nikki" and "Raiya," respectively. She remembered having had a dog named "Sabi" (Figure 8-5), and that she had lived in a place called "Riskrai."

Figure 8-5: Akane's drawing of her dog from her past life.

She described her former house as being two stories, having pink walls, a lion-shaped knocker on the front door, and a triangular flag on the top of the roof (Figure 8-6).

Figure 8-6: Akane's former house.
(drawn by the author by following Akane's instructions)

There had been a supermarket named "Efex" and another one named "Mishin." Her father had worked at a company named "Nushinama." Her mother had been very beautiful and had appeared on TV;[47] and had once been hospitalized because of high fever.

Akane had pyrophobia to the extent that she was unable to enter a restaurant with a decorative fire at the entrance. Her mother first noticed Akane's fear of fire when she took her to a night show at Tokyo Disney Sea Park. When fireworks started to be launched, Akane went into a panic and they had to leave the show. When Akane was almost four, a news program reported a house fire on TV. Watching the house on fire on the television screen, Akane started to scream in a panicked voice: "Nakebo! Nakebo!" When the surprised mother asked what she meant, she said: "Fire! Fire!"

The mother said that Akane disliked men wearing glasses. Fortunately, that feeling had subsided by the time of the interview, and my wearing glasses did not appear to have any negative effect.

The cause of Akane's pyrophobia was discovered after she turned four. She said: "I died in a fire. A man wearing glasses fell in love with my mother, and set fire to our house. I died with my mother. I remember seeing my mother's scorched body. I wiped her scorched face [non-physically?]. From the sky I saw the house burning and the other family members crying."

Verification

The information Akane gave was too unspecific to identify the people and the place she had been talking about, but consulting four graduate students from India[48] revealed that most of the information Akane gave was consistent with a typical Hindu community in India, as outlined in the table below:

---

[47] She did not say whether she appeared just once or more than once.

[48] They are Molli Shylaja Devi, Messrs. Amit Kumar Mishra, Govindam Venkata Siva Sudhakar, and Kamidi Boudha Aradhana. They were all graduate students of Nagoya University and I visited them there. I am grateful to KASHIMA Tanomu of Nagoya University for arranging the meeting.

Table 8-1: Indian Evaluations of Akane's Statements

Statements	Comments
Akane's Past-Life Personality: "Radhi" (or "Ladi," "Ladhi," etc.)	"Radhi" is quite common as the shortened form of "Radhika."
Father: "Rai Heiz" (or "Lai Heiz," etc.)	"Rai Hesu" is a real Indian name.
Mother: The name "Taiyre" (or "Tyre," "Taire," etc.)	"Tara" is a common name.
Brother: "Nikki" (or "Mikki")	Both are common names.
Sister: "Raiya" (or "Laiya," etc.)	"Rya" and "Laya" are common names.
Dog: "Sabi"	Unknown (but any name can be possible for a dog)
Place Where She Had Lived: "Riskurai" (or "Liskrai," "Lisklai," "Risklai," etc.	Perhaps "Rishikesh" in the Northern India?
Super Market: "Efex" ("FX?")	Unknown
Super Market: "Mishin"	Possible if "Mi" + "Singh"
Hospital: "Okoshin"	Possible if "Oko" + "Singh"
Father's Company: "Nushinama"	Unknown
Word Uttered When Akane Saw Fire: "Nakebo"	Perhaps "Nakaro," meaning "Don't?"
House with Pink Walls	Common
Triangle Flag on the Roof	Common, but usually on religious buildings, so perhaps a very religious family?

Akane and her mother had never been to India and had no connection with the country or people. The comments by the Indian graduate students on Akane's statements suggest that Akane may have had some paranormal knowledge concerning a life in India.

As for the reason she was born in Japan, Akane said, "I chose to be born in Japan. It was not a good choice to have been born in India because women were not treated nicely there. So I decided to come to Japan, where women were treated nicely. I heard mom's voice [= a woman's voice] calling me, so I went to her, and was born."

Interestingly, her mother did "call her" when Akane was in a life-between-life state: "I desperately wanted a girl. So shortly before my pregnancy, I had prayed and prayed for a girl, saying: 'Please come to me!'"

Unfortunately, I have lost contact with Akane's mother, so I am unable to report on her later development here. While there are some intriguing elements to the case, without being able to identify individuals associated with Akane's, it remains inconclusive.

9

I Came Back to Make Mom Happy This Time: The Case of Kazuya

~

How I Came to Investigate the Case

This is a case in which a young man who had passed away by committing suicide appears to have come back to his mother by being born to his half-sister. I came to know of the case through a Japanese documentary movie titled *Kamisama tono Yakusoku* (*A Promise with God*), featuring children claiming to have prenatal memories including life-between-life and past-life (Ogikubo (Director), 2013). In the film, 9-year-old Kazuya talked about his experiences after he died in his previous life (Figure 9-1).

Figure 9-1: *Kamisama tono Yakusoku* movie (2013).

I am one of the researchers appearing in the film, and the producer/
director OGIKUBO Norio, allowed me to watch the original interview
video with Kazuya, which lasts about two hours. In the video, Kazuya did
not talk about his past-life memories in detail, focusing instead on his
life-between-life memories. The main source of information about his
past life was a book written by Kazuya's grandmother, MINAMIYAMA
Midori (hereafter Midori), who is a counselor and therapist. The book
(Minamiyama, 2014) collects accounts of children claiming to have
prenatal memories.

After Skyping twice with Midori and once with Kazuya, I interviewed
them in person in 2016, when Kazuya was 10 years and 10 months old.
On the same day, I also interviewed Kazuya's mother Izumi, along
with three other children and their mother "Ms. T." These children,
M. (male, born in 2002), H. (female, born in 2004), and S. (male, born
in 2008) are of no direct relevance to Kazuya's past-life memories, but
they claim to have been with Kazuya in the life-between-life state. Their
accounts will therefore be discussed in the section on Kazuya's life-
between-life memories later in this chapter (two of the three children,
M. and H., also appeared in the documentary).

After the above-mentioned interviews, I heard from Midori that Kazuya had met two women whom Kazuya's past-life personality had trained in basketball when they were sixth-graders. I had another telephone interview with Kazuya about this part of the case, as well as with the two women.

The Story of Jun

Jun was the second son of Midori and her first husband, born in September 1975. Their first child, Jun's elder brother Makoto, had been born two years earlier. Soon after Jun was born, Midori divorced and her parents (Jun's grandparents) helped Midori raise Jun and Makoto. Because of this, Jun particularly loved his grandparents. Midori later remarried and a daughter, Izumi, was born in February 1980.

When Jun was 5 years old, he collapsed from an epileptic seizure and started taking medication, which he continued to take for the next 15 years. In 1997, when he was 21, he tried to help Izumi's classmates when they got into trouble with delinquents associated with the yakuza and were badly hurt in a fight.[49] After that, Jun began to reluctantly associate with the gang. His family, especially Midori, made every effort to put an end to it and persuade Jun to stop hanging around such bad influences. Jun promised Midori that he would break off his friendship with them, but the promise was not fulfilled.

On December 19th, 1997, Jun again promised to put an end to his association with the yakuza and he went off to meet them. At that time, Midori had changed jobs and started working in a work-skill training institute. While there, she received a telephone call from a man who had claimed that he would be able to help Jun leave the gang. He was with Jun when he had tried to leave, and explained to Midori that the attempt was unsuccessful. Midori was upset and sent a message to Jun via the man, telling him to come to the institute to discuss the issue with her. When Jun reluctantly arrived, Midori criticized him severely. Overwhelmed by her fury and his own sense of guilt, Jun dashed away from the institute.

That night, Midori received a telephone call from the police, who told her that Jun had committed suicide by jumping from a bridge over a highway. The estimated time of his death was 11:45 pm.

---

[49] The children were all students of a private school Midori managed at that time.

139

Some Incidents Suggesting the Survival of Jun's Consciousness

After Jun's death, Midori was suffering from a deep sense of remorse, believing that her words had triggered her son's suicide. She even thought, "I would willingly sell my soul to the devil if I could see Jun again."

On the seventh day after Jun's death, a little past 11:00 pm, Midori heard a loud knocking at the front hall door. The dog she had at the time dashed under Midori's bed, shaking with fear. Midori felt instinctively that Jun had come back. Despite herself, she said: "Jun, go back. This is not where you belong." Midori, who had been so longing to see Jun, did not understand why she had said that. As if responding to her words, the loud knocking ceased. After the incident, Midori became overwhelmed by an additional sense of guilt: she felt that she had severed the tie with her son for the second time.

About half a year after Jun's death, he began to appear to Midori in her dreams and admonish her. Night after night he said: "You should forgive them. You should not blame anyone."

Her reply in her dream was always, "No, I can't forgive them."

"You should forgive them," Jun would reply. "It was my own fault that I committed suicide, not theirs. Seeing you lament like that makes me sad, and I can't go back to the Light. So, please don't blame anyone."

Midori did not remember when the conversations with Jun in her dreams ended, but she said that his words had gradually calmed her down.[50]

Kazuya's Statements and Behaviors

In April 2005, Midori's daughter Izumi (Jun's half-sister) gave birth to Kazuya. He was almost two months premature, weighing only 1,198 grams (2 lbs. 10.5 oz.), and was immediately admitted to the neonatal intensive care unit. After 50 days, Kazuya was discharged but was asthmatic as well as atopic (developing allergic hypersensitivity reactions) and had to see a doctor regularly. He also had cryptorchidism

---

[50] Midori wrote about her dream in her 2013 book. Kazuya's statements and behaviors (2), (7), (10), (11), and (13) in Table 9-2 below were also reported in the book.

(failure of the testes to descend into the scrotum) and underwent surgery when he was one year old. Shortly after Kazuya was born, he and Izumi went to live with Midori, so Midori has had ample opportunity to observe Kazuya's development.

From a very young age, Kazuya began to show behaviors that perhaps suggested they had originated with the previous personality of Jun. Shortly after, he began making statements consistent with him.

At around 11:45 p.m. on December 9th 2004, the day and the estimated time of Jun's death seven years earlier, 8-month-old Kazuya, who was held by his mother Izumi, started to cry. With a gesture, he urged her to take him upstairs to the room where Jun had lived. Perplexed, Izumi took him to the room, at which point Kazuya stopped crying and smiled. Izumi felt that Jun had come back.

At the age of one, when Kazuya was crying, he was shown a drawing of a scene from a picture book titled *Suho's White Horse*. He suddenly stopped crying and appeared to recognize it. It was drawn by Jun when he was in second grade.

Before Kazuya turned one year old, he started to show great affection for his great-grandfather and great-grandmother. At that time his great-grandfather was in a hospital and Kazuya visited him and wiped his face every day (Figure 9-2). His visit continued for a year and two months until his great grandfather passed away.

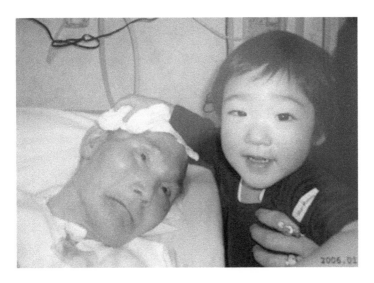

Figure 9-2: Kazuya (9 months) wiping his great-grandfather's face.

Kazuya refers to his family members in a way that is unusual for a son of Izumi, but to be expected as Jun. For example, Jun had called his grandfather (Kazuya's great grandfather) *otosan* meaning "father," and his grandmother (Kazuya's great grandmother) *okasan* meaning "mother." He had called Midori (Kazuya's grandmother) *mama*. For Jun, his grandfather and grandmother were like his actual father and mother, so he called them *otosan* "father" and *okasan* "mother," respectively. He chose another expression referring to one's mother, "mama," to call his actual grandmother (Midori.) Jun had called his sister Izumi (Kazuya's mother) *Ii-chan* ("Ii" is the lengthened first sound of "Izumi" and "-chan" is an honorific marker). Kazuya referred to them in the same idiosyncratic way as Jun did. Izumi recalled that, when Kazuya started calling his grandmother Midori *mama*, she said, "This [Midori] is your grandmother, not mother. I am your mother." But Kazuya protested, saying: "This is *mama*," and Izumi eventually yielded.

The expressions Jun and Kazuya used and those expected to be used by him are shown in the following table:

Table 9-1: Expressions Kazuya Actually
Used and Those Expected to Be Used[51]

Family Members	Expression Jun and Kazuya Used	Expression Kazuya Was expected to Use
Jun's grandfather (Kazuya's great grandfather)	*otosan*	*o-ojīchan*
Jun's grandmother (Kazuya's great grandmother)	*okasan*	*o-obāchan*
Jun's mother (Kazuya's grandmother)	*mama*	*obāchan*
Jun's sister (Kazuya's mother)	*Ii-chan*	*okasan* or *mama*

---

[51] The macron is used in "o-ojīchan," "o-obāchan," and "obāchan" to distinguish them from the corresponding words without a long vowel: "o-ojichan (great uncle)," "o-obachan (great aunt)," and "obachan (aunt)."

Another episode related to the ways in which Kazuya referred to people seemed to be further indication that he was the reborn Jun. One of Jun's best friends was named Yumi (pseudonym). She visited the house on every anniversary of Jun's death. Kazuya, when he was only two years old, first met Yumi on the tenth anniversary. Although nobody told him her name, he called her correctly by her name. Furthermore, the way Kazuya pronounced the name was quite unusual (putting strong accent on -*mi* in *Yumi*) – exactly how Jun had pronounced it. Neither Midori nor Izumi talked about the possible reincarnation of Jun, but hearing Kazuya pronouncing her name in the same way that Jun had, Yumi could not hold back tears. Midori and Izumi, who were present, also shed tears.

As mentioned, Kazuya was asthmatic and atopic and had to see a doctor regularly. When Kazuya was two years old, during an asthma attack, Midori, who was taking care of him, was surprised to hear him say: "I can't breathe, but I won't die. I will live this time."

One crucial incident, especially to Midori, happened when Kazuya was three years old. Midori had thought – but had not felt entirely certain – that Kazuya was the reborn Jun. After much hesitation, she finally asked him, "Were you Jun?"

Kazuya replied, "When I was born from *mama* [= Midori], I was Jun. But now I am Kaju [attempting but unable to pronounce 'Kazu']. I am Kaju, now."

Because of the statements and behaviors Kazuya had made so far, Midori now became almost convinced that Kazuya was Jun reborn. Kazuya's statements seemed to validate Midori's conviction, but at the same time reminded Midori of the fact that Kazuya is not Jun and that she should treat him as an independent person.

There were additional minor episodes that helped confirm to Midori and Izumi the already strong conviction that Kazuya was the reborn Jun. Because of his physical conditions, Kazuya had to ingest a couple of different medications. When he was five years old, Midori noticed that Kazuya kept drugs organized in a very similar way that Jun had organized his own drugs.

The way Kazuya accepted and coped with his disease was admirable to Midori and Izumi. They came to know the reason when they heard Kazuya say, "I could have died of a disease, but I wanted to die early. I didn't face my disease at that time, so I'm now facing it."

As mentioned above, Kazuya showed great affection for his great grandmother (Figure 9-3) as well as for his great grandfather. When

Kazuya was 10 years old, his great grandmother passed away. After the funeral and cremation, he insisted on carrying the cremation urn until he and his family arrived back home. He said, "I have finally fulfilled the promise with her which I couldn't fulfill before." When Jun had been alive, he had promised his grandmother that, when she became too old to walk, he would carry her on his back. This promise had not been kept because of his early death. Now, as Kazuya, by carrying her ashes in the urn, Jun fulfilled the promise.

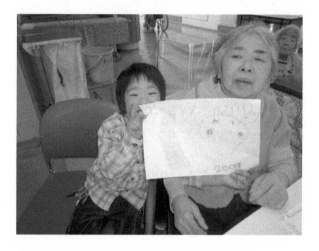

Figure 9-3: Kazuya (4 years and 2 months) celebrating his great-grandmother's birthday.

Kazuya's statements and behaviors related to his past life are summarized in the following table:

Table 9-2: Statements and Behaviors Related to Kazuya's Past Life

	age	statement/behavior
(1)	8 months old	On December 9th, 2004, at around 11:45 p.m. (the day and the estimated time of Jun's death), Kazuya started to cry. With a gesture, he urged his mother to take him upstairs to the room where Jun had lived. When taken there, he stopped crying and smiled.
(2)	1 year old	Suddenly stopped crying when he saw a drawing of a scene from a picture book titled *Suho's White Horse*, drawn by Jun when he was in second grade.
(3)	Around 9 months to 2 years old	Showed much affection for his great-grandfather, reminding Midori and Izumi of the affection Jun had showed him. From around 9 months old until the great-grandfather's death, Kazuya visited him in the hospital every day and wiped his face.
(4)	1 year to 2 years old	Called his great grandfather *otosan* meaning "father," as Jun had called him.
(5)	1 year to 10 years old	Showed great affection for his great-grandmother, reminding Midori and Izumi of the affection Jun showed to her. Also see item (14) below.
(6)	1 year to 10 years old	Called his great grandmother *okasan* meaning "mother," as Jun had called her.
(7)	1 year to present	Calls Midori (Jun's mother/Kazuya's grandmother) "mama," not "grandmother" as expected. When told by his mother that Midori was his grandmother, he insisted that she was his mother.
(8)	1 year to present	Calls Izumi (Kazuya's mother/Jun's half-sister) *Ii-chan* as Jun called her, not "mama" as expected.
(9)	2 years old	When Kazuya met Jun's best friend, who visited his home every anniversary of his death, he called her by the same nickname with the same unusual accent as Jun had done.

(10)	2 years old	During an asthma attack, he said to Midori: "I can't breathe, but I won't die. I will live this time."
(11)	3 years old	In response to Midori's question: "Were you Jun?" he said, "When I was born from *mama* [= Midori], I was Jun. But now I am Kaju [attempting but unable to pronounce "Kazu"]. I am Kaju, now."
(12)	5 years old	Kept his drugs organized in a way that reminded Midori of Jun's way of organizing his drugs.
(13)	9 years old	Said: "I could have died of a disease, but I wanted to die early. I didn't face my disease at that time, so I'm now facing it."
(14)	10 years old	After the funeral and cremation of his great-grandmother (February 2016), he insisted on carrying the cremation urn until Kazuya and his family arrived back home. He believed that he now "fulfilled the promise" that Jun had made to her: that he would carry her when she grew too old to walk.

Kazuya's Life-Between-Life Memories

More persistent were Kazuya's memories of the life-between-life place where he had stayed after the death of his past personality; that is, during the period between his death in his past life and the conception of his current self (Ogikubo, 2013). At the time of the interview, he still had the memories and recounted them to me:

> After I died, I regretted committing suicide and entered the 'reflection room,' a dark room for the dead who regret what they have done while alive. I was there for a while, reflecting on my past conduct, and when I felt I would be able to start over again [in a new life], I decided to be born to my mama. I have come here to give "presents" to those who I had hurt before [that is, to make them happy].

Midori also recalled that when they went to Asahina Kiridoshi, a sightseeing spot in Kamakura, for the first time, Kazuya said to Midori,

"Here, here. I was looking at this place from the sky!" He also said, "I have been here before."[52] Kazuya was three years old at the time. When he was five years old, Midori again took him to the place and he repeated that he had been looking at the place from the sky.

Another interesting feature of Kazuya's life-between-life memories is that the three children I interviewed all claimed that they had been with Kazuya in that state and had promised one another to be together again when they were reborn. Although neither Midori nor Ms. T. (the mother of the three children) remembered exactly when, by July 2008, when Kazuya was three years old, he had met the three children. Midori and Ms. T. remembered that when they had all first met, possibly at a seminar for counselors which Midori held, M. (the eldest of the three children) first said, "When we were up there, we promised to be together [on Earth]," and the other three seemed to agree with him. According to Midori, Izumi, and Ms. T., they are very close to each other, and the three children regularly visit Midori's house to be with Kazuya. When I spent over 6 hours together with them, I noticed that they all seemed very happy about being together.

Although this promise to be together on Earth did not have any verifiable elements, two of the three children also had memories comparable to Kazuya's. Just like Kazuya, M. (13 years and 9 months old at the time of the interview) and H. (12 years and 1 month old) claimed that before they met in the life-between-life place, they had spent some time in the "reflection room." They talked in detail about this in the 2013 documentary film, but at the time of the interview their memories appeared to have faded and they had only a fragmentary impression of the dark place and a sense of guilt due to misconduct in their past-lives.

In the movie, H. (female) talked about her past-life memories as an egoistic woman living in an Asian country, possibly Mongolia. She recalled being particularly interested in spending money to dress herself up, and she did not care about her family members at all. After her death, she saw that no one in her family was mourning her, and regretted the life she had led. She therefore entered the "reflection room" and reflected on her conduct. When she felt she should start over again, she decided to be reborn. She also talked about coming to her mother with "presents" to please her. Indeed, according to her mother, when H. was a small child, she was always trying to please her by giving her "presents" such as beautiful leaves, flowers, and stones.

---

[52] Midori had been to the place a number of times with Jun, so his remark here might have meant that he had been here in his past life as Jun.

In the movie, M. (male) did not talk about his past-life memories but talked about the "reflection room" in detail. He emphasized that nobody is forced to enter the room but those who feel that they did something wrong deliberately enter it to reflect on their conduct. At the time of the interview, he said that he vaguely remembered that he had participated in combat during a war in his past-life, and what he had done there would probably have been the cause of his entering the "reflection room." Neither H. nor M. remembered whether the present mother has any connection with somebody in their past-lives.

Kazuya's Birthmark

Children with past-life memories often have birthmarks and birth defects corresponding to wounds, often fatal ones, or other marks on the past-life body (Stevenson, 1997). Kazuya had a clear birthmark on his left arm, which was still visible at the time of the interview (Figure 9-4).

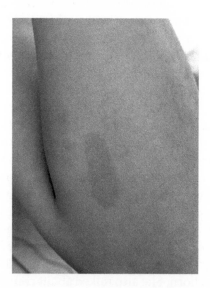

Figure 9-4: Kazuya's birthmark

According to Midori, the place of the birthmark corresponds to a burn that Jun suffered when he accidentally touched the exhaust pipe of a motorbike at the age of 18 or 19. Kazuya himself did not have any memory of the event (it is not known whether he had had the relevant memory when he was younger since Midori had never asked him about the birthmark).

"Reunion" with Former Students

Jun was a good basketball player and when he was a high-school student, once or twice a week he went to his former elementary school to train school children in basketball. Among the students trained by Jun in 1994 were twin girls named Mikoto and Tomomi, who were sixth-graders at the time. They both greatly admired Jun, who didn't treat them as small children, as most adults around them did, but as independent persons. Tomomi was especially fond of him and carried a picture of him as a kind of good-luck charm. After graduating from the elementary school, they no longer had the chance to meet with Jun. Naturally, they were greatly shocked when they heard from their mother in 1997 that he had committed suicide. Tomomi continued to carry the picture until she was 19 years old (in 2001). At that time, the girls did not know Midori, and Midori only indirectly knew them: her first son was a classmate of their older brother, and Midori's mother worked at the same hospital as their mother.

In July 2016, Mikoto, one of the twins, who was now 34 years old, had a "welcome baby" class held at a clinic where her son had been born two days earlier. Midori, a counselor and a therapist, was in charge of the session. In a chat with Midori after the class, Mikoto realized that Midori was Jun's mother and talked about her memories of Jun when she was a sixth-grader. Midori talked about the story of Jun and Kazuya.

Mikoto owns a farm, and invited Midori and Kazuya for a visit that September. In a telephone interview a month later, Mikoto described the meeting to me. "I was told by Midori that Kazuya was Jun reborn," she said, "but it was unbelievable. Jun was tall, and Kazuya is a sixth-grade kid. They were just so different. But during a chat, when I looked closely at Kazuya's eyes, I felt I knew them. It was overwhelming and I was unable to continue looking at them. I was convinced that Kazuya was Jun."

Regarding this meeting, Kazuya told me, "When I first met Mikoto, she told me, 'It's nice meeting you.' I didn't say that to her because I thought I had met her before. I didn't recall details, but I felt I knew her very well."

When Mikoto's farm held a harvest festival in September, her twin sister Tomomi as well as Kazuya and Midori visited her. In a telephone interview the following month, Tomomi told me, "I met Kazuya for the first time, but I felt I knew him very well. It might have been because I was told that Kazuya was Jun reborn. But it was such a strange feeling. After the meeting, I did something very strange. It was October. I had a chance to visit the city where Kazuya's school is located. I went to the school to meet Kazuya and gave him my contact information. I'm an artist. I like being alone and I don't usually give my address to anybody, but this time I felt I had to stay connected with him." Kazuya was only 11 years old at the time.

In relation to their meeting, Kazuya told me, "When I first met Tomomi at Mikoto's farm, I felt I knew her, just like I felt when I first met Mikoto. But I deeply felt so when Tomomi told me to come to her to take a picture." As for Tomomi's visit to his school, Kazuya said, "Teachers were making a fuss. An unknown woman, who is not a relative of mine, came to meet me. They asked her many questions, but when I entered the room where Tomomi was questioned, the teachers fell silent, and it was funny. The meeting with Tomomi was natural to me."

Although Kazuya did not give specific pieces of information that only his previous personality could have known, Mikoto and Tomomi's reactions are noteworthy. This is especially the case given that neither Mikoto nor Tomoi had ever been acquainted with real cases suggestive of reincarnation.

In this connection, it is worth pointing out that Kazuya, who had never been trained in basketball, is an unusually good basketball player. According to him, he was often asked by his friends why he was so good at the game.

The Case of Kazuya and Other Cases Involving Suicide

At the time of the writing of his 2001 book, Ian Stevenson had investigated 23 suicide cases. Concerning these cases, he wrote: "If we regard reincarnation as the best interpretation for these cases, they disprove the belief expounded in some religions that persons who commit suicide live in Hell for centuries or even for eternity" (Stevenson, 2001, p. 220). The case of Kazuya presents another piece of evidence against the "eternally live in Hell" theory.

Stevenson also pointed out that "the memory of the suicide did not necessarily extinguish the inclination to suicide" (Stevenson, 2001, p. 220). Kazuya's case, in which the memory of the suicide appears to contribute to strengthening his will to live, seems to be more in line with "unfinished business" cases than with suicide cases. Stevenson pointed out that the previous personalities associated with children who express past-life memories often have "unfinished businesses," by which he meant "someone like a mother who dies and leaves an infant or small children needing her care" (Stevenson, 1980, pp. 355-358) or "some persons who had debts to pay (or to collect) when they died" (Stevenson, 2001, p. 212). It seems that Kazuya's emotions can also be classified as an instance of "unfinished business": As Jun, he had not shown enough affection towards those who were close to him. He had also hurt them badly through his misconduct culminating in his suicide, and had not reconciled with them. His sense of "unfinished business" seems to be especially apparent in the episode of insisting on carrying the cremation urn of his great grandmother after her funeral and cremation.

Haraldsson and Matlock (2017, chapter 29), who analyzed in some detail 10 suicide cases reported by Ian Stevenson, German researcher Dieter Hassler (2013), and a case they came to know through Facebook, pointed out that the intermission period (from the death of the past-life personality to the birth of the subject) in most suicide cases is relatively short: 2 days, 4 weeks, 5 weeks, 4-8 weeks, 8 weeks, 4 months, 10 months, 17 months, 18 months, and 5 years and 9 months. In Kazuya's case the time was longer than any of these, at 7 years and 8 months. This longer intermission period may be because Jun wanted to come back to Midori, and had to wait for his half-sister's pregnancy.

Life-between-life memories in reincarnation cases, especially those with verified elements, might be regarded as providing a reliable source of information about what happens when we die, supplementing the bulk of information obtained from mediumistic communications[53] and near-death experiences. None of the suicide cases collected by Ian Stevenson and his colleagues report memories in the life-between-life state. This also holds true of the other suicide cases analyzed by Haraldsson and Matlock (2017, Chapter 29). Thus, the case of Kazuya presents a unique piece of information about what might happen between lives after suicide.

---

[53] See Heath and Klimo (2006) for a collection.

10

A Japanese Voice from Russia: The Case of Dr. Tatyana Snitko

~

In the majority of cases, past-life memories of children tend to fade by the time they reach the age of six or seven. In some cases, however, the memories are retained even after the person in question becomes an adult. The case of Dr. Tatyana Snitko is such an example.

It is also an international case like those of Tomo (Chapter 4) and Akane (Chapter 8). However, here the person in question, Dr. Tatyana Snitko, is a Russian, and the past-life personality or personalities is/are Japanese.

In international cases the person in question often shows a desire to go to the country associated with their past life, adores the country, and has skills related to the culture of the country. The present case has all of these features. Dr. Snitko has unusually deep affection for Japan and Japanese cultures, and shows outstanding skills in Japanese arts such as calligraphy, composing Japanese poems, the theatrical tradition Noh (Nogaku) and the martial art Aikido. She also has a good command of the Japanese language.

I interviewed Dr. Snitko three times in 2023, twice via Skype and once in person. I also consulted works published by her (Snitko, 2014a; 2015; 2017), her web page (https://tasnitko.com), and books that mention her (Kouki Shohokai, 2016, pp. 117-118; Yasue and Yamamoto, 2015, pp.

137- 138), but all the descriptions in these sources were double-checked either via the interviews or e-mail exchanges.

Dr. Snitko's Background

Tatyana Snitko was born in 1955 in Krasnodar, in the then Union of Soviet Socialist Republics (now the Russian Federation). Her father was a botanist and her mother was a pianist who also taught at a music academy. She taught her students not at school, but at home, as she had a very good grand piano. At one time, she taught as many as 18 students. The young Tatyana herself studied music under her mother. In the group of eight solfege students of her generation, six continued to pursue music as their career. Tatyana was one of the remaining two who did not do so.

Her paternal grandfather was a German and her grandmother a Ukrainian. Her maternal grandparents were Russian, but they also had some Turkish blood if you go back far enough. Her maternal grandfather taught Ancient History and Classics, Greek and Latin at the university, but lost his life in a forced labor camp (the Gulag system) during the rule of Joseph Stalin. One of her mother's cousins, who was a musician, was subjected to forced labor for 10 years. Her father was one of the grand-disciples of Nikolai Vavilov (1887-1943), a botanist who died in prison during the Great Purges by Stalin, and was also a victim of the Holodomor, a deliberately induced famine in Soviet Ukraine which began in 1932, and which is widely considered to be genocide. Tatyana's maternal great-grandfather was the head priest in the Russian Orthodox Church of Novocherkassk Cathedral in Rostov Oblast. He died in 1910 and thus escaped the fate of being killed during the 1917 Revolution. The family moved to a new location to escape the oppression of the Russian Communist Party, and survived the famine of the 1920s and 1930s by selling orthodox priest vestments (with embroidery, gem-stones etc.), Bibles and religious icons. Dr. Snitko remembered a shocking story she heard from her aunt that illustrates the level of deprivation and trauma the family suffered: in the 1930s they took in an orphan who was dying, the aunt thought that the purpose was to eat the orphan after she died. The family lost its roots in the Russian Orthodox Church due to state policy, and they had to lead a non-religious life. Tatyana herself spent her childhood without any connection to the Bible or church. Because of these experiences, no one in her family became a member of the Communist Party.

The above descriptions clearly show that Tatyana Snitko has no connection to Japan, either genetically or in terms of the environment in which she was brought up.

Figure 10-1: The young Tatyana Snitko
with Her Mother and Brother.

Dr. Snitko's Thoughts on Japan and Her Educational and Research Career

Beginning in her childhood, Tatyana felt a great sense of discomfort with her parents and the environment around her. She said: "Not this house. Not these broken roads. Are these people really my parents?" She kept thinking, "How did I get here? How did I get here?" She not only asked herself this, but also asked her perplexed parents.

155

Her loving parents had given her a variety of dolls, but she had no interest in Western dolls. She had a clear image in her mind of the doll she wanted, but the girl's limited vocabulary could only describe it as "a little doll with a pretty face." When her father tried to fulfill his daughter's wish by buying her a small German doll, she said, "No, no! No! [This is not what I want.]" A few years later she learned that the doll she wanted was a Japanese doll. In other words, she had a clear image of *hina* dolls (Japanese dolls) that she had never seen before. Figure 10-2 below is a picture of a Hina doll which Dr. Snitko found on the Internet upon my request to find an image of a doll closest to the one she wanted as a child.[54]

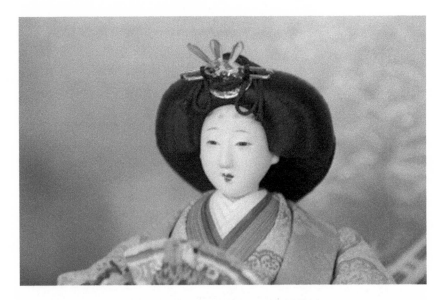

Figure 10-2: A Type of Hina Doll Dr. Snitko Had in Mind.

When she was in elementary school, Tatyana posted a map on the wall above her bed, but it was a map of Japan, not of the Soviet Union. She also wanted to correspond with Japanese people, but this was at a time when exchanging letters with a foreign country was unthinkable. So, she chose an elementary school shown on a map of Sakhalin (Karafuto), a Russian island in the Pacific, north of Japan, and she sent a letter. The name of the town she chose

---

[54] The picture is from the doll-making company called Ajioka Ningyo, whose website is: https://ajioka.net. It is reproduced courtesy of the company.

was Tomari. Located in the southwestern part of the island, the town was called "Tomari-cho" ("Tomari-o-ru-cho") until the Soviet Union took effective control after World War II. The criterion for the selection was "a town with a beautiful-sounding name," and she felt that "Tomari" fell into this category. As she later learned, Tomari was the only town on Sakhalin to retain its Japanese name. However, there were no Japanese in Sakhalin at the time, so she began correspondence with a Russian student at the elementary school in Tomari, which continued for several years.

When the time came for her to decide which university to attend, she wanted to enroll at the Institute of Asian and African Studies affiliated with Lomonosov Moscow State University, to study the Japanese language. However, to enter the institute, she needed a letter of recommendation from the Regional Committee of the Communist Party, which she was unable to obtain since no one in her family were Party members. So, in August 1972, she entered the Germanic Faculty of Rostov State University to study English and German.

Around the same time, her family was sent books from a deceased relative's personal library. Among them was a Japanese language self-study textbook for Russian merchants trading with Japan.[55] Someone also gave her a cassette tape of *enka* songs (a genre of Japanese music). So she began to spend her days listening to *enka* songs and learning Japanese for merchants in parallel with her university studies.

Later, she obtained a textbook for Japanese language learners,[56] and through her father, she came to know a Japanese resident of Rostov (a university teacher specializing in engineering), who greatly facilitated her learning.

Another interesting episode illustrates her admiration for Japan. At one time, she was involved with a man from the Cherkess region and even wanted to marry him, but she was not allowed to do so by her relatives for historical reasons: Cherkess people had been forced by the

---

[55] *Самоучитель японскаго языка* (*Japanese Self-Instruction Manual*) by KURONO Yoshifumi, a Japanese language teacher at the University of Petersburg, published in 1913. However, many of the example sentences in Japanese written in Cyrillic letters were quite old-fashioned and impractical.

[56] Written for second-year students (supervised by Golovnin) by the Ministry of Higher Secondary Specialized Education of the Soviet Union; the textbook for first-year students was not available. The grammar was well explained in detail, but the lack of explanation on the writing order of Chinese characters was a drawback, according to Dr. Snitko.

Russians to leave their ancestral lands. One of the main reasons she was attracted to the man was that he looked Japanese.

After graduating from the university in 1977, she started to teach English at the State University of Rostov while honing her Japanese language skills with the Rostov Oblast Technical Translation and Correspondence Course for four years (1980-1984). She earned a doctorate in linguistics in 1987, while simultaneously becoming a lecturer at the Pyatigorsk State Linguistic University and in 1989, an assistant professor. In 1994, she began teaching Japanese at the Pyatigorsk lyceum (secondary school), where two of her students won prizes in the All-Russian Japanese Speech Contest.

In 1996, with the title of Japanese Language Teacher at a junior and senior high school in Pyatigorsk, she came to Japan for the first time and took Japanese language classes at the Japan Foundation Japanese Language International Center in Kita-Urawa. This was the first time she formally learned Japanese in a classroom setting. Her stay in Japan at that time was for two months.

In 1999, she entered the Institute of Asian and African Studies, affiliated with Lomonosov Moscow State University, which was her long-cherished dream. Upon graduating from the University, she earned Habilitation, the highest degree at a European university. Then in 2000, she obtained Habilitation in Theoretical Linguistics, Comparative Linguistics and Linguistic Typology.

After teaching at the State Rostov University of Economics from 2000, she came to Japan in 2006 on a research fellowship from the Japan Foundation and served as a visiting professor at the University of Tokyo for two years. There she taught at several universities while engaging in translation, training, and other duties.

Due to her upbringing and educational background, Dr. Snitko is fluent in English, Japanese, German, French, and Ukrainian, as well as her native Russian. As a researcher, she has written numerous articles on linguistics and cultural theory, published a book on concepts of the ultimate level of abstract thinking in Western and Eastern linguocultures (Snitko, 2014b), a handbook of Russian (in Japanese; Kumanoya and Snitko, 2019), and is currently working on an English-language book on the Japanese Noh theater tradition.

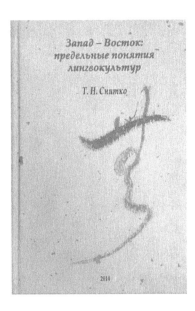

Figure 10-3: A Book Published by Dr. Snitko in Russian.

Dr. Snitko's Experiences Related to Her Past Lives

As shown above, Dr. Snitko was born and raised in a non-religious environment. Despite this, she has always felt since her childhood that reincarnation is real. She also feels a real connection with "gods," and according to her acquaintances, she has psychic abilities such as diagnosing and healing remotely.[57]

Although Dr. Snitko herself did not have detailed memories that would allow her to identify persons from her past lives, she was provided with relevant information on three occasions.

The first was in Russia. One day, Dr. Snitko, who was in her twenties, visited a friend's house, where a female fortune teller, who was an acquaintance of her friend, gave her a free reading. At that time, she was told that her past life was that of a Japanese named Ono no Komachi. Ono no Komachi (c. 825-c. 900) was a master of Japanese poetry or *waka* (Figure 10-4).

---

[57] Testimony by Ms. H, who experienced Dr. Snitko's abilities in close proximity for over 10 years. Also, as mentioned below, calligrapher YAMAMOTO Mitsuteru also acknowledges Dr. Snitko's psychic abilities.

Figure 10-4: Ono no Komachi.

At that time, Dr. Sunitko had no knowledge of the person and when she heard the word "Ono" could only think of ONO Yoko, the Japanese artist, and John Lennon's wife. Naturally, she did not take the reading seriously.

Around 2007 or 2008, Dr. Snitko began studying calligraphy with Ms. M in Tokyo. Ms. M was so amazed by Dr. Snitko's calligraphy that she repeatedly asked her where she had learned it. She was surprised to hear Dr. Snitko continuously say, "I have never learned calligraphy." So, Ms. M visited a psychic and with Dr. Snitko's permission asked for a reading of her. The psychic told Ms. M that Dr. Snitko's past-life personality was Ono no Komachi. Upon hearing this, Dr. Snitko recalled the reading she had received in Russia.[58]

A third psychic reading was done in 2009, by a well-known fortune teller named Rana Onsa. Dr. Snitko was told that she had multiple past lives of Japanese people, including Ono no Komachi. This was the third time she had heard this, from three different psychics. Rana Onsa further told her that Ono no Komachi was the past life most closely influencing her current life. According to the psychic, the last past life of Dr. Snitko

---

[58] Dr. Snitko herself was not present. I attempted to obtain information about the psychic, but was unsuccessful because I found that Ms. M was too ill to communicate.

was that of a five- or six-year-old girl who was incinerated in an instant by the atomic bomb in Hiroshima. As for Ono no Komachi, she thought: "If I *was* Ono no Komachi, it is not surprising since I do not feel I am a foreigner when I am in Japan." As for the girl, Dr. Snitko just felt that she was born again in about 10 years (in Russia after she had died in Hiroshima) and that it was rather a short period of time to be reborn.

Sometime later, however, Dr. Snitko realized that the reading about the girl who died in the atomic bombing in Hiroshima seemed to explain the strange experiences she had when she visited Hiroshima in 1996 and 2000.

In 1996, during Dr. Snitko's first visit to Japan, a group she was involved with had the opportunity to visit the Hiroshima Peace Memorial Museum. Normally, Dr. Snitko would not cry at the sight of tragic photos, but as soon as she saw photos of children who were victims of the atomic bomb, she burst into tears and almost fainted. So intense was her reaction that she had to leave the memorial and wait for the group to finish the tour.

She had an opportunity to visit again in 2000, but this time she could not even enter the Memorial Museum and had to spend several hours on a bench nearby until the group finished the tour.

It was a reaction that made sense to her when she thought that it was due to her past life as a girl who lost her life in the atomic bombing.

Later, although the exact year is unknown, Dr. Snitko experienced a sudden recall of the name of the girl in question while riding a train in Tokyo. A group of boys in a sports team, who appeared to be high school students, boarded the train car in which she was riding. One of the names on the back of their shirts caught her eye. At that time, the idea of her past lives was the furthest thing from her mind, but when she saw the name "Miyamoto" written on the back of a boy, she was convinced that her name (the name of the girl in Hiroshima) had been "Miyamoto." She felt that was certain.

In 2018, she and a friend had visited Onomichi in Hiroshima prefecture, where her friend's relatives lived. At that time, she again visited Hiroshima Peace Memorial Museum, and when she told the information desk that she was looking for a girl with the surname "Miyamoto" who died at the hypocenter when she was about 5 years old, she was told that the information could be retrieved on the computers in the basement. While searching for victims with the surname "Miyamoto," a photograph of a young girl caught her attention. The details about her in the database read:

MIYAMOTO Katsumi
Age at the time of the bombing: 5 years old
Place of exposure: Higashikan'non-cho, Hiroshima City (now Nishi Ward, Hiroshima City)
Address at the time of the bombing: Higashikan'non-cho, Hiroshima City
Occupation at the time of the bombing: infant
Radiation exposure: instantly burned to death because of proximity to the hypocenter. Her remains were in ashes.

Dr. Snitko was surprised to find that the girl matched the person she had "imagined" as her past life personality, but she did not have any other strong feelings about her. She just looked at the girl's eyes and thought, "Maybe those were my own eyes." In trying to recall the circumstances of her death, she felt that she had looked up at the sky and that she had found herself in a different place (the place she had gone after her death). In her search she also found the girl's mother, but looking at the picture did not bring up strong emotions to her.

Tastes and Skills that May Be Related to Dr. Snitko's Past Lives

As mentioned, Tatyana had a strong preference for Japanese dolls and other Japanese objects from childhood. It is worth emphasizing how she also learned and mastered many quintessential Japanese cultural arts and crafts at a high level:

1. Japanese Literature
Dr. Snitko has read numerous works by Japanese authors and many books about Japan, including such classics as *The Tale of the Heike*, *The Tale of Genji*, and *Makura no Soshi*, all in Russian translation. *Makura no Soshi* is one of her favorites, and she has read it to the point of memorization.

2. *Zazen*
Dr. Snitko began practicing *zazen* (Buddhist meditation) around 1985 while living in Russia. A friend taught her about *zazen*, along with various meditation and healing techniques. From 2007 to 2010, she participated in five- or ten-day *zazen* retreats several times a year at Chokoku-ji Temple,

a branch of Eihei-ji, the head temple of the Soto sect of Zen Buddhism. From 2011 on, she has been practicing zazen at Tosho-ji Temple. Although the temple is of the Soto sect, it has adopted the *koan* of the Rinzai school of Zen Buddhism, and offers *dokusan*, a private interview between a teacher and a student for spiritual development of the latter. "Zazen is essential for mastery of any path," says Dr. Snitko.

3. Calligraphy

Dr. Snitko first encountered calligraphy in 2007, when she visited an acquaintance in Kyushu. At that time, her acquaintance's wife, who is a calligrapher, taught her how to hold a brush. As mentioned earlier, upon seeing Dr. Snitko writing letters, the calligrapher was astounded and asked Dr. Snitko where she had learned it. The woman was even more surprised when Dr. Snitko replied that she had never studied calligraphy. So, the calligrapher advised her to study it upon her return to Tokyo. She followed her advice and began studying calligraphy under the aforementioned Ms. M. After five years of practice, she obtained the third *dan*, the eighth of the 24 levels. Her work was exhibited at a calligraphy exhibition at the Tokyo Metropolitan Art Museum (Figure 10-5).[59]

Figure 10-5: Snitko's work displayed at the 2009 calligraphy exhibition at the Tokyo Metropolitan Art Museum.

---

[59] Her calligraphy teacher invented the name "Tasha" instead of her real name "Tatyana." Dr. Snitko also uses this name for her aikido uniform.

Dr. Snitko's outstanding skills in calligraphy, as well as her psychic abilities, are noted by YAMAMOTO Koki, who created a special type of calligraphy called "Iroha Hifumi Kokyu Shoho" ("Iroha Hifumi Breathing Calligraphy"). He describes Snitko as a "Russian linguist and spiritualist, who pointed out the mechanisms related to the peculiarities of the calligraphy" (Kouki Shoho-kai, 2016, p. 117).

4. *Waka* Poems

In 2017, at the request of an acquaintance, Dr. Snitko began composing poems in a Japanese style called *waka* after participating in a *waka* recitation group called Hoshi to Mori Hikou Gakkai (Hoshi and Mori Hikou Study Group).[60] The following are two representative poems that Dr. Snitko has composed.

Title: "Fuyu no Hana (Winter Flowers)"[61]

Yumi no Na wo
Moteru Mayumi wa Usubeni yo
Hi ni Kagayakeri
Fuyubana Shugyo

A pale red Mayumi flower
Whose name is the name of a (Japanese) bow[62]
Is brightly lit by the sun
Winter ascetic practice of a flower

---

[60] The webpage for the Hoshi to Mori hiko study group study session is as follows: https://hikou.jp/. An acquaintance of Dr. Snitko was scheduled to take an exam at the Hoshi and Mori Hiko Study Group and needed to be accompanied by someone who had no knowledge of the Hiko. Therefore, the acquaintance asked Dr. Snitko to accompany her.

[61] A poem composed at Mukojima Hyakkaen Gardens. The mayumi tree (a species of flowering plant, Hamilton's spindle tree in English) in the winter garden was likened to a *zazen* practitioner, and the flower to enlightenment attained through ascetic practice.

[62] "Yumi" means "bow" in Japanese.

Title: "Asobi (Amusement)"[63]

Natsu no Umi
Mana-zuru-misaki[64]
Chitose-dori[65]
Maiasobi tari
Kami zo Medetaki

The summer sea
Off 'White-naped Crane' Cape
A millennial bird
Is circling in the sky
Kami (gods) are amusing themselves

In the original language, these waka poems are outstanding, aesthetic, and sophisticated, and I believe far beyond the quality of ordinary Japanese people (at least the present author) could make.

5. Noh

Dr. Snitko has been studying Nohgaku under YASUDA Noboru, a Noh performer (*Waki-kata*[66]) of the Shimogakari-hosho-ryu School since 2011, and from KATO Shingo, a Noh performer (*Shite-kata*[67]) of the Kanze School since 2015. She has performed such classic pieces as *Tsurukame* (2018) and *Soshiarai Komachi* (2020), and is currently practicing *Hagoromo*.

In a seminar hosted by YASUDA Noboru, Dr. Snitko had a strange experience related to Ono no Komachi, her possible past-life personality. The topic of the seminar at that time was "Sotoba Komachi," a work by Kan'ami (1333-1384) featuring Ono no Komachi. During the seminar, KATO Shingo, who would later become her teacher, showed Dr. Snitko

---

[63] A poem dedicated to the women who work at the Irifune Ryokan in Manazuru Fishing Port, which she has visited several times on an acquaintance's yacht. It is dedicated to the gods who dance and play at Mitsuishi (three stones) at the tip of Cape Manazuru, a famous power spot where the gods are said to dwell. The poem incorporates the Chitose-tori (crane), a symbol of good fortune and the eternal, perpetual flow of time.

[64] "Mana-zuru" means "White-naped Crane."

[65] "Chitose" means "one thousand years."

[66] *Waki-kata* are actors who play the "side" role.

[67] *Shite-kata* are actors who play the "main" role.

a Noh mask for the role of Ono no Komachi. The Noh mask is seen as a vessel for the soul of the character, and it is said that a Noh performer who holds a mask can feel the souls of the previous Noh performers who have worn them for hundreds of years. When Dr. Snitko held the mask of Ono no Komachi, she felt that the souls of the performers as well as the soul of Ono no Komachi had entered her Heart Chakra.[68]

Figure 10-6: Dr. Snitko Performing Noh

6. Aikido

Dr. Snitko received aikido instruction from MATSUMOTO Teruo at the Kishinkan Dojo for 10 years, from 2008 to 2018. Mr. Matsumoto was an excellent student of TOHEI Koichi, who received the highest rank of 10th dan from UESHIBA Morihei, the founder of Aikido, and later founded Shin Shin Toitsu Aikido.

---

[68] *Chakra*, meaning "wheel" in Sanskrit refers to (usually six or seven) energy centers in our body assumed to exist in meditative practices, especially yoga. Heart chakra or *Anahata* is regarded as the place where the true self or pure consciousness resides and is often associated with love.

Dr. Snitko's Skills and Her Past-Life Memories

Dr. Snitko's preference for Japanese culture and her high skills in Japanese arts seem to strongly suggest the influence of a past life (or past lives). Ono no Komachi, one of the Six Immortal Poets, appears a number of times in Dr. Snitko's life, and her past life as Ono no Komachi could explain her high abilities in *waka* poetry and calligraphy.

However, since the biographical information of Ono no Komachi is largely unknown,[69] there is no way to verify this possibility at this point. *Noh* and aikido were established much later than the Heian period (794-1185), when Ono no Komachi was active, so it is difficult to imagine that Dr. Snitko's tastes and skills in these areas were influenced by her past life as Ono no Komachi.[70] If there is any past life influence, it is likely to be one or more of the multiple past lives as a Japanese as told by the psychic Rana Onsa.

This chapter reported on the experience of Dr. Tatyana Snitko as a case study of a foreigner with past life memories as a Japanese. Her strong preference for Japanese culture and her outstanding skills in the arts and crafts, which can be called the essence of Japanese culture, make her a unique and valuable example of a possible case of the reincarnation type.

---

[69] See Katagiri (2015).

[70] However, according to Zeami, the source of Noh dates back to the time of Emperor Suiko (554-628), and if we focus on this point, the chronological discrepancy concerning Noh disappears (Zeami, 1958, p. 10).

PART THREE

Lives-Between-Lives and Other Prenatal Memories

11

I Found You and Decided to Come to You, Mom: Children with Life-Between-Life and Other Memories

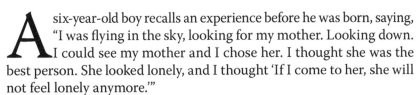

A six-year-old boy recalls an experience before he was born, saying, "I was flying in the sky, looking for my mother. Looking down. I could see my mother and I chose her. I thought she was the best person. She looked lonely, and I thought 'If I come to her, she will not feel lonely anymore.'"

A nine-year old girl describes the place where she was before she came to her mother's tummy: "There were many children, or souls, and a god, an entity with authority."

"Is he like a school teacher?" I asked.

"No, no, no! He is much more generous," she said, "he was looking after us, like a counselor."

There are many children who claim to remember such life-between-life experiences. The phenomenon itself is not new. One of the earliest examples is the case of Katsugoro, reported in Chapter 2, who said that after his death, he had been guided to a beautiful field by a man with long white hair and that, after spending some time there, he had been led by that man to his present house and was reborn. Contemporary Japanese children with past life memories such as Tomo (Chapter 4), Kanon (Chapter 7), Akane (Chapter 8), and Kazuya (Chapter 9) also talked about their life-between-life memories. Many examples were also reported by Ian Stevenson, and by Poonam Sharma and Jim B. Tucker (2004).[71]

In contrast to the cases investigated by these previous researchers and those explored earlier in this book, however, the present chapter deals with cases that share a strikingly notable characteristic: children who claim to have life-between-life memories, but do *not* have memories of an associated past life. In other words, they remember *only* states of being prior to being born in their present body and do not show characteristics of a past personality. Whether some children actually had such memories and forgot them, or if they never had them in the first place, is impossible to determine.

In this chapter, I will discuss the phenomenological properties of these cases – the descriptions of the experiences themselves – and suggest an analytic framework (as described in the Introduction) that incorporates not only past-life and life-between-life memories, but also womb and birth memories. It is my contention that the existence of such cases would not be unexpected if the survival of consciousness and reincarnation are real.

Survey of Children's Womb and Birth Memories

Inspired by studies undertaken by David Chamberlain, Thomas Verny (Chamberlain 1988, 1998, Verny and Kelly 1981, and Verny & Weintraub 2002), and others concerning children claiming to have womb or birth memories, Dr. IKEGAWA Akira conducted a questionnaire-based survey in 2003 (Ikegawa 2005). The questionnaire, which was distributed to 3,601 parents through nursery schools and kindergartens in two cities in Central Japan, contained questions about whether their children had ever reported womb or birth memories, either spontaneously or

---

[71] For example, the cases of Puti Patra and Veer Singh (Stevenson, 1975); the cases of Disna Samarasinghe and Lalitha Abeyawardena (Stevenson, 1977b); and the case of Nasir Toksöz (Stevenson, 1980). Numerous other examples are given in Stevenson (1983, 1997).

in response to questioning. The number of questionnaires answered was 1620, giving a response rate of 45.0%.

The survey showed that 38 children (2.3%) talked about womb memories spontaneously, without being asked, and as many as 496 children (30.5%) talked about such memories after being asked. Thus, the number of children with womb memories amounts to 534 (33%). As for birth memories, 22 children (6.6%) made spontaneous statements and 313 (19.3%) made statements after being asked, the combined number being 335 (20.7%).[72] So, the survey revealed that a fairly large number of children had womb and birth memories.

Although there were no questions about life-between-life and past-life memories in the questionnaire, some of the parents reported that their children talked about these memories as well. This is how the existence of Japanese children with life-between-life and past-life memories came to our attention.

Investigated Cases

In a follow-up study, Dr. Ikegawa and I investigated a total of 21 children with life-between-life memories. Some of them originated with Ikegawa's questionnaire-based survey, while others came from parents who contacted us directly or were introduced to us by early childhood educators.

The questionnaire consisted of three sections. The first contained questions about the child's background, including their handedness, the age when they first uttered a word and a two-word sentence, the family's religion, the parents' educational background, and the presence or absence of complications during the pregnancy. The second section contained questions concerning life-between-life memories, as well as questions about womb memories, birth memories, and past-life memories. We asked the parents if the child had these memories and if they did, to describe what the child said about them.

---

[72] From these figures, we cannot know how many children were asked and said nothing.

Questionnaire on Life-Between-Life Memories

1. The age when the child started talking about life-between-life memories
2. If there is any particular time or occasion when the child talks about the memories
3. If there is any change in the child's state (for instance, being dreamy, extremely active, etc.) when they talked about the memories
4. The reaction of the parents to the memories
5. How the child describes the life-between-life state or place
6. Whether there was a person or an entity there, and if there was, the role that person or entity played
7. The feeling the child had while in the life-between-life state
8. Whether the child was able to see people and events on Earth
9. Whether the child says they chose their parents; and if so, which parent they chose first
10. Whether there is a particular reason why the child was born, and if so, what the reason is
11. How and when the child entered their mother's womb
12. Whether the child made any statement that matches an event before they were born

The age range of the children at the time of the investigation was from 4 to 14 years old, with a mean of 7 years old. Only mothers replied to the questionnaire. After completing it, in 13 cases the mothers judged that their children would talk to us about their memories, enabling us to also conduct interviews with them. All but one of the interviews were in-person (the remaining one was on Skype).

Results

The average age when the children started talking about life-between-life memories was around 3 ½ years old.[73] The mothers of 14 of the children stated that their children talked about the memories during relaxed times such as bedtime or while taking a bath.[74] Ten of the mothers noticed some changes in the child's communication, such as becoming eloquent, speaking very clearly, and with much concentration. One mother reported that her child, who suffered from a stutter, became fluent only when he talked about life-between-life memories. Another stated that she was initially disturbed by her child's words, and that it took her some time to realize that they were talking about life-between-life memories and that he did not necessarily have mental health problems. While only one mother expressed a lack of interest in her child's claims, only two of the children's fathers were interested.

In analyzing the answers to questions 6-12 in the table above, it is useful to adopt the method used by Sharma and Tucker (2004) in their research into life-between-life memories of Burmese children. They proposed a framework which divides the memories into three stages: Stage I is a transitional one, illustrated by memories such as the child seeing their body or funeral, being taken away from weeping relatives, being directed to a different place, etc. Stage II is characterized by marked stability, meaning that the descriptions are highly similar between each child. They are typified by memories of staying in a particular non-earthly place, and being involved in various activities while in spirit-form. Finally, Stage III includes memories of choosing parents, being directed to them, and other considerations about the child's new incarnation.[75] It is interesting to note that of the 21 children who remembered life-between-life states, only two recalled the Stage I transitional phase, while twelve recalled Stage III. Four of

---

[73] This is based on 17 responses, though most parents do not remember the exact age when their children started talking about life-between-life memories and estimated "about two years old," or "probably three years old" etc. In such cases we counted them as the estimated age.

[74] In Japan, young children usually bathe with their parents and the family bathtub is often an important place for parent-child communication.

[75] As stated in the Introduction, they use the term "intermission memories" but do not appear to include memories of being in the womb, which are included in Stevenson's definition.

the 21 children claimed to have past-life memories. One was Tomo, the subject of Chapter 4, who talked about the funeral of the previous personality. Another was Akane, discussed in Chapter 8, who talked about seeing the burned house in which the previous personality and her mother died.

Let us now consider the children's Stage II and Stage III memories in detail. Thirteen of the children described the life-between-life place as "cloud or sky," and three of them as "light." The remaining eight described it variously as "a wide space where you can see the Earth," "a place like a star," "a place where there are a number of levels," "up there," and "a place in the shape of a long ellipse."[76]

All 21 children said they were not alone in the life-between-life state, and 14 claimed there was a god or god-like entity. They described the entity as being like a counselor, making suggestions about their future parents or giving permission to be born to the parents they chose. Twelve children claimed that they had been with their current family members (mostly brothers or sisters) or/and friends in the other realm. One child said that there were many "light balls" present but that it was difficult to say who they were, although he believes some of them were people close to him in his current life.

Eight of the children said that they felt "peaceful" or "calm," and two said they were "joyful" or "excited." The remaining three said "difficult to describe," "not different from what I feel now," and "lonely."[77]

Fifteen of the children said they were able to see "earthly affairs" from the life-between-life place, but their memories were limited, relating only to their new parents and their households. Seventeen children said that they chose their parents – nine choosing only their mothers, and eight choosing both parents. Of those eight, four said that they chose their fathers and mothers simultaneously,[78] and four said they chose their mothers first.

Thirteen children said they remembered why they decided to be born. Their reasons were: to meet or help their mothers (3); to help

[76] This child might be describing "in the womb" memories. However, since he talked about other Stage II memories, we classified this statement as an example of life-between-life memories.

[77] It is difficult to understand this claim because the child also said he was with his cousin.

[78] One child said she chose her father first because she saw him slightly earlier than her mother. We interpreted this statement as "simultaneous."

other people (5); to become happier than they were in their previous lives (2); and to enjoy life (3). One child said he forgot the reason when he was born, but that his forgetting was in order to rediscover the reason in the current life.

Twelve children recalled entering their mother's womb. Three of these said that somebody (a god, a shining ball, an angel-like entity) helped them to do so.

Three of the 21 children described things that happened before they were born, and those memories were supported by their parents. The first was a little girl who, when she was five or six, said to her mother, "When you were young, I frequently came to you." This statement matches her mother's experiences before she got married: she often felt that a small child (or a child-like entity) was looking at her and bustling around her.

The second child, who started talking about her life-between-life memories at the age of five, said to her mother, "I saw you in a gorgeous white dress. You were holding a dog." The mother had indeed held a dog while wearing her wedding dress. After the wedding ceremony, she had entered a room where the dog had been waiting for her return. She clearly remembered this experience because holding a dog in a wedding dress is not something you are supposed to do (wedding dresses are usually rented, so extra care is necessary and holding a dog might damage it).[79]

The third child, who was 6 years old at the time, drew a picture of a four-story building surrounded by mountains and said, "This is where you lived. I saw you there." Her mother was astounded because, as a child, she lived in a four-story building from which she could see the surrounding mountains (Figure 11-1).

---

[79] There exists a photograph of this event. Her mother emphasizes that the child had never seen the picture before the statement.

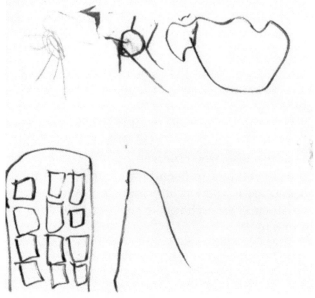

Figure 11-1. A child's drawing of a house in which her mother had lived.

Lending credibility to these claims by Japanese children is the case of an American child named James Leininger, who made statements similar to those discussed here. When his father, Bruce, told 4-year-old James how happy he was to have him as a son, James replied, "That's why I picked you: I knew you would be a good daddy."

Perplexed, Bruce asked, "What did you say?"

James replied, "When I found you and Mommy, I knew you would be good to me."

Bruce then asked, "Where did you find us?"

"Hawaii," James explained. "It was not when we all went to Hawaii. It was just Mommy and you. I found you at the big pink hotel."

Bruce and his wife had indeed stayed at a pink hotel in Hawaii, where James was apparently conceived (Leininger and Leininger with Gross 2009, pp. 153-154).[80]

---

[80] Jim Tucker pointed out that the stories told by two of the three Japanese children here are different from those told by other children who remember past lives, because the events they described took place long before conception. This raises the question about when children choose their parents (if they actually do so, as they claim), which we will not explore here (Tucker, August 13, 2013, personal communication).

The nature of the evidence for possible survival of consciousness after death presented by life-between-life cases alone is admittedly weak, and one might argue that such memories in children without associated past-life memories have little evidential value. Indeed, one might even argue that investigations should be limited only to children with past-life memories since they can at least be tested and validated. We should point out, however, that there does not seem to be notable differences between the life-between-life memories of the four children with past-life memories and those of the remaining 17 children without such memories. It is hoped that further investigation will reveal the existence of cases with stronger evidence.

Comparison of Japanese and Burmese Cases

There is an interesting cultural difference between Burmese and Japanese children with respect to Stage II memories (being in a non-earthly place while in spirit form). In their investigation, Sharma and Tucker (2004) found 19 cases in which Burmese children described the life-between-life state or the place itself. Nine said that they had stayed in a tree, four in a pagoda, and two remained near the place of death. In contrast, in our study, the places described by the Japanese children were in the "sky or cloud" (13), in the "light" (3), and in other various non-earthly locales (5).

This difference might be due to differences in religious backgrounds.[81] In the majority of the Burmese cases, the religion was Buddhism combined with native animism. They believed that death initiates a new birth into one of 30 nonhuman realms. During the period in which a person lives as a discarnate entity, prior to rebirth, he or she may be assigned a task such as guarding temples or treasures (Stevenson 1983, pp. 209-210). In contrast, in the Japanese cases only three parents said their religion was Buddhism. One said Christian, and the remaining

---

[81] In his research on NDEs in indigenous societies, Shushan (2018: 221ff) found that instead of rushing through a tunnel, people described walking along a road to the other world. Also, they went sometimes to earthly (or quasi-earthly) other worlds like volcanoes and mountains. This might apply to Burmese people with animistic beliefs, especially if they are not very Westernized or industrialized.

17 said "no religion."[82] Though it is significant that the three-stage model of Sharma and Tucker (2004) proposed for the Burmese life-between-life memories can be applied to the Japanese cases, there is an important difference that seems to reflect cultural differences between the two nations.

Our investigation suggests that there are many children who claim to have life-between-life memories but no past-life memories. If the life-between-life memories reported by children *with* past-life memories were completely different from those reported by children with *no* past-life memories, these two variants might need to be treated separately. However, since the life-between-life memories reported by the two groups are so similar, we believe that we are justified in studying all such memories as essentially the same phenomenon.

At the time of their writing, Sharma and Tucker (2004, p. 102) reported that 217 out of 1107 cases (19.6%) in the computerized database of the University of Virginia Division of Perceptual Studies include life-between-life memories. We suspect that the actual figure might be higher because at least two factors could have contributed to them being underreported. First, because their main concern has been verifiable aspects of children's alleged reincarnation memories, researchers have not always asked if the children also had life-between-life memories. Second, many of the cases were investigated after the children stopped talking about past-life memories, so the data inevitably relies only on witnesses' statements (parents, siblings, etc.). It would be reasonable to assume that there are at least some cases in which the children would have talked about life-between-life memories had they been asked when they were still young.

Womb and Birth Memories

From the perspective of survival research, womb and birth memories are of lesser value since these memories are from the period when the relevant person has a physical body, although in a premature form. However,

---

[82] According to a survey conducted by Gallup in 2006-2008, Japan is ranked the 8th least religious country among 143 countries, with only 25 percent of people answering "yes" to the question "Is religion an important part of your daily life?" (Crabtree and Pelham 2009). See also the "Note on Japanese Religion" section in the Introduction.

they share important properties with life-between-life memories and past-life memories as shown below, suggesting the necessity of treating the former together with the latter. This section demonstrates this by citing the results of an Internet-based survey I conducted, using an online marketing research company Rakuten Research that had around 2.2 million panels at the time of the survey (July 2014) (Ohkado, 2015).

In the survey, ten thousand randomly selected Japanese women aged 20s to 50s answered an online questionnaire about their children's unusual memories.[83] The results were that 974 (16.2%) children had birth memories, 1905 (28.1%) had womb memories, 369 (13.3%) had life-between-life memories, and 96 (4.0%) had past-life memories.[84] Of these respondents, 984 provided sufficient information for further analyses and the data were examined with respect to whether the four types of memories were present or absent.[85]

Although there were a number of exceptions, the overall picture obtained from the examination was in accordance with the following conjecture: (i) a child retaining past-life memories is likely to retain the other three types of memories; (ii) a child with life-between-life memories, but no past-life memories is likely to have womb and birth memories; (iii) a child with womb memories but no past-life nor life-between-life memories is likely to have birth memories; and (iv) the number of children only with womb memories is likely to be larger than that of the other patterns. This conjecture was based on the assumption that, generally,[86] stronger retentive faculty is needed

---

[83] The total number of respondents varied because those unfamiliar with the memory in question did not answer the relevant question: 6,025, 6,786, 2,784, and 2,382, respectively.

[84] The figures concerning birth and womb memories are slightly smaller than those given by Ikegawa (33.0% for womb memories, and 20.7% for birth memories; Ikegawa, 2005), but the ratio of the percentages (birth memory/womb memory) in both surveys is close: (3.7 / 6.3) [16.2 / 28.1] in Ohkado (2015) and (3.9 / 6.1) [20.7 / 33.0] in Ikegawa (2005).

[85] In the study, the cases in which children talked about the memories spontaneously and those in which children did so when asked are treated separately. For the sake of simplicity, the two are combined here.

[86] "Generally" applies to cases in which all the experiences more or less have the same impact on the experiencer. The "unexpected" patterns will be accounted for by the presence of unusually impressive experiences: for instance, past-life memories involving traumatic deaths are likely to be retained even if the other three types of memories are not retained.

to remember past-life memories than the other three memories, to remember life-between-life memories than the other two memories, and to remember birth memories than womb memories. Although there are many exceptions, the observed patterns appear to show that this conjecture seems to be on the right track.

The more fundamental assumption of the above conjecture is that the four types of memories are basically of the same character, reflecting a unified continuous stream of consciousness, which seems to be supported by the following facts.

First, in the case of life-between-life, womb, and birth memories, the number of children who talk about these memories is highest at age five or six and tends to decrease as children mature, as shown in the following figures ("YO" stands for "Year Old.").

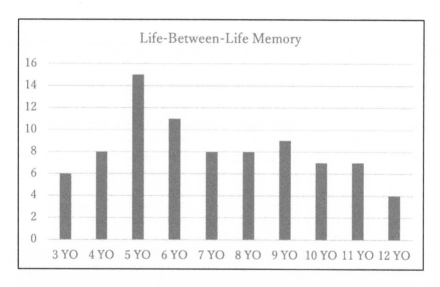

Figure 11-2. The age when children still talk about life-between-life memories.

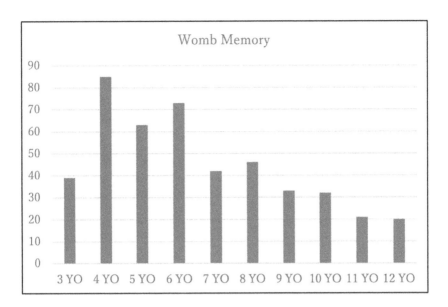

Figure 11-3. The age when children still talk about womb memories.

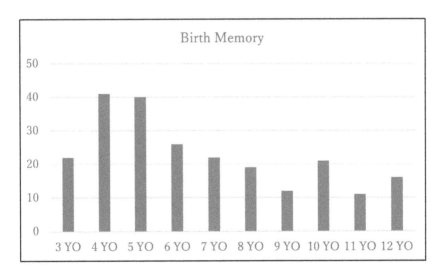

Figure 11-4. The age when children still talk about birth memories.

Although the tendency for memories to fade as children mature is apparently observed, the number of respondents to the internet-based survey on past-life memories was too small for a firm conclusion to be drawn (N = 37). However, in the DOPS database of children with past-life memories, we do observe a similar pattern. The Figure below shows the year when the children stopped spontaneously talking about their past-life memories.

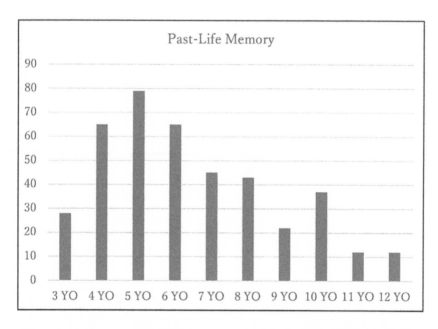

Figure 11-5. The age when children stop talking about past-life memories.

These various different analyses look at the same phenomena from different angles, though all indicate that children with these kinds of memories tend to lose them as they mature.

The second similarity observed in the examples involving the four types of memories is that the children tended to talk about them under similar circumstances: the most frequent time for children to talk about the memories is bedtime, ranging from 42 percent to 54 percent.

Third, many of the parents believed that their children's memories were real because they contained verified elements. The percentages of memories with verified elements are: 78.0 (128 out of 164) for birth memories; 64.3 (178 out of 277) for womb memories; and 35.9 (14 out of 39).

As for the past-life memories, verifiability depends on finding an actual historical past-life personality. Of the 26 respondents, only two said the person was identified, in which case both said the child's memories were real. Even in the remaining 26 cases, 8 (33.3%) believed the child's memories were real.

These considerations suggest that the existence of children with past-life memories, already a powerful piece of evidence for the survival of consciousness, is a portion of a much larger picture of memory retention phenomena demonstrating the validity of the survival hypothesis even more strongly.

Life-Between-Life Memories and Near-Death Experiences

Sharma and Tucker (2004) also demonstrated that life-between-life memories of children share a number of important features with near-death experiences. Especially noteworthy are the similarities between features observed in the otherworldly Stage II and those observed in the "transcendental" component of near-death experiences (see Greyson 1983, and also Ring 1980). These include (1) entering an unearthly world or dimension; (2) encountering a mystical being or presence; and (3) seeing deceased or spirits or religious figures. Such features are found in NDEs all over the world. Kellehear (1993) analyzed NDEs from China, India, Western New Britain, Guam, Native North America, Aboriginal Australia, and Maori New Zealand, and found that most featured these types of experiences in varying combinations, expressed in culturally varying ways (also see Shushan 2018). Life-between-life memories reported here also share these features – and cultural variations. This suggests that the realms in the life-between-life state described by the children investigated here may be the same as those described by many NDErs.

Matlock and Giesler-Petersen (2016, p. 26), who compared life-between-life memories between Asian and Western children, wrote that they "believe that the cross-cultural commonalities in intermission memories [life-between-life memories] hint at universal processes in reincarnation, and the similarities between them and NDEs suggest that these phenomena should be considered part of the same continuum of experience." I believe that the evidence presented in this chapter supports their conclusion. For further discussions on similarities and differences between life-between-life memories and near-death experiences, I refer readers to the work of Gregory Shushan (2022, pp. 127-158).

12

her Words Changed My Worldview: Spiritually Transformative Experiences Induced by a Child's Prenatal Memories

~

The term "Spiritually Transformative Experience," or "STE," is often used to describe a variety of life-changing phenomena such as near-death experiences, shared-death experiences, deathbed visions, meeting with deceased people, mystical experiences, and the recall of past lives.[87] Children's statements about prenatal memories, utterly unexpected by their parents, sometimes induce STEs – especially in mothers. This chapter introduces one such example, the case of Natsuki and Makiko.

---

[87] The American Center for the Integration of Spiritually Transformative Experience (ACISTE) and The Eternea: The Convergence of Science and Spirituality for Personal and Global Transformation were founded in 2009 and 2012, respectively. In the latter year, Nancy Clark published a book describing varieties of STE titled, *Divine Moments: Ordinary People Having Spiritually Transformative Experiences*. In 2012, 2013, and 2014, *The Journal of Near-Death Studies* published special issues dealing with the ACISTE conferences.

Natsuki was born in October 2010 to her mother Makiko and her father Keisuke. She has a younger brother, Koki, who was born in 2013. After a couple of exchanges via Facebook messenger, I conducted interviews with Makiko, Natsuki, and Koki via Zoom, and one phone call with Keisuke.

How to Raise a Child

After studying political science at university, Makiko started working in marketing. She married Keisuke, who worked for a bank. They then moved to Singapore where Natsuki was born. Makiko had experienced two miscarriages before that.

Makiko, who had built a successful career for herself, also had a clear vision of how children should be raised: she believed that discipline and education are of primary importance and that children will develop in accordance with good standards if they are taken care of properly.

Contrary to her expectations, however, Natsuki did not respond to her parenting as Makiko believed she would. Natsuki was hypersensitive and once she had started crying, she would not stop for hours. Despite Makiko's belief that breastfeeding is the best way to nourish children, she was unable to do so. She began to think, "I am not qualified to be a mother."

Pregnancy of Triplets?

In the spring of 2012, due to Keisuke's job, the family moved back to Japan. Intending to continue working, Makiko looked for a new job and found a very good one. Then, however, she found herself facing an unexpected pregnancy. Makiko, who had been looking forward to demonstrating her skills in business, was greatly shocked and thought, "Why now!?"

When examining the fetal ultrasound scan, the doctor was perplexed. "It looks like triplets," he said, "but chances of having triplets in natural pregnancy is rare. So, let's wait and see." According to Dr. IKEGAWA Akira, the scan *may* show three fetal sacs, but the areas could also be interpreted as endometrial bleedings or structural abnormalities (Figure 12-1).

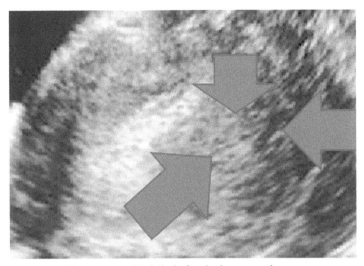

Figure 12-1: Makiko's fetal ultrasound scan
(arrows added by Dr. IKEGAWA Akira)

After returning home from the hospital, Makiko experienced slight bleeding and felt that something was wrong. As if confirming her hunch, in the next examination the doctor said, "You have twins" (Figure 12-2). Hearing the doctor's words, Makiko felt that one of the triplets had been miscarried.

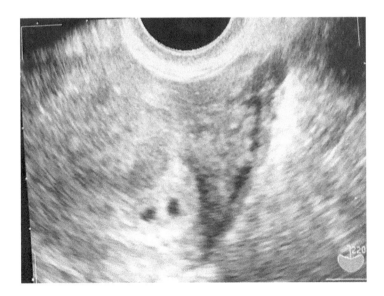

Figure 12-2: Makiko's fetal ultrasound scan showing twins

Shortly after the examination, Makiko experienced heavy bleeding and the doctor urged her to have abortion for her own safety. Makiko protested, and asked the doctor to wait a few days and see what would happen. When she returned for another fetal ultrasound scan, it showed that only one fetus was left (Figure 12-3).

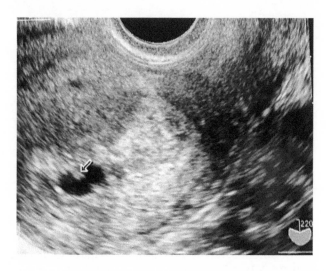

Figure 12-3: Makiko's ultrasound scan showing one fetus.

Hearing the doctor's words, she felt relieved, though at the same time guilty, wondering if her thought of "Why Now!?" might have led to the miscarriages of two of the three fetuses. She now determined to give birth to the remaining baby no matter what would happen. Since the doctor diagnosed that Makiko had a high risk of miscarriage and recommended her to keep quiet in bed, she moved with Natsuki to her parents' home.

Fortunately, the fetus developed properly and a baby boy, who was named Koki, was born in January 2013. Yet, the tense relationship between Makiko and Natsuki remained.

Natsuki's Life-Between-Life and Past-Life Memories

One morning in the spring of 2014, Natsuki refused to go to kindergarten and started crying uncontrollably. In frustration, Makiko exploded and said to Natsuki, "I was waiting for you to come to me for a long time!" – implying, *and all you do is cry!*

Natsuki's response was a decisive moment for Makiko, completely changing her worldview.

Natsuki said, "Me, too! I was watching you from above the clouds in the sky for a long time. And then, I jumped to you, saying 'I love you, Mom!' but I went back once, and then came here again." Makiko took this to mean that Natsuki was going to be born as the child from an earlier pregnancy, before she miscarried. With that baby no longer available to Natsuki's soul or spirit, she had to wait until Makiko was pregnant again to enter the viable baby's body. Of course, Natsuki could have no way of knowing about the two miscarriages before she was born.

Makiko was moved to tears. Natsuki held her and consoled, "Mom, don't cry. I'm here. I love you so much."

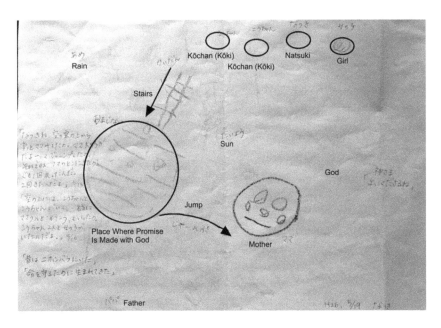

Figure 12-4: The world above the clouds, as drawn by Natsuki

The next day, Makiko asked Natsuki about the world above the clouds. Natsuki responded, "Above the clouds were Ko-chan (her would-be brother) and Ko-chan (a different boy with the same name), and we said to each other, 'Let's go to that mom together.' Ah, there was another girl as well." These remarks gave another shock to Makiko since she interpreted the second "Ko-chan" and "another girl" as referring to the two fetuses she had miscarried before Koki was born.

Three days later, Natsuki drew a picture of the world above the clouds, in which appear Natsuki herself, "Ko-chan," the second "Ko-chan," "another girl," "Mom," and "God." (Figure 12-4). She was 3 ½ years old at the time.

Natsuki also said that in the world above the clouds, there is a place where one makes promises with God. Souls come down the stairs from above and if they can make a promise with God [that is, come to an agreement with God about what they will do on Earth], they can jump into their mothers.

The following month, Natsuki made the following impressive statements:

"Before I was born, I had been helping dead people in the place called Nihonbara."[88]

"In my past life, I had helped people in a hospital. I was born to help people."

"In my past life, I was the mother of mom [Makiko]. I came to you because I had been worried and worried about my child [Makiko]."

"I was born [before Koki] because Koki said, 'After you.'"

These remarks completely changed Makiko's worldview concerning children. She now believed:

- There is a world beyond our physical body.
- Children, who are independent souls, come from that world to their parents.
- They have their own purposes of life.
- Parents do not have to teach them. Rather, children are trying to teach their parents something.
- Reincarnation is possible.

In one of our interviews, after explaining the concept of STEs, I asked Makiko if her change of worldview could be considered an example of an STE. She said that her experience was indeed best described by that expression.

Her newly embraced worldview was strengthened when she saw the movie *Kamisama tono Yakusoku* (see Chapter 9) shortly after Natsuki's remarks. It reinforced her belief that Natsuki was similar

---

[88] The literal translation would be *Nihon* "Japan" + *bara* (the *rendaku* form of *hara*, "plain"), so "Japan Plain." There is a place with the name in Okayama prefecture, but the relationship with her account is not clear.

to the children in the film – that she had prenatal memories of a life-between-life and of a past-life.

Koki's and Natsuki's Prenatal Memories

Around a year later, when he was just over two years old, Koki sat in the bath telling Makiko about his womb memories. "I was in mom's tummy," he said. "I went through a tunnel and came here." He then added something that made a profound impact on Makiko: "I came here because mom lost her mind. I was unable to enter mom's mind."

Koki's words immediately brought back Makiko's memories of her pregnancy with Koki (and the other two souls). She had been having a hard time with Natsuki and felt that she literally had "lost her mind." She could not help but think that Koki came to her because he was worried about her.

In 2017, Makiko got acquainted with parents of twins. The children often reminded her of her miscarriages and depressed her greatly. One day when Makiko was with Natsuki and Koki in the living room, she was thinking of the miscarriages and blaming herself for them.

As if responding to her thoughts, Koki, who had been playing alone, said, "Mom, those girls asked me if I can get along with the elder sister [Natsuki]. I said: 'Yes, I can.' Then, they said: 'Then, you can go.' And they let me be born. They said: 'We will go back to the sky and go to a different mom. So don't worry.'"

Hearing Koki's words, Natsuki, who had also been playing alone, responded, "The two girls said, 'We are happy with Koki and me getting along together.'"

Koki replied, "Yes. Only I was able to come, but it is okay."

"Yes, it was nice that they let you come," agreed Natsuki

"Yes, I was happy," replied Koki. "They died in mom's belly, but after going back to the sky, we will be able to see them."

Makiko was moved by this conversation, and asked the children if she could write about it on Facebook, to which they agreed. Reading Makiko's post, a number of her friends expressed their gratitude for sharing the story.

When Makiko told Natsuki and Koki that those who read the post had thanked them, they looked puzzled and asked, "Why did they thank us?"

Makiko explained, "I think because it is rare to hear stories of the souls of babies who died in the belly, so they were happy to have been able to hear your story. I was also happy!"

Showing their surprise, Natsuki and Koki asked, "Can't they!? People don't know that!?" They seemed to have thought that talking with spirits is a common thing, and the fact that there are people who cannot do so apparently astonished them.

In this connection, it is worth pointing out Koki's interesting remarks when I asked him (via Makiko) if I could interview him. Makiko had said, "A university professor wants to hear the story of your experience in the world above the clouds. Could you talk to him?"

Amazed, Koki replied, "He is a *professor*, but he doesn't know (about the world above the clouds)!?"

As seen in previous chapters, even children with strong prenatal memories tend to forget them before they become adults. Natsuki gives us a dramatic example of a child on the verge of losing life-between-life memories.

Later that year, I interviewed Natsuki via Skype and showed her the picture of the world above the sky that she had drawn three years earlier (Figure 12-4). Natsuki explained excitedly how she came to Makiko. Because she talked about the place where babies make a promise with God, I asked Natsuki what promise she made, expecting that she would talk about one or more of the statements she had made before. She started to say, "My promise was...." and then she stopped. After a while, she said in a sad voice, "I forgot."

Makiko's STE as Measured by Greyson and Ring's Scale

As a way to measure the impact on Makiko of hearing about Natsuki's and Koki's past-life and life-between-life memories, I used the Life Changes Inventory-Revised (LCI-R). The LCI-R was developed by two leading researchers of near-death experiences, Bruce Greyson and Kenneth Ring (2004), to assesses the aftereffects of near-death experiences. It is composed of 50 items which measure if there was an increase, decrease, or no change in one's attitudes and values such as "desire to help others," "concern with the material things of life," "concern with spiritual matters," "personal sense of life," "fear of death," and "conviction that there is a life after death."

When we apply this schema to Makiko's case, we find that she scored highly in items concerning appreciation of life, self-acceptance, quest for meaning and sense of purpose, concern for others, spirituality, and appreciation of death including a conviction that there is a life after death. These scores show that Makiko's experience of her children talking about past-life and life-between-life memories had a great impact on her world view, comparable to the commonly-recurring effects of other STEs like near-death experiences.[89]

Parents often report to me that their children's statements drastically changed their worldview. Although I have not conducted any systematic research using the LCI-R, an Internet based survey I conducted in 2014 in Japan suggests that such tendencies are common (Ohkado, 2015). In the survey, I asked mothers of children aged 3 to 12 how children with prenatal memories affected their worldview. Some of the mothers had children of their own with prenatal memories, though others had merely heard about such children.

Roughly 70 percent of the mothers of children with prenatal life-between-life, womb, and birth memories responded that the memories had either a "positive" or "very positive" effect on them. As for past-life memories, the figures are lower, but still about 40 percent of the mothers said that the children's memories had similar effects on them. It might be conjectured that the difference is because some people connect past-lives with karma (in the negative sense). Interestingly, a comparable percentage of mothers whose children had *not* talked about these memories said that just knowing about the existence of such children had a "positive" or "very positive" effect on them. It seems that a good portion of those mothers with children talking about these memories had STEs just like Makiko did.

---

[89] For details, see Ohkado (2018).

13

facial features Reflecting Past-Life memories?

Birthmarks and Other Signs of Reincarnation

In his two-volume book, *Reincarnation and Biology: A Contribution to the Etiology of Birthmarks and Birth Defects*, Ian Stevenson (1997) assessed more than 200 cases to demonstrate that various physical features of a child with past-life memories may be linked to the person identified as the child's previous personality. The relevant features are birthmarks, birth defects, internal diseases, abnormalities of pigmentation, physique, facial features, postures, gestures and other unconscious movements.

For instance, a Turkish boy named Necip, who had past-life memories of having been stabbed to death in a quarrel, had eight birthmarks that seemed to correspond to the wounds noted in the autopsy report of the person identified as his prior identity (Stevenson, 1997, pp. 430-455).

An example of extreme birth defects is found in the case of Lekh Pal of India. He was born without fingers on his right hand. He had past-life memories of a child whose right hand was chopped off in an accident involving a fodder-chopping machine (Stevenson, 1997, pp. 1186-1199).

Marta, a girl from Brazil, suffered from frequent bronchitis and laryngitis. She remembered a past life as a person who died of pulmonary tuberculosis, and her diseases appeared to be linked to the physical conditions of that person (Stevenson, 1974b, pp. 183-203; Stevenson, 1997, p. 1657).

There are also compelling examples of abnormalities of pigmentation in Asian children who were identified as having been white and British or American in their past lives. They were all extremely fair in hair and skin complexion, and most of them had light-colored irises (Stevenson, 1997, pp. 1757-1758).

Stevenson classified facial features into four categories:

a. faces modified by birth defects corresponding to wounds and diseases in a previous personality;
b. faces showing features uncharacteristic of the subject's race or nation, but characteristic of the race or nation of which he or she claims to have been a member in a previous life;
c. cases in which the subject's face, although not abnormal, showed a noticeable correspondence to the previous personality's face;
d. similarities and differences between the faces of identical twins.

The focus of this chapter is the second type.

Burmese Claiming to Have Past-Life Memories as Japanese Soldiers

In his book, Stevenson gave five examples of Burmese cases of the reincarnation type with the second feature described above (Stevenson, 1997, pp. 1913-1915). One of them claimed to have past-life memories as an Indian pony-cart driver. The form of his eyes conformed more to the Caucasian type consistent with Indian physiognomy, than to the Mongolian type characteristic of Burmese physiognomy. The remaining four people claimed to have past-life memories as Japanese individuals. According to Stevenson's informants and interpreters, these four people seemed to have Japanese rather than Burmese faces. Pictures of the four people are shown in his book so that "interested readers may compare the faces of these subjects with those of other Burmese subjects who remembered previous lives as Burmese persons" (Stevenson, 1997, p. 1913).

I conducted an experiment to explore this point. Stevenson and his colleagues found no fewer than 24 Burmese people who claimed to remember past lives as Japanese soldiers who died in Burma (present-day Myanmar) during the Second World War (Stevenson and Keil, 2005). When they were young, many of them showed a number of traits typical among Japanese, but usually not observed among Burmese. For example, they complained about the hot climate and the spicy cuisine of Burma. They would not wear Burmese clothes (*longi*), and would not observe Burmese style postures in rituals. They also showed a strong desire to go (back) to Japan. As stated above, some of them were said to look more Japanese than Burmese. Since Stevenson and his colleagues took pictures of many of them, we can systematically investigate whether they really did look Japanese as claimed by people whom Stevenson consulted.

For the investigation, I used the case data Stevenson had filed at the Division of Perceptual Studies at the University of Virginia. Of the 24 Burmese people who claimed to have past-life memories as Japanese soldiers, the files for 18 of them included photos. I used all these photos, calling them collectively the "Japanese-Burmese" group. As a control group, which I called the "Burmese-Burmese" group, I chose 18 pictures of Burmese people who claimed to have past-life memories as Burmese. There were 39 pictures available for this group. In order to avoid a possible bias in selecting pictures for the control group, I matched up the same combination of sex in past and present lives, as well as the age when the pictures were taken. In other words, I made pairs of "Japanese-Burmese" pictures and "Burmese-Burmese" pictures based on these two features so that they corresponded to each other as closely as possible. The attempt to choose pictures for the "Burmese-Burmese" group closely corresponding to those of the "Japanese-Burmese" group significantly reduced possible choices (when there was more than one possible choice for the "Burmese-Burmese" group, I made a random selection based on case numbers). This procedure yielded the 18 pairs.

My research plan was to show the 18 pairs of pictures at random to Japanese people and asked them to judge how "Japanese-like" each picture looked. To protect the confidentiality of the Burmese people, I took the following measures: (1) The pictures were shown to the Japanese without giving them any information about the people in the pictures other than their ethnicity; (2) The pictures were edited using an image manipulation program so that neither hairstyle, clothes, nor background would give any clue as to the identity of the person (all images were converted to black and white, and the background and clothes were made to match the color of the person's hair); and (3) Each of the edited pictures were shown on a computer screen for only 10 seconds, during which time participants focused on judging how "Japanese-like" the pictures looked to them. Furthermore, the pictures were taken more than 20 years ago, so the people in the picture would not be recognizable to anyone who does not know them well (see Figure 13-1. The original picture may be found in Stevenson, 1997, p. 1914).

Figure 13-1: A person in the "Japanese-Burmese" group.

I recruited 46 Japanese people living or staying in Charlottesville, Virginia, to participate in the study. Twenty-one were males and 25 were females, with ages ranging from 28 to 63 (mean age was 39.8). They were shown a computer display on which the faces of the 36 Burmese appeared one by one, with the age when the pictures were taken. The pictures were ordered according to the numbers that had been randomized by a computer program, and made into a PowerPoint slideshow. The timer feature on the program ensured that each picture was shown for exactly 10 seconds. Using a five-point scale, the participants were asked to rate how Japanese-like the faces were: (1) not Japanese-like at all; (2) not very Japanese-like, (3) neither Japanese-like nor not Japanese-like; (4) Japanese-like; and (5) very Japanese-like. Before the actual rating started, five pictures of Burmese not involved in the two groups were shown for practice.

Remarkably, the participants tended to rate the pictures of the "Japanese-Burmese" group higher for Japanese-likeness than those of the "Burmese-Burmese" group. The score difference was statistically significant.[90] (To me, the "Japanese-Burmese" group also looked more Japanese than the "Burmese-Burmese" group, but this impression should be discounted since I knew the "answer.") Thus, we now have some grounds to suggest a correlation between past-life memories and facial features attributed to nationality. Ideally, the experiments would also have been conducted from the perspective of Burmese people, in the sense that judgement about the facial features would also be made by Burmese. Unfortunately, I was unable to conduct that experiment because I could not find a sufficient number of Burmese in Charlottesville.

Another limitation of the investigation was that I relied on the subjective judgments of the participants. This raises an important but difficult question as to individual differences in perception and judgment. One possible solution for future studies might be to use rapidly developing facial recognition technology (Akamatsu, 1999; Burt and Perrett, 1997; Cosmides et al. 2003; Dupuis-Roy et al., 2009; Hosoi, et al. 2003; Lu et al. 2005; Yamaguchi, 2002; Yoshikawa, 1999). Especially promising for this type of investigation might be a new form analysis for identifying differences among Asian faces specifically (Akiba 2011). I hope to explore such possibilities in the future.

---

[90] For statistical analyses of the data, see Ohkado (2014, pp. 600-601).

14

Speaking an Unknown Language: The Case of Risa

The case reported here differs from others in this book in two
respects. First, the person in question is not a child, but an adult
(the other exception being the case of Dr. Snitko in Chapter
10). Second, the person did not spontaneously start talking about her
past-life memories. Rather, the past-life recall was induced by hypnotic
regression therapy.

Ian Stevenson (and others) have been quite critical about the use of
hypnotic regression to obtain reliable information concerning past-life
memories. However, Stevenson (1994, p. 192) also stated:

> ...rarely – very rarely – something of evidential value emerges
> during attempts to evoke previous lives during hypnosis. I have
> myself published reports of two cases in which hypnotized
> subjects spoke responsively in foreign languages that I am
> convinced they had not learned normally (Stevenson, 1994, p.
> 192).

The case presented here is, I believe, a third with some evidential value.

Risa (pseudonym) is a housewife who lives in central Japan. She was born in 1958, and her native language – indeed her only language – is Japanese. She majored in home economics at college and had some experience working as a dietician. Due to various physical problems and difficulties in her household, she sought the help of INAGAKI Katsumi, a hypnotherapist living nearby.

During a 70-minute hypnotic regression session conducted in June 2005, she was regressed to two past lives. One was that of a 16-year-old woman of 18th century Japan (the Edo period), who was drowned as a human sacrifice. Later, Inagaki attempted to verify the statements Risa made about this alleged individual and found that some of them matched events described in historical documents. However, he could find no record of the woman Risa described in the session.

The other life Risa recalled was that of a village chief in Nepal. Risa was able to provide two personal names as well as some names of Nepalese food items. She also said that the villagers had not used a calendar, and that they had not known how to write. In response to the hypnotherapist's request to speak in Nepali, she uttered two non-Japanese sentences. After the session, Inagaki consulted some experts, but after hearing recordings of the sentences they said, "The sounds are too indistinct to analyze," or "They are not Nepali."

In early 2009, I was searching for any examples of xenoglossy cases induced by a hypnotic regression therapy. "Xenoglossy" (from *xénos* "foreign" and *glôssa* "tongue" in ancient Greek) is a phenomenon in which a person is able to speak in a language of which they had no knowledge, and could not have acquired by normal means. The term was coined by Charles Richet (1850-1935), a French physiologist and psychical researcher, to differentiate between cases in which the authenticity of the language is demonstrated and cases of "glossolalia," or "speaking in tongues" (*glôssa* "tongue" and *laliā* "talking") – a phenomenon generally found in religious contexts.

As I stated in the Preface, my background is in linguistics, and I had been working on language within the framework of generative grammar, which presupposes the genetically endowed innate knowledge of language in the brain (Chomsky, 1965). I gradually became disillusioned with the idea that linguistic capacity is confined to the brain, an idea which is rooted in the assumption that consciousness is the product of the brain.[91] Reading reports by doctors and therapists working in past-life regression therapy, I found that xenoglossy occasionally takes place during the sessions. For example, Dr. Brian Weiss claimed, "Some of these patients could speak foreign languages in their past lives that they'd never learned or studied in this one" (Weiss, 2004, p. 8). However, few researchers have actually examined any "foreign language" uttered by a patient. The notable exceptions are the two cases reported by Ian Stevenson (1974a, 1984) and the two cases reported by Whitton and Fischer (1986). I contacted Whitton, Weiss, and Jim Tucker, the successor of Ian Stevenson's work, and asked if I could examine the linguistic data, hoping that they would allow me to analyze them for authenticity. To my disappointment, none of them had the data (anymore).[92]

I then came across INAGAKI Katsumi's 2006 book, in which he discussed the case of Risa and her memories of two past lives. Despite his remarks about the experts' judgements that the woman's utterances were not Nepali, I felt I had to examine them linguistically. I therefore contacted Inagaki, who gave me access to the original audio recordings.

At that time, an anthropologist named Khanal Kishor Chandra was in the same department as I was at Chubu University in Kasugai, Japan. Dr. Chandra is from Nepal and works on ethnic minorities in that country.

One evening I visited his apartment, intruding on his family time, and asked him to listen to the audio data to see if he could identify the language. After intensely listening to the recording through a headset a couple of times, he exclaimed, "This is Nepali!"

I still vividly remember the scene: in front me was Khanal Kishor Chandra wearing the headset and his wife holding their young son. I had mixed feelings of surprise, though also that I had expected it, combined with being sorry for my intrusion. Asking him to analyze the data when possible, I quickly left the apartment, feeling *something* was happening.

Later, Dr. Chandra sent me his analysis of the data:

---

[91] It is noteworthy that a prominent linguist, Mark C. Baker (2010), deviated from this standard assumption and, from a perspective of generative grammar, argued for the independence of the core part of consciousness, which he called the "soul."

[92] Shortly before I contacted Jim Tucker, the Division of Perceptual Studies had moved to a new building and many of the data collected by Ian Stevenson were still unpacked.

1. *Aru Vanda Eni Yada Aucha*
   "It reminds me more of her than another."

2. *Ma Aja Kathmandu magai Mugulin*
   "Today I go to Kathmandu and Mugulin."

He and other Nepali speakers[93] also agreed that some of the proper names Risa gave, such as the name of her past-life personality, "Rataraju," were familiar to them.

A New Regression Experiment

When I told Inagaki and Risa of these astonishing results, they naturally became curious. They agreed to do another regression to see if the past-life personality would appear again and give more detailed information. The session took place in May 2009 at Sakae Clinic, Nagoya. In addition to Risa, Inagaki, and myself, those present were SUETAKE Nobuhiro, a medical doctor of the clinic; OKAMOTO Satoshi, a scholar of Japanese literature who is knowledgeable about paranormal phenomena; an assistant of Dr. Suetake; and a Nepali speaker, Paudel Kalpana, a graduate student at Asahi University.[94]

This team of researchers observed as Risa was successfully regressed to her past-life in Nepal, as a village chief named "Rataraju." Paudel Kalpana, the Nepali speaker, spoke to Rataraju in Nepali, asking, "*Tapaiko nam ke ho?* (What is your name?)" To this Risa/Rataraju responded, "*Mero nam Rataraju* (My name is Rataraju)." The conversation between Risa and Kalpana lasted for 24 minutes, and was entirely in Nepali – albeit not good, fluent Nepali. Kalpana and Dr. Chandra, who later listened to the audio recording, judged that while Risa did have some command of the language, it was clearly not at the level of a native speaker.

The recording was then transcribed and grammatically analyzed by a linguist, KIRYU Kazuyuki, from the point of view of Nepali linguistics.

[93] Two more Nepali speakers listened to the same data. Their analyses differed only slightly from that of Khanal Kishor Chandra, and were essentially the same.

[94] Khanal Kishor Chandra was not available, so he recommended Paudel Kalpana to us.

Concerning her past life as a Nepali village chief, Risa gave the following clear information:

Table 14-1: Information Risa gave about her past life as "Rataraju."

Category	Information
Name	Rataraju
Name as a Boy	Kira
Wife's Name	Rameli
Son's Name	Kujaus
Daughter's Name	Adis
Father's Name	Tamali
Name of Tribe	Tamang
Familiar Food	lenti, rice, millet
Number of Village Households at the Time	25
Age When He Died	78
Funeral	Himalaya, Cremation (Risa seemed to say people go to Himalaya for cremation.)

When Kalpana asked "How did you die?" Risa's reply was to repeat, "Disease...disease" (*rog... rog*).

Risa/Rataraju did not know the answers to some questions, though did know how to express that this was the case. When asked if Rataraju's wife was at home, for example, the reply was "*Bujina* (I don't know)." When asked his age, Ris/Rataraju apparently didn't hear and asked, "*Ke?* (What?)."

In still other instances, Risa/Rataraju's reply included Nepali words, but were not appropriate to the questions asked. For example, when Kalpana asked "What do you eat at home in the morning?" Risa/Rataraju muttered something about Shiva (one of the main Hindu deities),[95] and *dharma* (often translated as "religion").

---

[95] Gregory Shushan has suggested that the word might be *shiba* meaning "alcohol" in Tamang as in item 8 in Table 14-3. If so, the utterance could be seen as a possibly appropriate response.

If calculated leniently, 75.7% of Risa's responses were judged to be appropriate to the questions. If calculated strictly, the figure is 38.6%.

We then calculated the number of words which Risa uttered first, in order to ensure that she wasn't merely repeating words Kalpana had spoken without understanding their meaning, thereby giving a false impression that she was successfully communicating in Nepali. For instance, even if Risa did not understand the question "*Kethibari chaina?* (Is there a field?)," Kalpana and the observers would have the impression that she did if she repeated either or both of the words. By counting only words Risa first uttered in the conversation, such a possibility can be excluded.

Proper nouns aside, the words Risa uttered first are:

Table 14-2: Words Risa uttered first.

No.	Word	Meaning
1.	*mero*	my
2.	*ke*	what
3.	*tiis*	30
4.	*ma*	I
5.	*bujhina*	I don't know
6.	*ho*	yes
7.	*kodo*	millet
8.	*shiba (shibo)*	alcohol (old expression of Tamang)
9.	*dharma*	religion
10.	*pachchiis*	25
11.	*(Nallu) gau. N*	(Nallu) village
12.	*peT*	stomach
13.	*duHkha hunchha*	hurt
14.	*rog*	disease
15.	*guhar*	help
16.	*aaTh*	8

17.	*satarii*	70
18.	*daal*	daal
19.	*khaanaa*	food
20.	*saathii*	friend

This table clearly shows that Risa did know a certain number of Nepali words.

It was also important to determine if Risa was familiar with contemporary formal Nepali, versus the dialectal form of the language as it was spoken at the time and place Rataraju allegedly lived. Thus, when Kalpana asked Risa if "he" (Rataraju) had a wife, using the standard Nepali word *"shriimati* (wife)," she appeared to be perplexed; but when he replaced the word with *"swaasni,"* an informal word with the same meaning, Risa quickly answered: *"Mero swaasnii naam raam raamel ... raamelii* (My wife's name, name, Raam, Raamel, Raamelii.)."

Risa also used Nepali grammar in a way that was appropriate to the past personality of Rataraju. Verbs in the language inflect in accordance with number, gender, status, person, tense, mood, and aspect. Risa apparently inflected the verb *hunu,* "to be," properly, depending on the subjects.[96] For example, when asked, "Are you Nepali?" she replied, *"mero buwaa taaman.ng hunuhunchcha"* (My father is a Tamang)." This is a rather complex usage very specific to Nepali, known as the third person singular low-respect form. While the second person form would actually have been the correct one in this instance, according to Chandra, using the third person singular form is quite common colloquially, especially among speakers whose first language is not Nepali (like Rataraju, who claimed to have belonged to the Tamang). Though technically "ungrammatical," Risa's usage actually makes more sense than the proper form. Furthermore, it is notable that in Risa's native Japanese, there is no such subject-verb agreement, and in fact, Japanese learners of languages with such a system tend to have considerable difficulty in acquiring this part of its grammar.

There are, however, some weaknesses to the case. Risa rarely initiated a conversation and her responses were relatively slow. Her limited vocabulary and sentence structure, and the spotty nature of

---

[96] For the conjugation of *hunu* "to be," for example, see the entry in Wiktionary: https://en.wiktionary.org/wiki/%E0%A4%B9%E0%A5%81%E0%A4%A8%E0%A5%81.

her responses, are also features of the two cases reported by Stevenson (Stevenson, 1974a, 1984). To some extent, this is understandable given that in general, speech in the state of hypnosis is typically slow and can be fragmentary.

But Risa's case differs from Stevenson's cases in one important way that potentially makes it stronger. Risa's native language, Japanese, is genealogically unrelated to Nepali, which is an Indo-European language. This is in sharp contrast with Stevenson's regression cases, in which the participants' native language (English) and the languages of their past-life personalities (Swedish and German) are all classified as Germanic languages and are genealogically very close to English. This makes it possible (even if not probable) that the participants were somehow able to utilize their linguistic knowledge, at least at the level of grammar, in speaking the "unknown" language – a possibility that can be excluded in Risa's case.

In addition, we might also point out the strong possibility that the Rataraju personality was not a native speaker of Nepali, since he referred to himself as belonging to the Tamang people, whose native tongue is in the Sino-Tibetan family. This could have contributed to the lack of fluency in his speech.

Because of these differences, the present case seems to be of stronger evidential value than the cases investigated by Stevenson.

It should be noted that Risa only had two sessions in which she communicated in her past-life language. In Stevenson's cases, one had eight sessions and the other had 19. In both of them, the past life languages seemed to improve from one session to the next, suggesting that past-life personalities need to "be brought out" a number of times for them to fully recover their original language. In Risa's case, the number of times the previous personality was called out was not enough to exhibit any great fluency in the language.

The most important point that remained to be determined is whether Risa had the opportunity to learn Nepali by normal means. She claims that she has never studied Nepali nor has she had contact with Nepali speakers. In order to confirm her claims, Inagaki, the therapist, investigated Risa's personal history, which led him to conclude that it is highly unlikely for her to have learned any Nepali. He then asked both Risa and her husband to sign an affidavit that she had never learned Nepali in her entire life, which the couple did willingly.

Risa even consented to a polygraph test, which was administered by ARASUNA Masana of the Houkagaku Kantei Center (Forensic Science

Investigation Center). Arasuna was chief of the Osaka Prefectural Police Criminal Investigation Laboratory and had conducted polygraph tests on more than 8,000 people. The test was conducted in August 2009 at Risa's home. She was asked three questions related to her ability to speak Nepali.[97] The first questions were whether she recognized two Nepali words, *"chimeki"* (neighbor) and *"chora"* (son), which she showed understanding of during the hypnotic session. No notable reactions were observed on the polygraph, and it was concluded that Risa did not recognize the two words. The third question concerned Nepali currency, which any person who had learned the language would be expected to know. Again, Risa's reaction showed that she lacked the relevant knowledge. It seemed clear that that Risa has never learned Nepali.

Verification of Statements

After considerable effort, we were able to verify some of the statements Risa had made in conversations. The Japanese language does not distinguish the "L" sound from the "R" sound. Although Risa's pronunciation of the village sounded like "NARU," we began to look for a village in Nepal named either "NARU" or "NALU." None of the Nepali people we consulted, including Khanal Kishor Chandra and Paudel Kalpana, said they had ever heard of the name. Nor could they find the name on the Internet. We contacted Kathmandu University and some Nepal media officials for information, but our queries were in vain.

Then, in late May, INAGAKI Katsumi found the name "Naru/Nalu" written in Japanese on a page of the volunteer program of the Japan International Cooperation Agency (JICA) (a government agency delivering Official Development Assistance for the Japanese government). The text on the page stated the village is located in the area close to Kathmandu. Using this information, we conducted another search to find that the name of the village is spelled "Nallu," not "Naru" or "Nalu," and is located about 25 kilometers north of Kathmandu. It is

---

[97] The type of polygraph test used required asking the same multiple-choice questions a number of times, very slowly to examine physiological reactions. In Risa's case, for instance, "Does the word 'Chora' mean A, B, C, D, or E?" was repeated again and again in order to determine possible differences in her reactions. In a one-hour session, three or four questions will thus be the limit.

interesting to note that the webpage Inagaki found had apparently not existed before May 21st, and was online only for a couple of months; nor did "Nallu" appear on Google maps at the time of his search.

According to the 2001 Nepal census data, this village had a population of 1,849 living in 320 individual households in 1991. There did not seem to be any other village of the same name, and more importantly, 96.7 percent of the villagers were reported to be Tamangs, the tribe to which the Rataraju personality claimed to belong.

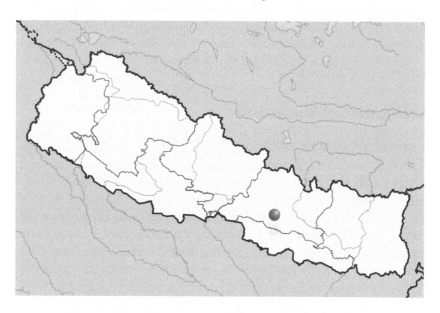

Figure 14-1: Location of the village of Nallu in Nepal.

With the village of Nallu located, we proceeded to attempt to track down the past-life personality by doing some fieldwork in the village. While under hypnosis, Risa had said "Rana" a number of times when asked "his" (Rataraju's) age. We reasoned that this likely referred to the Rana dynasty, which ruled the Kingdom of Nepal from 1846 to 1951. I spent a week in the village in August 2010, accompanied by Khanal Kishor Chandra who served as guide and interpreter. We conducted in-depth interviews with seven people: a 38-year-old elementary school teacher; the secretary and vice secretary of the Village Development Committee (VDC); the oldest man in the village (103) and his 78-year-old son; the 53-year-old former village chief; and the 65-year-old former secretary of the VDC. The villagers we interviewed suggested two people as possible candidates for Risa's past life: Ratnaraj Shapkota and Rana Bahadur. However, the names of their wives and children are different from those listed in Table 14-1, so neither of them could have been Rataraju.

Figure 14-2: The author with villagers

The investigation was further complicated by the fact that the village did not keep written records before 1950, and that all the documents kept by the VDC had burned in 2003 at the time of the People's War. The only relevant record we found was the electoral roll of 1994 stored at the Election Commission of Nepal. Rataraju himself would not be listed in the document as a voter as he would have long been dead, but we hoped that we might be able to find the names of a son or daughter. However, among the 1,643 voters (plus corresponding "guardians" for women) listed in the document, we were unable to find any of the names Risa had mentioned. While a few could be considered close ("Ratnaraj Shapkota" instead of "Rataraju"), the people whose names are close to "Adis" or "Rameli" did not have husbands or fathers whose names were close to "Rataraju."

213

Thus, neither the interview-based nor the document-based research was able to identify the people Risa had mentioned.

On the other hand, Risa's remarks about food and funerals turned out to be correct. Lentil and millet are both principal foods in the village, and rice is also eaten on special occasions. More compellingly, the funeral reference to the "Himalayas," which all the Nepalis we consulted in Japan said they did not understand, seems to indicate a funeral custom specific to the village. Bodies are brought to a mountain from where the Himalayan mountain range can be seen so they can be cremated within its view.

Risa's remarks about the number of villagers at the time of her claimed previous life also appear accurate. According to former village chief Krishna Bhadur Tamang, the village used to be divided into 25 small groups (however, it is not the case that there were only 25 households, as far as the former chief knows).

But perhaps the most intriguing discovery related to the case concerns Risa/Rataraju's way of expressing numbers. When asked about the age he died, Risa answered *"at satori"* – "eight and seventy," rather than "seventy-eight" (that is, placing the single-digit number before the double-digit number). All the Nepali speakers we consulted in Japan commented that this was "unnatural." In some languages, such as German, the single digits in a number are said before the double digits, but Nepali is not such a language. However, this way of expressing numbers used to be common in Nallu village – especially before education became widespread. The village elder, Jaya Bahadur Ghalan, unintentionally showed us this custom when we asked him how old he was. Since he can no longer speak, he communicated with gestures. In answering our question, he first showed "three" and then "100" in accordance with the old custom in the village.

Figure 14-3: Jaya Bahadur Ghalan, aged 103.

Prior Knowledge, Possession, Superpsi, or Reincarnation?

As the JICA webpage calling for volunteers in Nallu village shows, it is not the case that Japan has no connection to the village. Indeed, a school in the village was built with the support of JICA members and a handful of Japanese volunteers visited the place once a year. However, according to the unofficial village chief and the people working with him, none of the Japanese coming to the village spoke Nepali, and very few of them, if any, spoke English to the level that made effective communication possible. It therefore seems extremely unlikely that Risa somehow obtained information about the village through a Japanese person who had been there.

There are many cases in which a regression subject's "past-life" recalls are to be regarded as products of their imagination (Baker, 1982; Spanos, et al., 1991; Stevenson, 1994; Venn, 1986). However, although it happens rarely, hypnotic regression seems to induce a state in some people that can only be accounted for paranormally, either as (1) possession, (2) super-psi (see Chapter 15), or (3) reincarnation.

215

I discount the possibility of possession on the grounds that our case as well as Stevenson's two cases are different from possession cases in at least three ways: (1) Personalities in possession tend to be more talkative, while the participants of the study in the three regression cases spoke only when questioned; (2) The participants seemed to understand their native languages (English in Stevenson's cases and Japanese in the present case), so the two personalities seemed to go hand in hand. In possession cases involving xenoglossy (such as the case of Sharada reported in Stevenson, 1984), the possessed person does not understand the language the possessor uses, nor does the possessor understand the language of the possessed; (3) The personalities were evoked only under hypnosis rather than appearing spontaneously.

I also discount the possibility of super-psi because, as argued in Ducasse (1962), Stevenson (1974a, 1984), and Ryle (1949), one must recognize the difference between "knowledge-that" and "knowledge-how" (skills), as Michael Polanyi put it. The former is information and could hypothetically be transmitted by telepathy or other psi abilities, but the latter is a skill and cannot be so transmitted. In order to converse in a language, one must practice it; it is not simply a matter of repeating a few words and phrases.[98] This issue will be explored further in the next chapter.

Risa's case falls short of a fully confirmed case of reincarnation, however, as her past-life personality was not identified. But given that she displayed some ability to converse in a language not known to her—one that was perhaps not even well known to her past-life personality, Rataraju—and that the statements she made matched the life and customs of the place where the past-life personality was considered to have lived, I believe that this case provides some potential support for the reality of reincarnation.

---

[98] Counterarguments for this interpretation are provided by Braude (2003), which we will discuss in Chapter 15.

PART FOUR

Challenges And Conclusions

15

Counterarguments

~

The cases presented in this book support the notion that past-life and related phenomena strongly suggest that human consciousness survives bodily death, a proposition commonly called the "survival hypothesis." There are two main arguments against such a hypothesis. One is the "living-agent psi hypothesis": that the phenomena can be explained by the psi abilities of living people. The other is the problem of auxiliary assumptions, as pointed out by philosopher Michael Sudduth. This chapter examines both types of counterarguments, especially in relation to the reincarnation evidence.

The Living-Agent Psi Hypothesis

The "living-agent psi hypothesis" – sometimes called the "super-psi hypothesis" – argues that phenomena apparently suggesting the survival of consciousness are actually due to exceptionally strong psi abilities of certain living people.

Proponents of the survival hypothesis tend to criticize the living-agent psi hypothesis on the grounds that there is little evidence for the existence of such strong psi ability. The psi that does occur is not powerful enough to explain the complex phenomena reported in cases such as those explored in this book. For instance, in the entry on "Super ESP [= psi]" in *The Encyclopedia of Parapsychology and Psychical Research*, Arthur Berger and Joyce Berger (1991, p. 421) wrote that there is "virtually no evidence that the limitless and staggering powers assumed by the Super ESP hypothesis exist." In assessing reincarnation phenomena, Robert Almeder argues that "we need to have some independent empirical evidence (which is not to say, necessarily, laboratory evidence) for the existence of super-psi in other contexts before we can appeal to it as a way of explaining those features of our alleged cases of reincarnation that do not fit into established (confirmed) views about the limits of psi" (Almeder, 1992, p. 53).

Stephen Braude, however, contends that (i) a substantial body of evidence exists showing fairly strong ESP (what he calls "pretty *dandy* psi"), as demonstrated in the literature of Edmund Gurney, Frederic W. H. Myers, Frank Podmore (Gurney, et al., 1886), Louisa Rhine (Rhine, 1981), and George Nugent Merle Tyrrell (Tyrrell, 1942/1961); and that, (ii) presently, we have a poor understanding of the exact nature of psi, so we have no principled reason to exclude the possibility of *unlimited* psi. He even mentioned the possibility of a "magic wand" version of the super-psi hypothesis, in which "even the most extensive or refined psi requires nothing more than an efficacious wish or desire, as if the subject simply waved a magic wand to achieve a desired effect" (Braude, 2003, p. 11). Alan Gauld, an eminent psychical researcher who was the President of the Society for Psychical Research from 1989 to 1992, agreed with this view, writing, "since we do not know the limits of ESP, we can never say for certain that ESP of the extraordinary extent that would often be necessary – 'Super ESP' – is actually impossible" (Gauld, 1982, p. 15).

Emily Williams Kelly and Dianne Arcangel (2011, p. 247) called the situation an "impasse" and attributed the decline of mediumship research to it, writing that "despite more than 50 years of high-quality research on mediumship, the research more or less ground to a halt, primarily because researchers had reached an impasse when it came to evaluating these alternative explanations [survival vs. super-psi]."

Let us examine whether such an assessment of the status of the two hypotheses is valid. First, we examine the data concerning mediumistic communications to show that even within this category, there are cases that can only be addressed properly by the survival hypothesis. We will then investigate data concerning children with past-life and other memories and show that our conclusions based on the mediumistic communication data is further confirmed.

Mediumistic Communication

In weighing the two competing hypotheses, we must keep in mind that in mediumistic communications, both hypotheses presuppose the existence of psi-mediated communication. In the living-agent psi hypothesis, the communication takes place (a) between the medium and other *living* people; (b) via psychic access to documents or records concerning the deceased; or (c) via access to a hypothetical cosmic reservoir of consciousness in which Earth's memories are stored. According to the survival hypothesis, on the other hand, the communication takes place between the medium and the surviving soul of a deceased person.

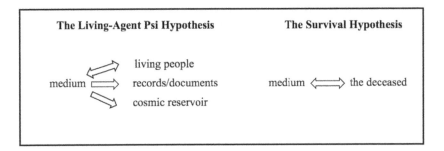

Figure 15-1. The difference between the survival and living-agent psi hypotheses.

Notably, in both cases communication between the medium and another human (either living or deceased) is bidirectional. In contrast, the "medium-records/documents" and "medium-cosmic reservoir" communication is unidirectional in the sense that the medium is the only active agent in gathering information.

It should be noted that psi abilities, the existence of which is well-established by telepathy and other ESP phenomena, are indispensable in mediumship communications even when arguing for the survival hypothesis. For mediums to be able to communicate with the surviving consciousness of the deceased, they would have to use psi abilities, not their normal senses. The question, therefore, is whether a given case can be accounted for by the living-agent psi hypothesis alone or if the survival hypothesis must also be invoked.[99]

[99] Julie Beischel of the Windbridge Institute, who has been a leading mediumship researcher in recent years, has noted some phenomenological

The problem with the living-agent psi hypothesis is not the assumption that it may work as a magic wand, but rather its limitations. Cases exist in which mediums fail to recognize a sitter appropriate to the situation, if we accept that the information source is a discarnate consciousness. Outstanding examples occur in the sittings of Leonora Piper (1859–1950), arguably the most thoroughly investigated medium by the Society for Psychical Research. In his address of the president before the Society for Psychical Research in 1896, William James (1842–1910), one of the founders of psychology in the United States, talked about Leonora Piper as follows:

> If you will let me use the language of the professional logic shop, a universal proposition can be made untrue by a particular instance. If you wish to upset the law that all crows are black, you mustn't seek to show that no crows are, it is enough if you prove one single crow to be white. My own white-crow is Mrs. Piper. In the trances of this medium, I cannot resist the conviction that knowledge appears which she has never gained by the ordinary waking use of her eyes and ears and wits. What the source of this knowledge may be I know not and have not the glimmer of an explanatory suggestion to make; but from admitting the fact of such knowledge I can see no escape (James, 2024, p. 73-74).

Some of the most compelling examples of Piper's sittings are those in which a deceased friend of Richard Hodgson, an acclaimed debunker of fraudulent mediums, appeared. The purported deceased communicator was George Pellew (G. P.), a writer who died in 1892.

In the session of January 7, 1897, G. P. failed to recognize a sitter, a young woman, although he showed some familiarity with the person, saying, "I do not recall your face. You must have changed. ..." When

---

differences between readings of the deceased and those of the living by mediums (Beischel, et al., 2009, Rock, et al., 2009). Among the important findings in her paper with Chad Mosher and Mark Boccuzzi, perhaps most interesting is that experiences of psychic connections during readings for the living included "nonspecific discarnates" as a source of information. This strongly calls into question theoretical frameworks that posit separating mediums' experiences into categories that do and do not involve communication with the deceased, as well as the continued use of terminology reflecting such a separation (Beischel, et al., 2017, p. 86). Eventually, it might turn out that some kind of discarnates are involved in every psychic communication.

Hodgson suggested the identity of the person, telling him the name of the person's mother and asking, "Do you remember Mrs. Warner?", he showed excitement and said, "For pity's sake, are you her little daughter? ...By Jove, how you have grown ... I thought so much of your mother, a charming woman." Then he gave some verified information concerning Mrs. Warner (Hodgson, 1898, pp. 324–325).

As Hodgson pointed out, what is most striking here is the lack of recognition of Miss Warner, who was a girl when G. P. had last seen her, and had grown by the time of the sitting: The sitting took place five years after the death of G. P. When Hodgson let him know who she was, G. P. showed his excitement and recognized that she was Miss Warner and how much she had changed. The combination of the nonrecognition and the recognition after Hodgson's explanation appears to be explained only by the survival hypothesis, unless we add to the living-agent psi hypothesis a highly ad hoc assumption that the information gathering by psi works in a way that only *looks* as if the relevant information is given by the deceased person.[100] In other words, the limitation rather than a feat of information gathering provides a strong argument for the survival hypothesis over the living-agent psi hypothesis. Such cases suggest that there was indeed a deceased communicator, capable of real-time interaction with a medium, and able to learn and process new information.

Children with Past-Life and Other Memories

Let us now turn to the cases of children with past-life and other prenatal memories, which pose even graver problems to the living-agent psi hypothesis. As a representative example, let us return to the case of Katsugoro (Chapter 2).

As previously described, Katsugoro was the son of an ordinary farmer. Although he appeared to be cleverer than other children, there was nothing extraordinary about him. It seems highly doubtful for such an ordinary child, even if he had had the "magic wand" version of super-psi,

---

[100] Other cases that might only be explained by the survival hypothesis are drop-in communications (mediumistic communications in which an unknown, uninvited "spirit" comes unexpectedly). As Stephen Braude suggests, "although the best cases are by no means coercive, the evidence for drop-ins, overall, seems to strengthen the case for survival" (Braude, 2003, p. 51).

to have used it to collect information about Tozo and identify him as his own past-life personality.

A possible line of reasoning for assuming the psi hypothesis might be to suggest that Katsugoro had personal motivations for concocting his story, such as a desire to gain his mother's attention. Katsugoro slept with his grandmother since his mother had to suckle her daughter and could not spend as much time with him. Feeling frustrated, perhaps Katsugoro used his psi ability to collect information about Tozo to attract his mother's attention. Such a speculation, however, does not account for Katsugoro's reaction to his sister's words when he first talked about his past-life memories. His surprise shows that he assumed everyone had past-life memories. Once he realized he was special, he asked his sister not to talk about his past-life memories to anyone else. This suggests that he had no intention of attracting his mother's or anyone's attention by talking about his unusual memories.

Furthermore, according to the report by Hirata Atsutane, Katsugoro desired to become a samurai. It is unthinkable that even if he had had any motivation – not to mention ability – to use super-psi ability to collect information, that Katsugoro would have used it to identify himself as a child of a farmer in a small village unknown to him or other members of his family. If his story was invented, one would have expected him to identify his past life as a samurai.

One could argue that, even if Katsugoro did not have such motivations, his family member(s) unconsciously induced him to use his "magic wand" psi ability. Judging from their reactions to his statements and reluctance to check them until virtually forced to do so by his incessant begging, this conjecture seems to be groundless.

Although one can always postulate "hidden, unconscious motivations" for any activity, there seems to be no evidence for assuming such motivations in the case of Katsugoro, either on his part or on the part of his family members.

Several additional features also cannot be accounted for by the living-agent psi hypothesis. First, it is crucial to note that Katsugoro talked about his past-life memories as a person who experienced them all himself.[101] They in no way resemble statements made by a psychic (or mental medium) talking about information concerning a dead person, or those by a trance medium through whom the alleged deceased person communicates. Katsugoro's statements were from a child talking about

---

[101] Also see Becker (1993, pp. 31-32) for this line of argument.

his *own* experiences – even though they were experiences apparently from when he was in a previous life.

Second, the content of his statements had appropriate limitations if we accept that they were based on actual past-life memories, but are unexplainable if they had been obtained by his psi ability. For example, his memories of his past-life ended when Tozo died, so he was unaware of the changes that took place after his death, such as the presence of the roof of the tobacco house and the tree. Had he obtained the information via his psi ability, he would have known about the changes. In contrast, the survival hypothesis presents a natural explanation for such limitations.

Third, Katsugoro showed no sign of having special psi abilities. He showed paranormal knowledge only in the area related to his past-life personality, Tozo. This fact is essential for the survival hypothesis argument, as pointed out by Ian Stevenson (2001, p. 159):

> ... the child subjects hardly ever show, or have credited to them by their families, any evidence of extrasensory perception apart from the memories of a previous life. I have asked many parents about such capacities in their children. Most of them have denied that the child in question had any; a few have said that their child had occasionally demonstrated some form of extrasensory perception, but the evidence they provided was usually scanty. I cannot understand how a child could acquire by extrasensory perception the considerable stores of information that so many of these subjects show about a deceased person without demonstrating–if not often, at least from time to time– similar paranormal powers in other contexts.

In the DOPS database, 693 cases had values for the variable "whether child exhibits ESP with subjects other than past-life memories," that is, whether the child in question showed any ESP power in areas other than those related to his or her past life. In 502 cases (72.4%), the "No" value is assigned. The other values are: "Yes, much and / or often" in 13 cases (1.9%), "Yes, significantly" in 52 cases (7.5%), and "Yes, slightly" in 126 (18.2%) examples. As Stevenson stated, while there are some cases in which the child showed ESP abilities, the majority did not. This invalidates the living-agent psi hypothesis to account for the phenomena in general, and in the cases of those reported in this book since none of the children showed ESP abilities.

Fourth, the emotional elements in the case are hardly accountable by the living-agent psi hypothesis. Why did Katsugoro show a strong desire to see the mother and stepfather from his past-life? Why did he repeatedly beg his family members to take him to Hodokubo village to visit the grave of his former father?

The features in the fifth argument are not apparent in Katsugoro's case but in many others. Personality traits such as phobias, philias, and unlearned skills are hard to explain by the living-agent psi hypothesis. As mentioned in Chapter 14, survivalists have claimed that a distinction should be made between "knowledge-that" and "knowledge-how" (skills) (Ducasse, 1962; Stevenson, 1974a; 1984; Ryle, 1949). The latter, which require a period of practice, cannot be transmitted by psi abilities; therefore a person with unlearned skills cannot have acquired them via psi. After all, while there is ample experimental evidence showing that information can be obtained by paranormal means, there is no such evidence for skills. However, Stephen Braude challenged this argument from a different angle by calling attention to the fact that (i) savants and prodigies often show astonishing skills, and that (ii) latent abilities can be suddenly manifested by hypnotic subjects. This casts doubts on the validity of assuming the subject does not have the "unlearned" skills. They may have just been hidden and were suddenly manifested (Braude, 2003).[102] Limiting one's attention to skills alone, one should admit that apparent paranormal manifestations of them can plausibly be accounted for by such reasoning. However, taking the whole picture of the phenomena into consideration, one faces the problem that it cannot account for why only the particular skills related to past-life personalities are evoked. For instance, why was the dancing skill manifested, among the countless possibilities of latent skills? Out of all the countless languages, why did the subject come to speak the particular unlearned language that corresponds to the language the claimed past-life personality spoke? The choice of particular skills fitting given past-life memories is what we can expect under the survival hypothesis, but is unaccountable under the living-agent psi hypothesis.

Sixth, the continuity of the memories – past-life, life-between-life, womb, and birth memories – is straightforwardly accounted for by the survival hypothesis, but not by the living-agent psi hypothesis. The latter must assume that somehow the subject obtained various

---

[102] Also, see Braude (2014, pp. 157-173) for an account of why having recourse to skills (alone) for the survival argument can be untenable.

pieces of information from the four different stages of the soul's life cycle and arranged them in the "correct" order. These considerations demonstrate that we have enough evidence for selecting the survival hypothesis over the living-agent psi hypothesis.

Auxiliary Assumptions

Philosopher Michael Sudduth (2016) advanced the survival hypotheses argument a step further by pointing out that its proponents should be aware of the problem of auxiliary assumptions. According to the so-called Duhem–Quine thesis, scientific hypotheses cannot be tested in isolation because they typically require auxiliary assumptions (Duhem, 1954; Quine, 1951). Elliott Sober, well-known for his work in the philosophy of biology and philosophy of science, argues that for a hypothesis to be tested, its auxiliary assumptions should be independently justified (Sober, 2008).

Since the postmortem state takes many forms, there are various possibilities. For instance, it can theoretically be possible that one's consciousness survived the bodily death, but lost the ability to communicate. Or, even if it retained the ability to communicate, it lost the desire or intention to communicate. For the survival argument to account for the phenomena apparently showing that the consciousness of the deceased actually survived death, the bare assumption that the consciousness survived death is not enough: It must be supplemented by auxiliary assumptions such as that the surviving consciousness retained the ability, desire and intention to communicate.

Sudduth argues that, although these auxiliary assumptions account for the phenomena in question, they are not independently justified. In other words, there is no evidence for them outside the contexts in which they are made. Therefore, the survival hypothesis is not a viable scientific claim.

We deal with this problem by examining the nature of the auxiliary assumptions allegedly necessary for the survival hypothesis.

As Sudduth says, his arguments concerning the survival hypothesis are comparable to Elliot Sober's (2008) arguments concerning the intelligent designer hypothesis (Sudduth, 2016, pp. 303–304). The intelligent designer is in a sense an alternative term for "God" and the hypothesis assumes that since the universe appears to be too complex to be created by a mechanical process, there must be or must have been an intelligent designer behind it.

As correctly pointed out by Sober, the intelligent designer theory, which posits the existence of a "creator" in the world, requires a set of auxiliary assumptions postulating what kind of properties the intelligent designer must have. For instance, it must have power which enables it to create the universe as it is structured now.

The parallelism between the survival hypothesis and the intelligent designer hypothesis, however, is only superficial. In the intelligent designer hypothesis, the core hypothesis merely postulates the existence of the intelligent designer. No one knows exactly what properties it has, so they have to be specified by adding auxiliary assumptions. In contrast, in the survival hypothesis, the properties the human consciousness has are already known unless its properties change after the bodily death. In other words, as pointed out by Edward F. Kelly (Kelly, 2016, p. 591), by adopting what R. W. K. Paterson calls "the least conjectural assumption," we can dispense with auxiliary assumptions that specify the properties of the human consciousness:

> I, therefore, suggest that the safest course is to assume that minds which function in a certain way when embodied will probably continue to function in a broadly similar way when they are disembodied, naturally making due allowance for the huge consequences which must be inseparable from the fact of disembodiment itself. Although we are admittedly engaged in conjecture, we ought to proceed on that assumption which is *the least* conjectural (Paterson 1995, p. 192).

On this, Sudduth remarks (Sudduth, 2016, p. 210):

> ... we might very well grant Paterson's general principle that patterns and processes of antemortem cognitive functioning will probably continue into the afterlife, but this is insufficient to underwrite several of his more specific claims about what we should expect of postmortem persons. The problem here is that Paterson is unjustifiably narrow in his conception of antemortem cognitive functioning. In this domain, we not only find the kinds of cognitive processes that Paterson notes but also – as Broad explained ... – dream-world experiences, a range of dissociative phenomena (including extreme dissociative pathology such as dissociative identity disorder), and various forms of amnesia.

Sudduth's criticism can be circumvented by expanding Paterson's "strong continuity" assumption so that it also includes "dream-world experiences and various forms of amnesia." Just as human consciousness can take various states while incarnate, it can take different states when it is discarnate. Just as incarnate consciousness has dream-world experiences or in the state of amnesia appears confused and unintelligible, the discarnate consciousness in such conditions appears confused and unintelligible, as illustrated in some mediumistic communications.

Moreover, even if we admit the necessity of the auxiliary assumptions for the survival hypothesis, we can say that they have some independent justification. Consider the phenomena of near-death experiences. Although the term implies that the person was near death but not dead, in many cases, the people *were* temporarily clinically dead, and Dr. Sam Parnia even proposes that in some cases, the term "near-death experience" be changed to "actual-death experience" (Parnia and Young, 2013, p. 149).

I believe that for research purposes in cases where people have suffered a cardiac arrest and been resuscitated, we need to change the term *near-death experience* to *actual-death experience* because, in the cardiac arrest phase, we can say exactly what is happening to the body's physiology. The idea that someone suffering from meningitis had the same experience as someone who had almost bled to death after a motor vehicle accident or someone with an actual cardiac arrest is not accurate and specific enough. For starters, the biology will be very different. There may be similarities, but they are not the same thing, just as to someone who has never seen an elephant, a rhinoceros, and a hippopotamus, the three share many similarities, but to those who have more knowledge, they are clearly different. This is why we need to clearly define what we are talking about.

One of the most impressive cases of near-death experiences during the clinically dead condition was Pam Reynolds, an American singer-songwriter (1956–2010). The case was reported by a cardiologist, Michael Sabom (1998). Thirty-five-year-old Reynolds was diagnosed with a giant basilar artery aneurysm at the base of her brain, the rupture of which would be fatal. The crucial point of this well-known case is that Pam Reynolds had profound experiences, some of which were verified, during the period when her body was "dead." In other words, her case demonstrates that consciousness can function while the body is dead.[103] Another extreme case is that of George Rodonaia, reported by P.M.H. Atwater, a three-time near-death experiencer, author, and researcher (Atwater, 2009, p. 15, pp. 73-76). Rodonaia was a communist dissident in Tbilisi, Georgia. In 1976, he was run over twice by a car driven by a member of the KGB in an attempted assassination. He was pronounced dead at a hospital, and his body was sent to the morgue. Following the standard procedure, the body was frozen immediately and kept in that state for three days. After three days, it went to the autopsy room. As one of the doctors started to cut into his body, Rodonaia opened his eyes. Thinking this a mere reflex, the doctor closed Rodonaia's eyes. When he opened his eyes again, the doctor closed them once more. When Rodonaia opened his eyes for the third time, the doctor jumped backward and screamed. Rodonaia was rushed immediately to emergency surgery. He remained hospitalized for nine months, but since he became so famous, the KGB, although keeping an eye on him, could not touch him again.

During the "death" state, Rodonaia experienced an encounter with light, and feelings of happiness. When he thought about his body, he was instantly back in the morgue, looking down at his frozen body. Though he did not want to be around it, he was forced to linger and look around by an unknown power. Then the memory of the accident (assassination attempt) came, and suddenly he felt as if the thoughts of everyone involved were inside him, and he could see them. Then he saw his wife go to the grave where he would be buried and saw her thinking about her future. Next,

> He returned to the morgue and was drawn to the newborn section of the adjacent hospital where a friend's wife had just given birth to a daughter. The baby cried incessantly. As if possessed of x-ray vision, Rodonaia scanned her body and noted that her hip had been broken at birth. He "verbally" addressed her: Don't cry. Nobody will understand you. The infant was so surprised at his presence that she stopped crying. "Children can see and hear spirit beings. That child responded to me because, to her, I was a physical reality" (Atwater, 2009, p. 75).

---

[103] For detailed descriptions and analyses of her verified statements and reply to critical evaluations of her experience, see Rivas, et al. (2016, pp. 95-103).

The intriguing aspect is not only that he was able to "read" the minds of other people, but he could communicate with the infant, which is comparable to mediumistic communication from the deceased.

Titus Rivas contacted Atwater, who had interviewed not just George Rodonaia, the experiencer, but also his wife, Nino, to verify the accuracy of the recorded statements. In an e-mail sent on July 28, 2015, from Atwater to Rivas, Nino said that George knew exactly what she had been thinking at the time of his being in the morgue, and she confirmed what had happened at the hospital of his friend's wife, who had just given birth to a daughter. Three days after coming back to life, when George was able to talk, he told the doctors to go to the maternity ward immediately and X-ray the baby's hip. George, who was also a doctor, described the condition of the baby in detail. The doctors X-rayed the baby and found the break exactly as George described. The nurse in charge of the baby confessed that she had dropped the baby and was immediately fired (Rivas, et al., 2016, pp. 129-132).

These cases suggest that consciousness retains the intention to communicate and can be successful, independently justifying the "auxiliary assumptions" for the survival hypothesis.

In summary, I hope the above discussions have demonstrated that neither the counterarguments in terms of the living-agent psi hypothesis nor those in terms of auxiliary assumptions undermine the survival hypothesis.

The Survival Hypothesis and Children with Past-Life and Other Memories

The above considerations show that, coupled with phenomena concerning mediumistic communications and conceptual considerations related to auxiliary assumptions, cases of children with past-life and other related memories present strong support for the survival hypothesis over living-agent psi hypothesis. The strength of the evidence posed by the children with prenatal memories is concerned with the selection of a person in question: Why do children with apparently no or little psychic abilities give detailed information concerning a specific person and behave in a manner appropriate to that person, even when there appears to be no psychological motivations for children to do so? In mediumistic communications, such motivations are often present with the exception of drop-in or similar cases. In that sense, the cases of children with past-life and related memories present stronger evidence than the cases of mediumistic communications. Moreover, such children with continuous memories as Katsugoro present even stronger evidence for the survival hypothesis.

16

Conclusions: Does Everyone Reincarnate?

Past-Life Memories

I believe that the existence of children with past-life and other prenatal memories is now firmly established. The follow-up question regards the prevalence of the phenomena. In other words, is it only people who have such memories who survive death and reincarnate, or do we all? It seems we can infer that the latter is the case.

Children with past-life memories are admittedly rare, which would seem to suggest that the number of people with past lives is relatively small. However, at least six facts suggest otherwise.

First, one of the most prominent features of reincarnation cases is that a disproportionately high percentage of subjects recall a life that ended violently. In the DOPS database, 64.4 percent of subjects reported unnatural death, mostly violent, as the following figures show.

Table 16-1. The Cause of Death in Children with Past-Life Memories.

Cause of Death		Number of Cases	Percentage
Unnatural	Intentional Shooting	205	10.8%
	Accidental Shooting	21	1.1%
	Stabbing	79	4.2%
	Drowning	109	5.8%
	Snakebite	34	1.8%
	Other Intentional Violent	236	12.5%
	Other Accidental Violent	488	15.8%
	Intentional Suicide	41	2.2%
	Medical Complications	4	0.2%
	Subtotal	1217	64.4%
Natural		674	35.6%
	Total	1891	

Likewise, the majority of subjects reported that they had unfinished business in their past lives, as shown below.[104]

---

[104] Some of the data overlap with the data concerning the mode of death.

Table 16-2. "Unfinished Business" in
Children with Past-Life Memories.

Presence of Unfinished Business		The Number of Cases	Percentage
Yes	Expressed by the past-life personality	16	11.0%
	Expressed by the subject	34	23.3%
	Expressed by both the past-life personality and the subject	2	1.4%
	Expressed by relatives	26	17.8%
	Identified by the principal investigator	41	28.1%
	Subtotal	119	81.5%
No		27	18.5%
	Total	146	

As Jim Tucker conjectures, these facts may show that only a portion of the whole population with relevant factors, such as having died in violence or having left some unfinished business, *remember* past lives, although every person *has* one (Tucker, 2005, p. 214).

> ... reincarnation may normally occur but without memories continuing from the previous life. In that case, we may all have had previous lives even though most of us do not remember them. If this is true, then the usual process may get disrupted either by a factor in the previous life like an unexpected death or by some factor in the next life. This may lead some memories to be present in the next life, and therefore, even though everyone may reincarnate, our cases are unusual because of the presence of the memories.

The second relevant fact is that most children forget their past-life memories before adulthood. This was seen in the case of Katsugoro, who said, "Until I was around four, I remembered my past-life in detail, but now I have forgotten many things." Considering all the cases in this book, the mean age when the children stopped talking about past-life memories was 7 years and 3 months (the median was 6 years). This may imply that many of us remember our past lives while young, but forget as we grow older.

This conjecture appears to be supported by the third fact: Adults, who think they do not have past-life memories or have never thought of the possibility of past-life memories, may recall past lives either spontaneously or under hypnotic regression.

A solid example of the former type is the case of Jeffrey Keene, an American firefighter who was born in 1947. In May 1991, when he visited a Civil War battle site called Sunken Road, something unusual happened to him:

A wave of grief, sadness, and anger washed over me. Without warning, I was suddenly being consumed by sensations. Burning tears ran down my cheeks. It became difficult to breathe. I gasped for air as I stood transfixed in the cold roadbed. To this day, I could not tell you how much time transpired, but as these feelings, this emotional overload passed, I found myself exhausted as if I had run a marathon. (Keene, 2003, p. 2)

The following year at a Halloween party, Keene met a palm reader named Barbara Camwell, who gave readings at the party. When his turn came, Keene asked about the strange experience at Sunken Road. Barbara said, "That's because you died there." She added, "When you were hovering over your body looking down, you were very angry and yelled NO!" For reasons unknown to Keene, he said to Barbara, "Not yet!" Barbara conceded, "Yes, like not yet, but you hung around for a long time" (Keene, 2003, p. 5).

Then, the next year, Keene started to read a magazine titled *Civil War Quarterly*, which he had bought at a gift shop during a trip to the Sunken Road but had not read for a year and a half. When he turned to the section on the Sunken Road, a two-word quote caught his attention, and the hair on the back of his neck stood up. "Not yet." It was the order given by the Confederate military leader John B. Gordon to the anxious members of the 6th Alabama Regiment who requested permission to fire. As Keene read the article, tears welled up in his eyes. When he saw a picture of Gordon, he was astounded. The face in the picture looked identical to his own.[105] (Apparently, Gordon had not died in the battle, and what Barbara described in the reading might have been his near-death experience.) From that time on, Keene undertook extensive research on the life of John B. Gordon and found striking similarities between Gordon and himself, including a birthmark and scars corresponding to the battle wounds Gordon suffered. Furthermore, with the help of a linguist, Miriam Petruck, Ph.D., Dr. Walter Semkiw analyzed the writing styles of John B. Gordon and Jeffrey Keene and pointed out their structural similarities.

To this category of spontaneous past-life memories in adults, we may add the case of William Barnes, who claimed he had memories of the life of Thomas Andrews, the British naval architect in charge of the Titanic plans (Barnes, 2000); or Bruce Kelly, who said he recalled memories of the life of James Johnson, an American submarine sailor (Brown, 1990); or Robert Snow, who allegedly had memories of the life of James Carroll Beckwith, an American painter (Snow, 1999).

Examples of adults recalling past lives under hypnosis are abundant as hypnotic past-life regression remains a popular form of therapy. As shown in Chapter 14, even Ian Stevenson, who is critical about the use of hypnosis in eliciting accurate past-life recalls, admitted that there are genuine cases. He provided two xenoglosssy cases he investigated as examples, and to these we may add the case of Risa. Stevenson also cited the case of Bridey Murphy in Bernstein's *The Search for Bridey Murphy* (Bernstein, 1956) as a possible genuine case (Stevenson, 1974a; 1984).

Fourth, as lucidly argued by Stevenson (1977a), the assumption that human consciousness survives bodily death and links to a new body may present a unified account for a variety of otherwise unaccountable phenomena as follows.

- Phobias and philias of childhood
- Skills possessed but not learned in early life
- Abnormalities of child-parent relationships
- Vendettas and bellicose nationalism
- Childhood sexuality and gender identity confusion
- Birthmarks, congenital deformities, and internal diseases
- Differences between members of monozygotic twin pairs
- Abnormal appetites during pregnancy

---

[105] The reader may check this in Keene's book (Keene, 2003).

In the "standard" assumption that human traits are determined either by nature (genes), nurture (environmental conditions), or the combination of both, there remain many unexplained facts. For instance, a study of 50 clinical cases of childhood water phobia by Ross G. Menzies and J. Christopher Clarke showed that "the majority of parents (56%) claimed that the child's concern had always been present, even on their first encounter with water (Menzies and Clarke, 1993)." The genetic factor did not seem to play a role, either. In such cases, one could speculate that the phobia was a reflection of a past-life experience of drowning – the difference between water phobic children and children with past-life memories being whether the child was consciously aware of the traumatic event, or only subconsciously affected by it (Stevenson, 2001, p. 184).[106]

In addition to the traditional two factors, the third one, the epigenetic factor (simply put, the interaction of genetics and environments), is now regarded as another critical influencer. Yet, as various twin studies show, there are still unknown factors, often called "noise" (Spector, 2012). The effect of past-life memories fits in nicely to fill the gap.

In addition, there are many people who claim to have past-life memories but who remain unnoticed by researchers. Whenever I present a talk about reincarnation, people always approach me to discuss their "secret" past-life memories, which they are afraid to reveal even to people close to them. There remains a stigma surrounding such notions, and people commonly fear being ridiculed or seen as "crazy." In recent years, however, thanks to the development of social media, it is becoming easier for such individuals to share their stories. One such Facebook group, *Signs of Reincarnation*, moderated by James Matlock, a research fellow of Parapsychology Foundation, has over 180,000 members, and some of the shared stories have been investigated by researchers.[107]

Finally, there appear to be many people who have past-life memories but, due to their lack of knowledge on the subject, are unaware that

---

[106] There are various theories for the etiology of phobias. See the study by Harald Merckelbach and others (Merckelbach, et al., 1996).

[107] The description of the group is as follows: "Over the last 60 years or so (since 1961) there has been a lot of serious research with people who remember previous lives without the aid of hypnosis, but it is not well known by the scientific community or general public. The purpose of this group is to make this research better known." https://www.facebook.com/groups/965923533422836 (retrieved 26 Nov., 2023).

they do. A striking example was the case of an 18-year-old woman who attended one of my presentations on past-life investigations. After the talk, she approached me and said, "I now understand what I have been wondering." An exceptionally vivid vision she remembered had been puzzling her. In the vision, she is in the schoolyard of an elementary school with one of her friends, handing a trash bag to a teacher who would burn it in the incinerator. Figure 16-1 is a picture the woman drew to describe the scene.

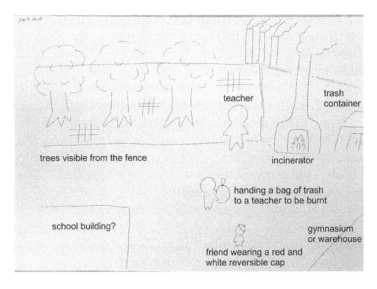

Figure 16-1: Picture Drawn by a Young Woman.

Interestingly, incinerators in the schoolyard in Japan were abolished in 1997, before the woman was born. In the vision, she was not a girl but a boy. Furthermore, she used to have a vivid dream of being stabbed by "his" (her previous self's) mother. After hearing my talk, she was convinced that she had past-life memories and the vision was a scene from that life.

Life-Between-Life and Other Prenatal Memories

Just like past-life memories, life-between-life memories are also sometimes recalled through hypnotic regression. Helen Wambach reported the results of her examination of 750 subjects who reported the pre-birth experience (the state between lives) under hypnotic regression (Wambach, 1979). Although she did not attempt to verify the participants' recalls, some subjective reports suggest that they reflect reality, such as when adoptive parents, not biological parents, were selected. Many claimed to have chosen to be born, or described an entity guiding their birth, similar to Katsugoro's memory of an old man leading him in his life-between-life state.[108]

Womb memory recalls under hypnosis were reported by Dr. David Cheek, an obstetrician. In one of the four cases he discussed in his 1992 article, a woman with a recurrent dream that her mother was trying to abort her with a button hook, an unlikely tool for the attempt, was hypnotized and recalled the following real event that took place around six months into the pregnancy (Cheek, 1992, p. 130):

[Subject]: It's before I'm born. My father is shouting, "I'm going to kill you." (A few seconds later, [Subject] began screaming. She pulled her legs up to her chest as though trying to get away from something very frightening) ... I saw that button hook coming up at me. I knew my mother was trying to get me out.
[Therapist]: Then what happened?
[Subject]: Nothing happened—only a little bleeding.

Astonishingly, after she had talked about these memories, her mother confessed that she actually had done just what the daughter described. It is highly improbable that the daughter had heard about the event from her parents or anyone else, suppressed it, then later recalled it under hypnosis. The more plausible explanation is that she had a genuine womb memory.

Moreover, the reliability of birth memory recollection under hypnosis was confirmed experimentally by one of the pioneers of birth psychology, David Chamberlain. In an article reporting one of his experiments, ten pairs of mothers and their children with no conscious memory of birth, were independently hypnotized and asked to recall what happened at the time of birth (Chamberlain, 1986). A comparison of the accounts

---

[108] Michael Newton's reports of those "experiencing" life-between-life states under hypnosis are more elaborate, including elements not observed in children's reports of life-between-life experiences (Newton, 1994; 2000). However, as James Matlock suggests, they may have been influenced heavily by the suggestible nature of the hypnotic state (Matlock, 2019).

made by the mothers and the children revealed matching statements, although there were some contradictions. A good example of matching statements is the following concerning the onset of labor:

Child (of Pair #10): Mother was in the bedroom resting. It's daytime. Contractions start at 1:10 pm. Mother called father and doctor and was advised to wait.
Mother (of Pair #10): At about one o'clock, I knew I was in labor and called my husband to come home. I telephoned the doctor; he advised waiting.

The total numbers of matches and contradictions obtained from 10 mother-child pairs examined by Chamberlain (1986) are: 137 matches versus 9 contradictions.

To sum, these six facts suggest that many more people have past-life memories, and some are concerned with life-between-life, womb, and birth memory phenomena. It suggests that the survival of consciousness after death is not a rare and exceptional phenomenon but a very common, and possibly universal one.

Afterword

My Daughter's Past-Life Memories (and My Own)

～

"**I** remember being crushed by a falling pillar," said my second daughter, hesitantly. She was 15 years old at the time.

Her words surprised me, but at the same time they presented a plausible explanation for her strange behaviors and characteristics she had shown ever since she was an infant.

She was and still is quite easily frightened. One of the most impressive episodes occurred when she was about two or three years old. It was before I came to know Ian Stevenson's work, let alone started investigating children with past-life memories.

Having a cotton blanket being thrown over her body and trying to get out of it was one of my older daughter's favorite games when she was two or three years old. Expecting my younger daughter to enjoy the same amusement, I threw a cotton blanket over her. Quite contrary to my expectation, she screamed, desperately got out of the blanket, rushed, and clung to me, crying and trembling. Her unexpected reaction shocked and perplexed me.

She showed similar reactions in similar situations, like when a sheet of cloth, cushions, or stuffed toys accidentally fell over her. These extreme reactions of my daughter, not shared with any of our family members, appeared utterly inexplicable to me.

A couple of years later, as an elementary school student, while watching a TV program with her mother (my wife), she muttered, "I remember being shaken by an earthquake." My wife later told me about these strange remarks, which neither of us understood at the time.

When I began investigating children claiming to have past-life memories and learned that many of them have phobias related to past-life experiences, I came to believe that our younger daughter's strange behaviors might be due to her past-life experiences.

Such considerations shed light on her other seemingly inexplicable characteristics, such as her excessive fondness of skulls and psychedelic colors and patterns (which later developed into an urge to go to Mexico), her phobia of knives which made her unable to cut or peel vegetables and fruits with a knife, and her muscular physique which made her the strongest arm-wrestler among classmates (including boys) throughout her elementary school years.

"She might have been a Mexican soldier who was stabbed to death by an enemy," was one of my imaginings.

More than once, I asked her if she remembered something that had happened before she was born, but she never gave a clear response.

Then, completely out of the blue, she said she remembered being crushed by a falling pillar. By that time, she knew to some extent that there are children who claim to have past-life memories and that I investigate such children.

"Why didn't you say that before?" was my initial response.

To which she replied, "I was too scared to talk about it."

I asked her if she remembered anything else, such as the person's name or where the person lived and so on. To my disappointment (as a researcher), although she had had other memories before, being crushed to death by a falling pillar was the only one that remained. Like other children with past-life memories, she seemed to have lost most of them around the age of eight.

Her story has no verifiable elements and is of little value as possible evidence for the reincarnation hypothesis. However, at the subjective level, it sounded real and genuine to the effect that I could not help but have pity for her, having suffered a tragic "experience."

Past-Life Regression Therapy Experience

In the summer of 2009, I attended a three-day conference of the International Society of Life Information Science (ISLIS) in Hakone, Japan. The ISLIS is a society of researchers focusing on parapsychological phenomena. Our team presented the case of Risa, the Japanese woman who spoke Nepali under hypnotic past-life regression therapy (Chapter 14). The conference participants were not just researchers but doctors, nurses, and practitioners of various therapies. In the evening, some therapists held sessions to give participants a chance to experience their treatments. One of them offered a hypnotic past-life regression session *a' la'* Dr. Brian Weiss, which I was willing to try. Since I had not been able to find a practicing therapist, I had purchased CDs by Weiss (2008a, 2008b, 2008c) and had tried to have a past-life regression experience for about a year without any luck. So this conference session was a golden opportunity.

The therapist was TAKEMOTO Ayaco, a student of OTSUKI Maiko, a leading hypnotherapist who had finished a training program at the Weiss Institute (see Chapter 3). Since I had no particular problems to explore through past-life regression therapy, I told the therapist, "I just want to experience the past-life, if any, which I should experience now."

In the session I was regressed to a girl living in the 16th-century. I was running on a grass field, towards my mother. I was embraced by her and felt ineffable happiness. I grew and married a man, with whom I had three children.

The first scene I saw in the hypnotic regression[109].

I then went through various losses: my second child seemed to have died from disease, and I saw a small coffin with flowers.

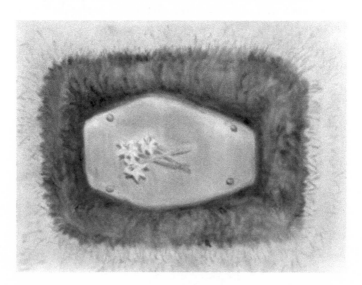

The coffin for the second child.

[109] The pictures in this chapter were drawn by the author.

I also lost my husband and another child, as well as a countless number of people in the city where I lived, possibly due to war. Especially shocking was that, in the latter scene, a tremendous number of the dead were small children.

The death of countless people.

"So many children who should have enjoyed their lives were killed," was my reply to the therapist, when asked what I thought when I was in the scene. It seemed to me that this "past-life experience" accounts for my strong urge to work with children. In addition to my university work, I served as PTA president in two elementary schools, and as a volunteer staff member in a kindergarten, and I read books to children at elementary schools as a volunteer.

Although I was well aware of the warnings from Ian Stevenson about "the dramatizing powers of the mind that hypnosis releases" and the "convincing appearance of realism," the experience was so overwhelming that it was hard to believe that my recollection was anything but a real past-life experience.

The death memory from the "past-life" was even more overwhelming. I was in bed, surrounded by neighbors. Then I left my body and floated for a while, looking down at the people around my body. The therapist asked me, "How do you feel now?"

I said, "I feel frustrated because I want to tell them that I am okay and that you don't have to lament, but I can't."

Then, drawn toward a light, I entered and was embraced by it. In the ineffably ecstatic feeling, I received a message: "You are heading toward the right direction." It was a profoundly important and pertinent message to me. As previously stated, during the conference, our team presented a talk on the case of Risa's xenoglossy occurring under hypnosis. It was my first parapsychological presentation. A study related to past lives is a topic my academic friends and colleagues, mainly linguists, would frown upon, and I was afraid of their reactions. Therefore, the message was a huge encouragement to me.

In her 1978 book, psychologist Helen Wambach reported the results of her systematic study of 750 subjects on the effects of hypnotic past-life regression. "There is no doubt from the report of my subjects after they awoke from the hypnosis that death was the best part of the trip. Again, and again, they reported how pleasant it was to die and what a sense of release they had after they left their bodies (87, p. 140)." I agree with Wambach's study participants.

The aftereffects of the experience were also profound. I felt my heart chakra was completely open, and I thought I was "love incarnate." Everything around me seemed to shine with life or love energy, and everything was embraced by it. Although those conditions lasted only for about a week, the effect of the experience is long-lasting.

This experience led me to conduct the investigation in which near-death experiencers and past-life regression experiencers were compared using the standard near-death scale developed by Dr. Bruce Greyson and the Life Changes Inventory-Revised developed by Drs. Kenneth Ring and Bruce Greyson to assess the aftereffects of near-death experiences (Ohkado and Greyson, 2018). We found that the scores of the two scales in "death" experiences are even higher than those in near-death experiences reported in one study, and concluded that the results appear to warrant further investigation of hypnotically-induced "death" experiences by using the scales designed for near-death experiences.

Concluding Remarks

I have been practicing *qigong* for more than 30 years, as well as other energy techniques such as Reiki and meditation for about ten years. But what I experienced in the past-life regression therapy was life-changing. Since the experience, I can easily undergo a similar sense of unity with the light (though not as strong as when I experienced the hypnotic regression therapy) during my meditation practice.

I have had two additional exceptional experiences during hypnotic sessions. The first was when guided by YOSHIDA Hiroko, the founder of the HPS Psychological Center, who developed a technique that enabled clients to "meet deceased loved ones" under hypnosis. In my session, I was able to see a friend of mine who had died 20 years ago. Although we exchanged no conversation, and I just felt his energy, the experience was convincing enough that I felt I had successfully contacted my friend. The second notable experience was when guided by NIJIIRO Rumika, a hypnotherapist offering a unique session in collaboration with "her deceased son" who committed suicide. During the session, I felt guided by the therapist's son and saw several other spirits guiding us.

The combination of these personal experiences and the knowledge acquired through my research is, for me, compelling evidence for the survival of consciousness after death. For those who judge the matter solely based on intellectual understandings, I suggest that they become familiar with *qigong*, meditation, hypnotic regression therapies, audio techniques such as Hemi-Sync provided by the Monroe Institute, or *Seeking Heaven* (Alexander, 2013), and other methods that enable practitioners to experience various altered states of consciousness suggestive of the continuity of consciousness beyond the body and possibly death.[110]

I would also like to remind readers to pay attention to children. You will then have a better chance of noticing when they are talking about

[110] For instance, by using specific patterns of sound waves, Hemi-Sync technology allows the listener to experience various state of consciousness, some of which are said to be that of death or beyond. Eben Alexander, one of the best-known profound near-death experiencers, states: "I believe Hemi-Sync has enabled me to return to a realm similar to that which I visited deep in coma, but without having to be deathly ill" (Alexander, 2012, p. 159).

their spiritual experiences.[111] Elizabeth Carman and Neil Carman (2019, pp. 23-26) list 12 indicators that lend credibility to children's prenatal memories.

1. Spontaneous, unprompted divulgence of memories
2. Consistency of the memory over time
3. Locked-in eye contact
4. Common elements
5. Age when memory is shared
6. Validation (memory matches a real event)
7. Matter-of-fact, confident, serious tone of voice
8. Parents intuit that their child is speaking the truth
9. Spontaneous drawings of prebirth
10. Spiritual progress and healing
11. Worldwide consistency
12. Consistency between children and adults

From an evidential point of view, items related to factual and universal features, that is, (1), (2), (4), (5), (6), (9), (11), and (12) will be more critical than others. From the personal point of view, however, (3), (7), (8) (if you are a parent), and (10) will be more essential. An eight-year-old girl Aya told me that she had no fear of death because she had died many times. Her past-life stories did not have many verified elements and, in that sense, were not very evidential, but her remarks on death, such as "I have no fear of death because I have died many times," made in a matter-of-fact tone of voice were unforgettable. Likewise, in an interview with a 5-year-old girl, Chihiro, her mother told me the story of when Chihiro's elderly relative was grieving the death of his sister. Chihiro said to him, "Don't worry. Granny will come back." Chihiro told me that she knew this because she had been in the Butterfly Island where spirits reside and from which they come back. Her detailed life-between-life story had few verifiable elements. Yet, her way of disclosing the story with her eyes locked on mine convinced me of its genuineness.

---

[111] Gary Schwartz of University of Arizona, who revived mediumistic research in 1990s by exploring mediums' abilities in laboratory settings, calls attention to the importance of exploring the possibility of the survival of consciousness after death, as a first step, by personal experiences with open mind (Schwartz, 2011). I feel that this approach, what Schwartz calls "self-science," should be put into practice by anyone interested in the topic.

An intriguing fact is that during interviews with children, they often say that they do not talk about their memories to their respective fathers. Typical reasons they give are, "He just would not listen," "He just would not believe it," and "He just dismisses it as fantasies or absurdity." As a result, there are many stories children share only with their mother, which saddens me for both the children and their fathers. There might be many cases in which only fathers accept their children's stories, though I know only a very few. I am also certain that there are many cases where children cannot share their stories with anybody, a great pity and loss for the world.

In the field of parapsychology, the importance of the experimentee's expectation (and possibly the experimenter's as well) is known as the "sheep-goat effect": sheep, those who believe the possibility of ESP tend to obtain higher scores in ESP experiments than goats, those who do not believe is such a possibility (Billows and Storm, 2015). This "sheep-goat effect" can be crucial in having experiences related to the possibility of the survival of consciousness, among which are children's past-life and other memories.

Japanese has an expression, "an old man of the age of three" to refer to an amazingly mature, wise child. It also has a proverb: "Children under the age of seven are within the realm of gods." In interviewing children for their past-life and other memories, I often recall these words and feel they capture the truth.

References

Abe, Saburo. 2015. *Tokko Yamato Kantai*. Tokyo: Shioshobo-Kojinsha.

Akamatsu, Shigeru. 1999. Computer recognition of human face: A survey. *Systems and Computers in Japan* 30(10), 76-89.

Akiba, Masakazu. 2001. *Race/Gender Perception of Faces and Extraction of Faces and Extraction of Facial Impression Feature*. PhD Dissertation, Yokohama National University.

Alexander, Eben. 2012. *Proof of Heaven: A Neurosurgeon's Journey into the Afterlife*. New York: Simon & Shuster (Kindle Edition).

Alexander, Eben. 2013. *Seeking Heaven* (CD). New York: Simon & Shuster Audio.

Almeder, Robert. 1992. *Death and Personal Survival: The Evidence for Life After Death*. Lanham, MD: Rowman & Littlefield.

Asano, Makoto. 2002. *Zensei (Past Lives)*. Tokyo: Tama Shuppan.

Asano, Makoto. 2003. *Zensei II (Past Lives II)*. Tokyo: Tama Shuppan.

Asano, Makoto. 2004. *Zensei III (Past Lives III)*. Tokyo: Tama Shuppan.

Asano, Makoto. 2005. *Zensei IV (Past Lives IV)*. Tokyo: Tama Shuppan.

Asano, Makoto. 2006. *Zensei V (Past Lives V)*. Tokyo: Tama Shuppan.

Atkins, Paul S. 2016. Shinkokin Wakashu: The New Anthology of Ancient and Modern Japanese Poetry. In Shirane, Haruo; Suzuki, Tomi; with Lurie, David. *The Cambridge History of Japanese Literature*, 230-237. Cambridge: Cambridge University Press (Kindle Edition).

Atwater, P. M. H. 2009. *Beyond the Light: What Isn't Being Said About Near-Death Experience: From Visions of Heaven to Glimpses of Hell*. Kill Devil Hills, NC: Transpersonal. (Original work published in 1994)

Baker, Mark. 2010. Brains and Souls: Grammar and Speaking. In Baker, Mark; Goetz, Stewart (eds.). *The Soul Hypothesis: The Investigations into the Existence of the Soul, 73-93.* New York: Continuum.

Baker, Robert A. 1982. The Effect of Suggestion on Past-Lives regression. *American Journal of Clinical Hypnosis,* 25, 71-76.

Barnes, William. 2000. *Thomas Andrews, Voyage into History: Titanic Secrets Revealed Through the Eyes of Her Builder.* Gillette, NJ: Edin Books.

Batchelor, John. 1901. *The Ainu and Their Folk-Lore.* London: Religious Tract Society.

Becker, Carl B. 1993. *Paranormal Experience and Survival of Death.* New York: State University of New York Press.

Beischel, Julie. 2014. *From the Mouths of Mediums, Vol. 1: Experiencing Communication.* Tucson, AZ: The Windbridge Institute.

Beischel, Julie; Mosher, Chad; Boccuzzi, Mark. 2017. Quantitative and Qualitative Analyses of Mediumistic and Psychic Experience. *Threshold: Journal of Interdisciplinary Consciousness Studies,* 1(2), 51–91.

Beischel, Julie; Rock, Adam J. 2009. Addressing the Survival vs. Psi Debate Through Process-Focused Mediumship Research. *Journal of Parapsychology,* 73, 71–90.

Berger, Arthur S; Berger, Joyce. 1991. *Encyclopedia of Parapsychology and Psychical Research.* New York: Paragon House.

Bernstein, Morey. 1956. *The Search for Bridey Murphy.* New York: Doubleday.

Billows, Helen; Storm, Lance. 2015. Believe It or Not: A Confirmatory Study on Predictors of Paranormal Belief, and a Psi Test. *Australian Journal of Parapsychology,* 15, 7–35.

Books Esoterica. 1994. *Hinzukyo no Hon (A Book of Hinduism).* Tokyo: Gakken Plus.

Braude, Stephen. 1997. *The Limits of Influence: Psychokinesis and the Philosophy of Science, Revised Edition.* Lanham, MD: University Press of America.

Braude, Stephen. 2003. *Immortal Remains: The Evidence for Life After Death.* Lanham, MD: Rowman & Littlefield.

Braude, Stephen. 2014. *Crimes of Reason: On Mind, Nature, and the Paranormal.* Lanham, MD: Rowman & Littlefield.

Brown, Rick. 1990. *The Reincarnation of James: The Submarine Man.* Glendora, CA: Rick Brown.

Burt, Michael D.; Perrett, David I. 1997. Perceptual Asymmetries in Judgements of Facial Attractiveness, Age, Gender, Speech and Expression. *Neuropsychologia* 35(5), 685-693.

Carman, Elizabeth; Carman, Neil. 2019. *Babies Are Cosmic: Signs of Their Secret Intelligence.* Austin, TX: Babies Are Cosmic.

Chabris, Christopher; Simons, Daniel. 2010. *The Invisible Gorilla and Other Ways Our Intuitions Deceive Us.* New York: Crown Publishers.

Chamberlain, David B. 1986. Reliability of Birth Memory: Observations from Mother and Child Pairs in Hypnosis. *Journal of the American Academy of Medical Hypnoanalysis,* 1(2), 89–98.

Chamberlain, David B. 1988. *Babies Remember Birth.* New York: Ballantine Books.

Chamberlain, David B. 1998. *The Mind of Your Newborn Baby.* Berkeley, CA: North Atlantic Books.

Cheek, David B. 1992. Are Telepathy, Clairvoyance, and "Hearing" Possible in Utero? Suggestive Evidence as Revealed During Hypnotic Age-Regression Studies of Prenatal Memory. *Pre- and Peri-Natal Psychology Journal,* 7(2), 125–137.

Chomsky, Noam. 1965. *Aspects of the Theory of Syntax.* Cambridge, MA.: MIT Press.

Clark, David; Takenouchi, Hirobumi. 2020. The Mitori Project: End of Life Care in the United Kingdom and Japan – Intersections in Culture, Practice and Policy. *Progress in Palliative Care,* 28(3), 189-191.

Clark, Nancy. 2012. *Divine Moments: Ordinary People Having Spiritually Transformative Experiences.* Fairfield, IA: 1stWorld Publishing.

Cockell, Jenny. 1993. *Yesterday's Children: The Extraordinary Search for My Past Life Family.* London: Piatkus.

Cockell, Jenny. 1996. *Past Lives, Future Lives.* London: Piatkus.

Cockell, Jenny. 2010. *Journeys Through Time: Uncovering My Past Lives.* London: Piatkus.

Cockell, Jenny. 2017. *Past Lives Eternal.* Scotts Valley, CA: CreateSpace Independent Publishing Platform.

Cosmides, Leda; Tooby, John; Kurzban, Robert. 2003. Perceptions of race. *Trends in cognitive sciences,* 7(4), 173-179.

Crabtree, Steve; Pelham, Brett. 2009. What Alabamians and Iranians Have in Common: A Global Perspective on Americans' Religiosity Offers a Few Surprises. *Gallup World,* February 9, 2009. <http://www.gallup.com/poll/114211/alabamians-iranians-common.aspx> Retrieved August 2, 2013.

Daher, Jorge Cecilio, Jr.; Damiano, Rodolfo Rurlan; Lucchetti, Alessandra Lamas Granero; Moreira-Almeida, Alexander; Lucchetti, Giancarlo. 2017. Research on Experiences Related to the Possibility of Consciousness Beyond the Brain: A Bibliometric Analysis of Global Scientific Output. *The Journal of Nervous and Mental Disease*, 205(1), 37–47.

Dalai Lama. 1962. *My Land and My People: Autobiography of the Dalai Lama.* New York: McGraw-Hill.

Ducasse, Curt J. 1962. What Would Constitute Conclusive Evidence of Survival after Death? *Journal of the Society for Psychical Research*, 41, 401–406.

Duhem, Pierre. 1954. *The Aim and Structure of Physical Theory.* Princeton, NJ: Princeton University Press.

Dupuis-Roy, Nicolas; Isabelle Fortin; Daniel Fiset; Frédéric Gosselin. 2009. Uncovering Gender Discrimination Cues in a Realistic Setting. *Journal of Vision* 9(2), 1-8.

Dyer, Wayne W.; Garnes, Dee. 2015. *Memories of Heaven: Children's Astounding Recollections of the Time Before They Came to Earth.* Carlsbad, CA: Hay House.

Ehara, Hiroyuki. 2010. *Zensei: Jinsei wo Kaeru (Past Lives: Change Your LIfe).* Tokyo: Tokuma Shoten.

Fan, Ying. 2013. *Sarashina Nikki* no Yume to Shinko: "Zensei no Yume" wo Megutte (Dreams and Faith in the *Sarashina Nikki*: Concerning 'the Dream about the Previous Life'). *Kokusai Bunka Kenkyusho Kiyo*, 18, 17-37.

Funahashi, Yutaka. 1990. *Kodai Nihonjin no Shizenkan: Kojiki wo Chushin ni (Ancient Japanese's View of Nature: With Special Reference to the Kojiki).* Tokyo: Shinbisha.

Gauld, Alan. 1982. *Mediumship and Survival: A Century of Investigations.* London: William Heinemann.

Golovnin, I. V. (Supervising Editor). 1973. *Learning Japanese: Ministry of Higher Secondary Specialized Education of the USSR.* Moscow: Ministry of Higher Secondary Specialized Education of the USSR. (Original text in Russian).

Greyson, Bruce. 1983. The Near-Death Experience Scale. *The Journal of Nervous and Mental Disease*, 171(6), 369-375.

Greyson, Bruce; Ring, Kenneth. 2004. The Life Changes Inventory-Revised. *Journal of Near-Death Studies*, 23(1), 41-54.

Gurney, Edmund; Myers, Frederic W. H.; Podmore, Frank. 1886. *Phantasms of the Living*, 2 Vols. London: Society for Psychical Research.

Hara, Katsuhiro. 2003. *Shinso: Senkan Yamato no Saigo (The True Account of the End of the Battleship* Yamato*)*. Tokyo: KK Bestsellers.

Haraldsson, Erlendur; Matlock, James G. 2017. *I Saw a Light and Came Here: Children's Experiences of Reincarnation*. Hove: White Crow Books.

Hassler, Dieter. 2013. A New European Case of the Reincarnation Type. *Journal of the Society for Psychical Research*, 77, 19-31.

Hearn, Lafcadio. 1897. The Rebirth of Katsugoro. In Hearn, Lafcadio *Gleanings in Buddha Fields*, 267–290. Boston: Houghton Mifflin.

Heath, Pamela Rae; Klimo, Jon. 2006. *Suicide: What Really Happens in the Afterlife?* Berkeley, CA.: North Atlantic Books.

Hirata, Atsutane. 1823. Edited and Annotated by Koyasu, Nobukuni. 2000. *Senkyo Ibun/Katsugoro Saisei Kibun*. Tokyo: Iwanami.

Hiroshima Peace Memorial Museum. n.d. <https://hpmmuseum.jp/?lang=eng> Retrieved August 6, 2022.

Hodgson, Richard. 1898. A Further Record of Observations of Certain Phenomena of Trance. *Proceedings of the Society for Psychical Research*, 13, 284–582.

Hosoi, Satoshi; Takigawa, Erina; Kawade, Masato. 2003. Ethnicity Estimation with Facial Image. *Technical Report of The Institute of Electronics, Information and Communication Engineers* 103(454), 19-24.

Iida, Fumihiko. 1996. *Ikigai no Sozo (Creating the Value of Life)*. Tokyo: PHP Kenkyusho.

Ikeda, Kanzan. n.d. *Katsugoro Saisei Zensho Banashi*. <https://www.wul.waseda.ac.jp/kotenseki/html/he13/he13_00361/index.html> Retrieved July 30, 2022.

Ikeda, Toshio (ed.). 2001. *Hamamatsu Chunagon Monogatari*. Tokyo: Shogakkan.

Ikegawa, Akira. 2005. Investigation by Questionnaire Regarding Fetal/Infant Memory in the Womb and/or at Birth. *Journal of Prenatal and Perinatal Psychology and Health*, 20(2), 121–133.

Inagaki, Katsumi. 2006. *Zensei Ryoho no Tankyu (Explorations in Past-Life Regression Therapy)*. Tokyo: Shunjusha.

Inyaku, Rio. 2012. *Jibun wo Erande Umaretekitayo (I Chose My Body Before I Was Born)*. Tokyo: Sunmark.

Ito, Shota. 2021 Inseiki no Tennou Zensei Setsuwa nituite (On Past-life Stories of the Emperors in the Insei Period). *Hokkai Gakuen Daigaku Jinbun Ronshu*, 71. 25-43.

James, William. 2024. *Mind Dust and White Crows: The Psychical Research of William James*. Ed. Gregory Shushan. Guildford: White Crow.

Katagiri, Yoichi. 2015. *Ono no Komachi Tsuiseki: Komachishu ni yoru Komachi Setsuwa no Kenkyu (Chasing Ono no Komachi: A Study of Komachi Setsuwa through* Komachishu). Tokyo: Kazama Shoin.

Kato, Shuichi, translated and edited by Sanderson, Don. 1997. A *History of Japanese Literature: From the Manyoshu to Modern Times.* Surry: Japan Library (Kindle Edition).

Katsugoro Umarekawari Monogatari Chosadan (ed.). 2015. *Hodokubo Kozo Katsugoro Umarekawari Monogatari Chosa Hokokusho.* Hino: Hino City Museum of Local History.

Kawabata, Yasunari; Keene, Donald; Miyata, Masayuki. 1998. *Taketori Monogatari – The Tale of the Bamboo Cutter.* Tokyo: Kodansha International.

Keene, Jeffrey J. 2003. *Someone Else's Yesterday: The Confederate General and Connecticut Yankee.* Nevada City, CA: Blue Dolphin Publishing.

Kellehear, Allan. 1993. Culture, Biology, and the Near Death Experience: A Reappraisal. *Journal of Nervous and Mental Disease,* 181(3), 148-156.

Kelly, Edward F. 2016. Book Review: A Philosophical Critique of Empirical Arguments for Postmortem Survival by Michael Sudduth. Palgrave Mcmillan, 2016. xv + 336 pp. £49.00 (hardcover). ISBN978-1-137-44093-8. *Journal of Scientific Exploration,* 30(4), 586–595.

Kelly, Edward F. 2021. Epilogue: Our Emerging Vision and Why it Matters. In Kelly, Edward F.; Marshall, Paul (eds.). *Consciousness Unbound: Liberating Mind from the Tyranny of Materialism,* 483–487. Lanham, MD: Rowman & Littlefield.

Kelly, Edward F.; Crabtree, Adam; Marshall, Paul (eds.). 2015. *Beyond Physicalism: Toward Reconciliation of Science and Spirituality.* Lanham, MD: Rowman & Littlefield.

Kelly, Edward F.; Kelly, Emily Williams; Crabtree, Adam; Gauld, Alan; Grosso, Michael; Greyson, Bruce. 2007. *Irreducible Mind: Toward a Psychology for the 21st Century.* Lanham, MD: Rowman & Littlefield.

Kelly, Edward F.; Marshall, Paul (eds.). 2021. *Consciousness Unbound: Liberating Mind from the Tyranny of Materialism.* Lanham, MD: Rowman & Littlefield.

Kelly, Emily Williams. 2007. Psychophysiological Influence. In Kelly, Edward F.; Kelly, Emily Williams; Crabtree, Adam; Gauld, Alan; Grosso, Michael; Greyson, Bruce (eds.). *Irreducible Mind: Toward a Psychology for the 21st Century.* 117–239. Lanham, MD: Rowman & Littlefield.

Kelly, Emily; Arcangel, Dianne. 2011. An Investigation of Mediums Who Claim to Give Information About Deceased Persons. *The Journal of Nervous and Mental Disease*, 199(1), 11–17.

Kinsey, Alfred C.; Pomeroy, Wardell B.; Martin, Clyde E. 1975. *Sexual Behavior in the Human Male*. Bloomington, IN: Indiana University Press.

Kiriyama, Seiyu. 1993. *Kimi wa Dare no Umarekawari ka (Whose Reincarnation Are You?)*. Tokyo: Hirakawa Shuppan.

Kouki Shohokai. 2016. *Iroha-Hifumi (Kotodama) Kokyushoho (Breathing Method of Iroha-Hifumi)*. Sakai: Gingashoseki.

Kumanoya, Yoko; Snitko, Tatyana. 2019. *Roshiago Hyogen Handobukku (A Handbook of Russian Expressions)*. Tokyo: Hakusuisha.

Kyokai, translated and annotated by Nakamura, Motomochi Kyoko. 1973. *Miraculous Stories from the Japanese Buddhist Tradition: The Nihon Ryoiki of the Monk Kyokai*. London: Routledge.

Leininger, Bruce; Leininger, Andrea; Gross, Ken. 2009. *Soul Survivor: The Reincarnation of a World War II Fighter Pilot*. London: Hay House.

Lewis, Candace R.; Preller, Katrin H.; Kraehenmann, Rainer; Michels, Lars; Staempfli, Philipp; Vollenweider, Franz X. 2017. Two Dose Investigation of the 5-HT-Agonist Psilocybin on Relative and Global Cerebral Blood Flow. *Neuroimage* 159, 70–78.

Lin, Pei-Ying. 2018. The Rebirth Legend of Prince Shotoku: Buddhist Networks in Ninth Century China and Japan: Buddhist Networks in Ninth-Century China and Japan. In Meinert, Carmen; Heirman, Ann; Christoph, Anderl (eds.). *Network and Identity: Exchange Relations Between China and the World*, 301-319. Leiden: Brill.

Lu, Xiaoguang; Chen, Hong; Jain, Anil K. 2005. Multimodal Facial Gender and Ethnicity Identification. *Advances in Biometrics*, 3832, 554-561.

Lurie, David. 2016. Myth and History in the *Kojiki, Nihonshoki*, and Related Works. In Shirane, Haruo; Suzuki, Tomi; with Lurie, David. *The Cambridge History of Japanese Literature*, 22-39. Cambridge: Cambridge University Press (Kindle Edition).

Martin, Michael; Augustine, Keith. 2015. *The Myth of an Afterlife: The Case Against Life After Death*. Lanham, MD: Rowman & Littlefield.

Matlock, James. 2017. Reincarnation Intermission Memories. *Psi Encyclopedia*. London: The Society for Psychical Research. <https://psi-encyclopedia.spr.ac.uk/articles/reincarnation-intermission-memories> Retrieved 14 May 2022.

Matlock, James. 2019. *Signs of Reincarnation: Exploring Beliefs, Cases, and Theory*. Lanham, MD: Rowman & Littlefield.

Matlock, James; Giesler-Petersen, Iris. 2016. Asian Versus Western Intermission Memories: Universal Features and Cultural Variations. *Journal of Near-Death Studies*, 35(1), 3–29.

Matsura, Seizan. Edited by Nakamura, Yoshihiko; Nakano, Mitsutoshi. 1977. *Kassiyawa, Vol. 2 (Stories Started to Be Written on the Night of the Day of the Wooden Rat)*. Tokyo: Heibonsha.

Matsushita, Kazuyo. 1984. Kakosei wa Sonzai suru (Past Lives Do Exist). *Religion and Parapsychology*, 28, 27-34.

Matsutani, Miyoko. 2003. *Gendai Minwako, Vol. 5 (On Modern Folklores)*. Tokyo: Chikuma Shobo.

Merckelbach, Harald; de Jong, Peter J.; Muris, Peter; van den Hout, Marcel A. 1996. The Etiology of Specific Phobias: A Review. *Clinical Psychology Review*, 16(4), 337–361.

Menzies, Ross G.; Clarke, J. Christopher. 1993. The Etiology of Childhood Water Phobia. *Behavior Research and Therapy*, 31(5), 499–501.

Mills, Antonia. 1994. Rebirth and Identity: Three Gitksan Cases of Pierced-Ear Birthmarks. In Mills, Antonia; Slobodin, Richard (eds.). *Amerindian Rebirth: Reincarnation Belief Among North American Indians and Inuit*, 211-241. Toronto: University of Toronto Press.

Minai, Utako; Gustafson, Kathleen; Fiorentino, Robert; Jongman, Allard; Sereno, Joan. 2017. Fetal Rhythm-Based Language Discrimination: A Biomagnetometry Study. *NeuroReport*, 28(10), 561–564.

Minamiyama, Midori. 2014. *Mama ga "Iiyo" tte Ittekureta kara Umaretekoretan dayo. (I Was Able to Be Born Because Mom Said "Yes.")* Tokyo: Zennichi Publishing.

Misumi, Yoichi. 1996. *Monogatari no Henbo (The Transfiguration of Stories)*. Tokyo: Wakakusa Shobo.

Moon, Christine; Lagercrantz, Hugo, Kuhl, Patricia K. 2013. Language Experienced *in Utero* Affects Vowel Perception After Birth: A Two-Country Study. *Acta Paediatr*, 102(2), 156–160.

Moriyama, Shigeki. 2007. Kosodate no Minzoku: Umarekawari wo Chushin ni (Folkways of Parenting: Focusing on Rebirth). *Tokyo Kasei Daigaku Hakubutsukan Kiyo*, 12, 27-40.

Motoyama, Hiroshi. 1987. *Karuma to Saisei (Karma and Reincarnation)*. Tokyo: Shukyo Shinri Shuppan.

Murasaki Shikibu, translated by Omori, Annie Shepley; Doi, Koichi; with an introduction by Lowell, Amy. 1920. *Diaries of Court Ladies of Old Japan*. New York: Houghton Mifflin Company.

Nahm, Michael; Greyson, Bruce; Kelly, Emily Williams; Haraldsson, Erlendur. 2012. Terminal Lucidity: A Review and a Case Collection. *Archives of Gerontology and Geriatrics*, 55(1), 138–142.

Nakamura, Hajime. 1984. *Budda no Kotoba: Sutta Nipata (Words of Buddha: Sutta Nipata)*. Tokyo: Iwanami.

Nakamura, Motomochi Kyoko. 1973. Translator's Preface. In Kyokai, translated and annotated by Motomochi, Nakamura Kyoko. 1973. *Miraculous Stories from the Japanese Buddhist Tradition: The Nihon Ryoiki of the Monk Kyokai*, v-viii. London: Routledge.

Newton, Michael. 1994. *Journey of Souls: Case Studies of Life Between Lives.* Woodbury, MN: Llewellyn.

Newton, Michael. 2000. *Destiny of Souls: More Case Studies of Life Between Lives*. Woodbury, MN: Llewellyn.

Nippon Gakujutsu Shinkokai. 1965. *The Manyoshu: One Thousand Poems with the Texts in Romaji*. New York: Columbia University Press.

Nitta, Akira. 2015. *Sansara: Rinne toiu Shinwa, Vol. 4, Part 4, Nihonbukkyo to Ingaoho, Vol. 1 (Samsara: The Myth of Reincarnation, Japanese Buddhism and Karma)*. Kanagawa: Texnai.

Nomura, Jiro. 1973. *Dokoku no Umi: Senkan Yamato Shito no Kiroku (The Wailing Sea: A Record of the Fight to the Death of Yamato)*. Tokyo: Yomiuri Shinbun.

Ochi, Keiko. 1999. *Inochi no Komoriuta – Namida to Warai to Odoroki no Kakosei Ryoho (Cradle of Life – Past-Life Therapies of Tears, Laughter, and Surprise)*. Tokyo: PHP Kenkyusho.

Ogikubo, Norio (Director). 2013. *Kamisama tono Yakusoku (Promise with God)*. Tokyo: Kumanekodo.

Ohkado, Masayuki. 2011. "Kakosei no Kioku" wo motsu Kodomo ni tsuite: Nihonjin Jido no Jirei (Children with "Past-Life Memories:" A Case of a Japanese Child). *Jintaikagaku*, 20(1), 33-42.

Ohkado, Masayuki. 2012. "Kakosei Kioku" wo motsu Kodomo – Indojin toshiteno Kioku wo motsu Nihonjinjoji no Jirei – (Children with "Past-life" Memories–A Case of a Japanese Female Child with "Memories" as an Indian). *Jintaikagaku*, 21(1), 17-25.

Ohkado, Masayuki. 2013. A Case of a Japanese Child with Past-Life Memories. *Journal of Scientific Exploration* 27(4), 625–636.

Ohkado, Masayuki. 2014. Facial Features of Burmese with Past-Life Memories as Japanese Soldiers. *Journal of Scientific Exploration*, 28(4), 597-603.

Ohkado, Masayuki. 2015. Children's Birth, Womb, Prelife, and Past-Life Memories: Results of an Internet-Based Survey. *Journal of Prenatal and Perinatal Psychology and Health* 30(1), 1–16.

Ohkado, Masayuki. 2016. A Same-Family Case of the Reincarnation Type in Japan. *Journal of Scientific Exploration*, 30(4), 524–536.

Ohkado, Masayuki. 2017. Same-Family Cases of the Reincarnation Type in Japan. *Journal of Scientific Exploration*, 31(4), 551–571.

Ohkado, Masayuki. 2018. Kodomo ga Kataru Tainaikioku ni Ysotte Yuhatsusareta Reitekihenyotaiken (A Case of Spiritually Transformative Experiences Induced by a Child's Prenatal Memories). *Jintaikagaku*, 27(1), 13-22.

Ohkado, Masayuki. 2021. Katsugoro (Reincarnation Case). *Psi Encyclopedia*. London: The Society for Psychical Research. <https://psi-encyclopedia.spr.ac.uk/articles/Katsugoro-reincarnation-case> Retrieved 6 May 2022.

Ohkado, Masayuki. 2023a. A Japanese Case of the Reincarnation Type with Written Records Made Before Verifications: A Child Claiming to Have Fought on the Battleship Yamato. Explore, 19, 153-159.

Ohkado, Masayuki. 2023b. Nihonjin toshiteno Kakosei-Kioku wo motsu Rosiajin no Saiseigata-Jirei (A Russian Case of the Reincarnation Type with Memories of a Past Life in Japan). Jintaikagaku, 32(1), 25-33.

Ohkado, Masayuki; Greyson, Bruce. 2018. *Journal of International Society of Life Information Science*, 36(2), 73-77.

Ohkado, Masayuki; Ikegawa, Akira. 2014. Children with Life-between-Life Memories. *Journal of Scientific Exploration* 28(3), 477–490.

Ohkado, Masayuki; Inagaki, Katsumi; Suetake, Nobuhiro; Okamoto, Satoshi. 2010. On Xenoglossy Occurring in Hypnosis and What It Suggests. *Journal of International Society of Life Information Science*, 28(1), 128-133.

Ohkado, Masayuki; Okamoto, Satoshi. 2014. A Case of Xenoglossy Under Hypnosis. *EdgeScience: Current Research and Insights*, 17, 7–12.

Omori, Annie Shepley; Doi, Kochi. 1920. *Diaries of Court Ladies of Old Japan*. Boston and New York: Houghton Mifflin Company.

Otsuki, Maiko. 2004. *Anata wa Motto Shiawase ni Nareru (You Can Be Happier)*. Tokyo: Seishun Shuppan.

Otsuki, Maiko. 2007. *'Zensei' karano Kosodate Adobaisu (Parenting Advice Book from Past Lives)*. Tokyo: Futami Shobo.

Parnia, Sam with Josh Young. 2013. *The Lazarus Effect: The Science that Is Erasing the Boundaries Between Life and Death*. London: Rider.

Paterson, R. W. K. 1995. *Philosophy and the Belief in a Life After Death*. New York: St. Martin's Press.

Pehlivanova, Marieta; Janke, Monica J.; Lee, Jack; Tucker, Jim B. (2018) Childhood Gender Nonconformity and Children's Past-Life Memories. *International Journal of Sexual Health*. doi: 10.1080/19317611.2018.1523266.

Quine, Willard Van Orman. 1951. Two Dogmas of Empiricism. *The Philosophical Review*, 60, 20–43.

Rhine, Louisa E. 1981. *The Invisible Picture: A Study of Psychic Experiences*. Jefferson, NC: McFarland.

Ring, Kenneth. 1980. *Life at Death: A Scientific Investigation of the Near-Death Experience*. New York: Coward McCann and Geoghegan.

Rivas, Titus; Carman, Elizabeth M.; Dirven, Anny Dirven. 2015. Paranormal Aspects of Pre-Existence Memories in Young Children. *Journal of Near-Death Studies*, 34(2), 84–108.

Rivas, Titus; Dirven, Anny; Smit, Rudolf H. 2016. *The Self Does Not Die: Verified Paranormal Phenomena from Near-Death Experiences*. Durham, NC: IANDS Publications.

Rock, Adam J.; Beischel, Julie; Cott, Christopher. 2009. Psi vs. Survival: A Qualitative Investigation of Mediums' Phenomenology Comparing Psychic Readings and Ostensible Communication with the Deceased. *Transpersonal Psychology Review*, 13(2), 76–89.

Ryle, Gilbert. 1949. *The Concept of Mind*. Chicago: University of Chicago Press.

Sabom, Michael. 1998. *Light and Death*. Grand Rapids, MI: Zondervan.

Sahara, Sakumi. 1998. *Nihon ryoiki* ni Okeru Tenseitan no Kozo (The Structure of the Reincarnation Stories in *Nihon ryoiki*). *Komazawa Tandai Kokubun*, 28, 1-16.

Saunders, Rebecca. 2017 Archaic Shell Mounds in the American Southeast. *Oxford Handbooks Online*. <https://www.oxfordhandbooks.com/view/10.1093/oxfordhb/9780199935413.001.0001/oxfordhb-9780199935413-e-75> Retrieved January 20, 2022.

Schwartz, Gary E. 2011. *The Sacred Promise: How Science Is Discovering Spirit's Collaboration with Us in Our Daily Lives*. Hillsboro, OR: Beyond Words Publishing.

Segawa, Takuro. 2016. *Ainu to Jomon: Mohitotsu no Nihon no Rekishi (Ainu and Jomon: Another History of Japan)*. Tokyo: Chikuma Shobo.

Sharma, Poonam; Tucker, Jim B. 2004. Cases of the Reincarnation Type with Memories from the Intermission. *Journal of Near-Death Studies*, 23(2), 101–118.

Shimamura, Naomi; Mikami, Hiroko. 1994. Acquisition of Hiragana Letters by Pre-School Children: In Comparison with the 1967 Investigation of the National Language Research Institute. *Japanese Journal of Educational Psychology*, 42(1), 70-76.

Shimonoseki Genbakuten Jimukyoku, (eds.) 2008. *Genbaku to Taisen no Shinjitsu (The Truth of Atomic Bombs and the World War)*. Shimonoseki: Choshu Shinbunsya.

Shirane, Haruo. 2016. Setsuwa (Anecdotal) Literature: *Nihon Ryoiki* to *Kokon Chomonju*. In Shirane, Haruo; Suzuki, Tomi; with Lurie, David. *The Cambridge History of Japanese Literature*, 280-286. Cambridge: Cambridge University Press (Kindle Edition).

Shotoku Taishi (translated by Nakamura, Hajime; Hayashima, Kyosyo). 2007. *Shomankyo Gisho, Yuimakyo Gisho (Sho)*. Tokyo: Chuokoron-Shinsha.

Shushan, Gregory. 2018. *Near-Death Experience in Indigenous Religions*. New York: Oxford University Press.

Shushan, Gregory. 2022. *The Next World: Extraordinary Experiences of the Afterlife*. Hove: White Crow Books.

Skulski, Janusz. 1988. *The Battleship* Yamato. Annapolis, MD: Naval Institute Press.

Snitko, Tatyana. 2014a. Tokyo no Gojigen (The Five Dimension of Tokyo). *Kan*, 59, 256-258.

Snitko Tatyana. 2014b. *Запад - Восток: предельные понятия лингвокультур. (West Versus East: Polar Concepts in Language and Culture)*. Moscow: Azbukovnik Publishing.

Snitko, Tatyana. 2015. 'Shi' ni Nozonde 'Mirai' wo Egaku Nihon (Japan Describing Its 'Future' in the Face of Its 'Death'). Fujiwara Shoten Henshubu, ed. *'Asia' wo Kangaeru 2000-2015 (A Thought on 'Asia' 2000-2015)*, 216-217. Tokyo: Fujiwara Shoten.

Snitko, Tatyana. 2017. Nihongo Dokugaku no 'Senri no Michi' ('A Thousand Miles' of Japanese Self-Study). *Kotoba to Bungaku (Language and Literature)*, July Issue, 76-85.

Snow, Robert L. 1999. *Looking for Carroll Beckwith: The True Story of a Detective's Search for His Past Life*. Emmaus, PA: Daybreak Books.

Sober, Elliot. 2008. *Evidence and Evolution: The Logic Behind the Science.* Cambridge: Cambridge University Press.

Spanos, Nicholas P.; Menary, Evelyn; Gabora, Natalie J.; DuBreuil, Susan C.; Dewhirst, Bridget. 1991. Secondary Identity Enactments During Hypnotic Past-life Regression: A Sociocognitive Perspective. *Journal of Personality and Social Psychology,* 61, 308–320.

Spector, Tim. 2012. *Identically Different: Why We Can Change Our Genes.* London: George Weidenfeld & Nicholson.

Stevenson, Ian. 1958. Scientists with Half-Closed Minds. *Harper's Magazine,* 217, 64–71.

Stevenson, Ian. 1960a. The Evidence for Survival from Claimed Memories of Former Incarnations: *The Winning Essay of the Contest in Honor of William James,* Part I.: The Review of the Data. *Journal of the American Society for Psychical Research,* 54, 51–71.

Stevenson, Ian. 1960b. The Evidence for Survival from Claimed Memories of Former Incarnations: *The Winning Essay of the Contest in Honor of William James,* Part II.: Analysis of the Data and Suggestions for Further Investigation. *Journal of the American Society for Psychical Research,* 54, 95–117.

Stevenson, Ian. 1974a. *Xenoglossy: A Review and Report of a Case.* Charlottesville, VA: University Press of Virginia.

Stevenson, Ian. 1974b. *Twenty Cases Suggestive of Reincarnation* (2nd and revised edition). Charlottesville, VA: University Press of Virginia.

Stevenson, Ian. 1975. *Cases of the Reincarnation Type, Vol. 1: Ten Cases in India.* Charlottesville, VA: University Press of Virginia.

Stevenson, Ian. 1977a. The Explanatory Value of the Idea of Reincarnation. *The Journal of Nervous and Mental Disease,* 164(5), 305–326.

Stevenson, Ian. 1977b. *Cases of the Reincarnation Type. Vol. 2, Ten Cases in Sri Lanka.* Charlottesville, VA: University Press of Virginia.

Stevenson, Ian. 1980. *Cases of the Reincarnation Type. Vol. 3, Twelve Cases in Lebanon and Turkey.* Charlottesville, VA: University Press of Virginia.

Stevenson, Ian. 1983. *Cases of the Reincarnation Type. Vol. 4, Twelve Cases in Thailand and Burma.* Charlottesville, VA: University Press of Virginia.

Stevenson, Ian. 1984. *Unlearned Language: New Studies in Xenoglossy.* Charlottesville, VA: University Press of Virginia.

Stevenson, Ian. 1994. A Case of the Psychotherapist's Fallacy: Hypnotic Regression to "Previous Lives." *American Journal of Clinical Hypnosis,* 36(3), 188–193.

Stevenson, Ian. 1997. *Reincarnation and Biology: A Contribution to the Etiology of Birthmarks and Birth Defects*, 2 Vols. Westport, CT: Praeger.

Stevenson, Ian. 2001. *Children Who Remember Previous Lives: A Question of Reincarnation*, Revised Edition. Jefferson, NC: McFarland.

Stevenson, Ian; Keil, Jürgen. 2005. Children of Myanmar Who Behave like Japanese Soldiers: A Possible Third Element in Personality. *Journal of Scientific Exploration*, 19(2), 171-183.

Sudduth, Michael. 2016. *A Philosophical Critique of Empirical Arguments for Postmortem Survival*. New York: Palgrave Macmillan.

Taiheiyo Senso Kenkyukai (ed.). 2002. *Nihon Kaigun ga Yokuwakaru Jiten (Encyclopedia of the Imperial Japanese Navy)*. Tokyo: PHP Kenkyusho.

Takekura, Fumito. 2015. *Rinne Tensei: "Watashi" wo Tsunagu Umarekawari no Monogatari (Reincarnation: Rebirth Stories of Linking "Me")*. Tokyo: Kodansha.

Takekura, Fumito. 2021. Reincarnation Revisited: An Inquiry into Three Types of Rebirth. In Kashio, Naoki; Becker, Carl (eds.). *Spirituality as a Way: The Wisdom of Japan*, 161-178. Kyoto/Tokyo: Kyoto University Press/Trans Pacific Press.

Totani, Noriko. 2012. *Kagero Nikki: Yojoron*. Ph.D. Dissertation, Kobe University.

Tucker, Jim B. 2005. *Life Before Life: Children's Memories of Previous Lives*. New York: St. Martin's.

Tucker, Jim B. 2013. *Return to Life: Extraordinary Cases of Children Who Remember Past Lives*. New York: St. Martin's.

Tucker, Jim B. August 13, 2013. Personal Communication via E-Mail.

Tucker, Jim B.; Keil, Jürgen H. H. 2013. Experimental Birthmarks: New Cases of an Asian Practice. *Journal of Scientific Exploration*, 27(2), 269-282.

Tyrrell, George Nugent Merle. 1942/1961. *Apparitions*. New Hyde Park, NY: University Books.

Uff, John. 2000. *The Southall Rail Accident Inquiry Report*. Norwich: HSE Books.

Umehara, Yuki; Kanda, Akira. 2014. *Chojo Gensho: Kagakushatachi no Chosen (Supernatural Phenomena: Challenges of Scientists)*. Tokyo: NHK Shuppan.

Venn, Jonathan. 1986. Hypnosis and the Reincarnation Hypothesis: A Critical Review and Intensive Case Study. *The Journal of the American Society for Psychical Research*, 80, 409–425.

Verny, Tomas; Kelly, John. 1981. *The Secret Life of the Unborn Child*. New York: Dell Publishing.

Verny, Thomas R.; Weintraub, Pamela. 2002. *Pre-Parenting: Nurturing Your Child from Conception*. New York: Simon & Schuster.

Wambach, Helen. (1978). *Reliving Past Lives: The Evidence Under Hypnosis*. New York: Harper & Row.

Wambach, Helen. 1979. *Life Before Life*. Toronto: Bantam Books.

Watanabe, Makoto. 2013. *Yomigaeru Jomon no Megami (Reviving Jomon Goddesses)*. Tokyo: Gakken Publishing.

Weiss, Brian L. (1988). *Many Lives, Many Masters*. New York: Simon & Schuster.

Weiss, Brian L. 2004. *Same Soul, Many Bodies*. London: Piatkus.

Weiss, Brian. 2008a. *Spiritual Progress Through Regression* (Audio CD). London: Hayhouse UK.

Weiss, Brian. 2008b. *Through the Mirrors of Time* (Audio CD). London: Hayhouse UK.

Weiss, Brian. 2008c. *Regression to Times and Places* (Audio CD). London: Hayhouse UK.

Whitten, Joel; Fisher, Joe. 1986. *Life Between Life*. New York: Warner Books.

Yamaguchi, Mami. 2002. *Kao no Tokucho Joho o Saguru Jikkenteki Kenkyu: Hyojo, Sei, Nenrei Joho wo Chushin ni*. Tokyo: Kazama Shobo.

Yamato Museum. n.d. About Yamato Museum. <https://yamato-museum.com/eng/. February 20, 2022> Retrieved

Yanagita, Kunio. 1964. *Teihon Yanagita Kunio Shu, Bekkan 3 (Standard Collection of Yanagita Kunio, Supplementary Vol. 3)*. Tokyo: Chikuma Shobo.

Yanagita, Kunio. 2013. *Shinban Tono Monogatari, Tono Monogatari Shui tsuki (The Stories of Tono, with Gleanings of the Stories of Tono)*. Tokyo: Kadokawa.

Yasue, Kunio; Yamamoto, Koki. 2015. *Kami ni Chikazuku niwa Hacho wo Awasereba Ii (Approaching Gods By Adjusting Your Wavelength)!* Tokyo: Fuunsha.

Yokoyama, Shigeru; Matsumoto, Ryushin. 1973. *Muromachi Jidai Monogatari Taisei 1 (Collection of Stories from the Muromachi Period, Vol. 1)*. Tokyo: Kadokawa Shoten.

Yoshida, Mitsuru, translation and introduction by Minear, Richard H. 2013. *Requiem for Battleship Yamato*. Annapolis, MD.: Naval Institute Press.

Yoshikawa, Sakiko. 1999 *Kao no Sainin Kioku ni Kansuru Jisshoteki Kenkyu*. Tokyo: Kazama Shobo.

Zeami. Edited by Nogami, Toyoichiro; Nishio, Minoru. 1958. *Fushi Kaden (Style and the Flower)*. Tokyo: Iwanami.

Some of the content in this book has been adapted, revised, and expanded from the following previously published articles (used with permission):

"'Kakosei Kioku' wo motsu Kodomo – Indojin toshiteno Kioku wo motsu Nihonjinjoji no Jirei" (Children with "Past-life" Memories–A Case of a Japanese Female Child with "Memories" as an Indian). *Jintaikagaku*, 21(1), 17-25. (2012).

"A Case of a Japanese Child with Past-Life Memories." *Journal of Scientific Exploration* 27(4), 625–636. (2013).

"Children with Life-between-Life Memories." *Journal of Scientific Exploration* 28(3), 477–490. (2014). (with Ikegawa Akira)

"A Case of Xenoglossy Under Hypnosis." *EdgeScience: Current Research and Insights*, 17, 7–12. (2014) (with Okamoto Satoshi)

"Children's Birth, Womb, Prelife, and Past-Life Memories: Results of an Internet-Based Survey." *Journal of Prenatal and Perinatal Psychology and Health* 30(1), 1–16. (2015).

"A Same-Family Case of the Reincarnation Type in Japan." *Journal of Scientific Exploration*, 30(4), 524–536. (2016).

"Same-Family Cases of the Reincarnation Type in Japan." *Journal of Scientific Exploration*, 31(4), 551–571. (2017).

"Kodomo ga kataru Tainaikioku ni Yotte Yuhatsu sareta Reitekihenyoutaiken" (A Case of Spiritually Transformative Experiences Induced by a Child's Prenatal Memories). *Jintaikagaku*, 27(1), 13-22. (2018)

"Katsugoro (Reincarnation Case)." *Psi Encyclopedia*. London: The Society for Psychical Research (2021). https://psi-encyclopedia.spr.ac.uk/articles/Katsugoro-reincarnation-case

"A Japanese Case of the Reincarnation Type with Written Records Made Before Verifications: A Child Claiming to Have Fought on the Battleship *Yamato*." *Explore*, 19, 153-159.

"Nihonjin toshiteno Kakosei-Kioku wo motsu Rosiajin no Saiseigata-Jirei" (A Russian Case of the Reincarnation Type with Memories of a Past Life in Japan). *Jintaikagaku*, 32(1), 25-33.

Image Credits

~

Figure 0-1. Life Cycle Assumed in This Book (by the author)

Figure 1-1: An Image of a Woman Drawn on a Pot Found in Todonomiya (courtesy of the Idojiri Archaeological Museum)

Figure 1-2: A Pot from Tsukimimatsu (courtesy of the Board of Education of Ina City)

Figure 1-3: A Pot from Tsuganegoshomae (courtesy of the Hokuto City Hometown Museum)

Figure 1-4: An Ainu man (Batchelor 1901, p. 9)

Figure 1-5: A Page from the Shinpukuji Manuscript of the *Kojiki* (public domain)

Figure 1-6: Manuscript page of the *Man'yoshu* (public domain)

Figure 1-7: Manuscript of *Kagero Nikki* (Center for Open Data in Humanities, http://kotenseki.nijl.ac.jp/biblio/200021025/viewer/5)

Figure 1-8: Murasaki Shikibu Nikki Picture Scroll (ColBase, https://colbase.nich.go.jp/)

Figure 1-9: Sarashina Nikki (public domain)

Figure 1-10: Izumi Shikibu by Utagawa Toyokuni (Ukiyo-e Portable Database, https://www.dh-jac.net/db/nishikie/results-big.php?f1=NDL-562-00-157&f11=1&enter=portal#)

Figure 1-11: *Nihon ryoiki* (Center for Open Data in the Humanities, http://codh.rois.ac.jp/pmjt/book/200019027/)

Figure 1-12: Hamamatsu Chunagon by Gakutei Harunobu (public domain)

Figure 1-13: A sample of Nara ehon, Kyushu University Collection (public domain)

Figure 2-1: A Letter of Tsuyuhime to Kanzan (National Archives of Japan Digital Archive https://www.digital.archives.go.jp/gallery/0000000064)

Figure 2-2: The Report by Okado Denhachiro (courtesy of Japan Psychic Science Association)

Figure 2-3: Report of Katsugoro by Hirata Atsutane (courtesy of Ms. KITAMURA Sumie)

Figure 2-4: Hirata Atsutane (public domain)

Figure 2-5: The Path Along Which Katsugoro Took Tsuya to Hodokubo Village (photo by the author)

Figure 2-6: Matsura Seizan [Kiyoshi] (public domain)

Figure 2-7: Report by Katsugoro Umarekawari Monogatari Chosadan, a Great Source of New Information About Katsugoro.

Figure 3-1: Yanagita Kunio (public domain)

Figure 3-2: Matsutani Miyoko (courtesy of her family)

Figure 4-1: Garlic Peeled by Tomo (courtesy of Tomo's mother)

Figure 4-2: Tomo Peeling Garlic Skin with His Left Hand (courtesy of Tomo's mother)

Figures 4-3 and 4-4: Pictures drawn by Tomo (courtesy of Tomo's mother)

Figure 4-5: A Map Drawn by Tomo as He Explained How to Get to the Hospital (courtesy of Tomo's mother)

Figure 5-1: The Yamato during sea trials (public domain)

Figure 5-2: The explosion of the Yamato (public domain)

Figure 5-3: The picture Takeharu drew when he was three years old (courtesy of Takeharu's mother)

Figure 5-4: The booklet Takeharu made (courtesy of Takeharu's mother)

Figure 5-5: Scale model of the battleship Yamato (photo by the author)

Figure 5-6: The cover of the book Takeharu wanted (Shimonoseki Genbakuten Jimukyoku, eds., 2008)

Figure 5-7: Takeharu explaining how the Yamato was attacked (photo by the author)

Figure 5-8: Picture drawn by Takeharu (courtesy of Takeharu's mother)

Figure 6-1: Sakutaro's drawing of his past-life accident (courtesy of Sakutaro's mother)

Figure 6-2: The Nintendo Famicom, 1983 version (public domain)

Figure 6-3: Sakutaro's accessory auricle (courtesy of Sakutaro's mother)

Figure 6-4 Chie and Sakutaro (courtesy of Sakutaro's mother)

Figure 7-1: Momoka, aged 2 years and 11 months (courtesy of Kanon's mother)

Figure 7-2: Kanon's Sylvanian Families toy rabbits (courtesy of Kanon's mother)

Figure 7-3: Momoka and her mother, Yoshie, after the successful operation (courtesy of Kanon's mother)

Figure 7-4: A portrait of Yoshie drawn by her husband (courtesy of Kanon's mother)

Figure 7-5: Kanon's handprint for his 4th birthday commemoration (courtesy of Kanon's mother)

Figure 7-6: Kanon's toy cosmetic set (courtesy of Kanon's mother)

Figure 7-7: Kanon wearing a ribbon (courtesy of Kanon's mother)

Figure 7-8: The wall color of the house (courtesy of Kanon's mother)

Figure 7-9: Kanon's letter echoing Momoka's words (courtesy of Kanon's mother)

Figure 8-1: Akane's birthmark (courtesy of Akane's mother)

Figure 8-2: Goddesses Akane met in the sky (photo by the author)

Figure 8-3: Gods Akane met in the sky (photo by the author)

Figure 8-4: Akane's drawing of her mother from her past life (photo by the author)

Figure 8-5: Akane's drawing of her dog from her past life (photo by the author)

Figure 8-6: Akane's former house (drawn by the author)

Figure 9-1: *Kamisama tono Yakusoku* movie (2013) (Ogikubo, 2013)

Figure 9-2: Kazuya wiping his great-grandfather's face (courtesy of Kazuya's grandmother)

Figure 9-3: Kazuya celebrating his great-grandmother's birthday (courtesy of Kazuya's grandmother)

Figure 9-4: Kazuya's birthmark (photo by the author)

Figure 10-1: The young Dr. Snitko with Her Mother and Brother (courtesy of Dr. Snitko)

Figure 10-2: A Type of Hina Doll Dr. Snitko Had in Mind (courtesy of Ajioka Ningyo, a doll maker)

Figure 10-3: A Book Published by Dr. Snitko in Russian (photo by the author)

Figure 10-4: Ono no Komachi (Public Domain)

Figure 10-5: Snitko's work displayed at the 2009 calligraphy exhibition at the Tokyo Metropolitan Art Museum (courtesy of Dr. Snitko)

Figure 10-6: Dr. Snitko Performing Noh (courtesy of Dr. Snitko)

Figure 11-1: A child's drawing of a house (courtesy of the child's mother)

Figure 11-2: The age when children still talk about life-between-life memories (by the author)

Figure 11-3: The age when children still talk about womb memories (by the author)

Figure 11-4: The age when children still talk about birth memories (by the author)

Figure 11-5: The age when children stop talking about life-between-life memories (by the author)

Figure 12-1: Makiko's fetal ultrasound scan (courtesy of Makiko)

Figure 12-2: Makiko's fetal ultrasound scan showing twins (courtesy of Makiko)

Figure 12-3: Makiko's ultrasound scan showing one fetus (courtesy of Makiko)

Figure 12-4: The world above the clouds, as drawn by Natsuki (courtesy of Makiko)

Figure 13-1: A person in the "Japanese-Burmese" group (courtesy of the DOPS)

Figure 14-1: Location of the village of Nallu in Nepal (https://en.wikipedia.org/wiki/Nallu#/media/File:Nepal_adm_location_map.svg)

Figure 14-2: The author with villagers (photo by the author)

Figure 14-3: Jaya Bahadur Ghalan (photo by the author)

Figure 15-1: The difference between the survival and living-agent psi hypotheses (by the author)

Figure 16-1: A Picture Drawn by a Young Woman (photo by the author)

About the Author

O hkado Masayuki is a parapsychologist and linguistics professor in the Graduate School of Global Humanics and the School of General Education at Chubu University in Japan. He has been a visiting professor at M.I.T, at the University of Amsterdam, and in the Division of Perceptual Studies, University of Virginia. Ohkado is active in Japanese parapsychological circles, and is an award-winning author of numerous articles and several books relating to reincarnation, xenoglossy, and near-death experiences. His books (all in Japanese) include *Scientific Study of Reincarnation* (2021), *Why Are We Born and Die?* (2015), *We Can Be Reborn* (2015), and *A Study of Spirituality, with Special Reference to Xenoglossy* (2011). Afterworlds Press is proud to publish his first book in English, *Katsugoro and Other Reincarnation Cases in Japan.*

Milton Keynes UK
Ingram Content Group UK Ltd.
UKHW011138220424
441551UK00006B/648